Primitive
Normativity

ELIZABETH W. WILLIAMS

Primitive
Normativity

Race, Sexuality, and Temporality

in Colonial Kenya

DUKE UNIVERSITY PRESS *Durham & London* 2024

© 2024 DUKE UNIVERSITY PRESS
All rights reserved
Printed in the United States of America on acid-free paper ∞
Designed by Matthew Tauch
Typeset in Garamond Premier Pro and Comma Base by
Westchester Publishing Services

Library of Congress Cataloging-in-Publication Data
Names: Williams, Elizabeth W., [date] author.
Title: Primitive normativity : race, sexuality, and temporality in colonial
Kenya / Elizabeth W. Williams.
Description: Durham : Duke University Press, 2024. | Includes
bibliographical references and index.
Identifiers: LCCN 2023014305 (print)
LCCN 2023014306 (ebook)
ISBN 9781478025498 (paperback)
ISBN 9781478020714 (hardcover)
ISBN 9781478027621 (ebook)
Subjects: LCSH: Sex customs—Kenya—History. | Sex customs—Great
Britain—Colonies—History. | Men, White—Sexual behavior—Great
Britain—Colonies—History. |
Indigenous peoples—Great Britain—Colonies—History. |
Race discrimination. | Great Britain—Colonies—Race relations—
History. | Great Britain—Colonies—Kenya. | Kenya—Race relations. |
BISAC: HISTORY / Africa / East | SOCIAL SCIENCE / Gender Studies
Classification: LCC HQ18.K4 W557 2024 (print) | LCC HQ18.K4
(ebook) | DDC 306.7096762—dc23/eng/20230609
LC record available at https://lccn.loc.gov/2023014305
LC ebook record available at https://lccn.loc.gov/2023014306

Cover art: Syowia Kyambi, *Traces of Her Walking into the Wall
(Chapter I Performative Marks)*, 2018. Ash and ivory and black
pigment with archival glue on acid-free paper, 170 cm × 328 cm.
Courtesy of the artist.

For Jesús Estrada-Pérez, who left too soon.

CONTENTS

....

ABBREVIATIONS

ADC	Assistant District Commissioner
BL	British Library, London, United Kingdom
BNA	British National Archives, London, United Kingdom
CNC	Chief Native Commissioner
DC	District Commissioner
EAINC	East African Indian National Congress
EAP	East African Protectorate
EAS	East African Standard
EAWL	East African Women's League
IPC	Indian Penal Code
KAR	King's African Rifles
KNA	Kenya National Archives, Nairobi, Kenya
LEGCO	Legislative Council
MP	Member of Parliament
PP	Parliamentary Papers
RH	Rhodes House Archive, Oxford University Libraries, Oxford, United Kingdom

ACKNOWLEDGMENTS

I always read the acknowledgments. From a practical standpoint, it's good to see the scholars that a book has been in conversation with, and the institutions and programs that have facilitated it. But mostly, I am interested in other things: I like to figure out who people are friends with, attempt to recreate the timeline of their love lives, suss out familial relationships, and ideally to hear some details about their pets. In other words, I read the acknowledgments in an attempt to find the person who exists beneath and within the text that will follow.

Perhaps because of my own (possibly prurient) interest in acknowledgments, my own have been challenging to write. I worry that I will leave someone out, that I will fail to do my duty by the friends and companions and mentors who have traveled with me over the decade it took me to complete this project. Writing these words also compels me to revisit the events of these past ten years, some of which have been magnificent and some of which have been almost unbearable. Here, then, is a necessarily incomplete but nevertheless heartfelt list of some of the folks who have made this book—and the years it took to complete it—possible.

This project has been supported by several grants and fellowships. I thank the Interdisciplinary Center for the Study of Global Change for a year of financial support, space to write, and a vibrant and eminently friendly intellectual community. A Doctoral Dissertation Fellowship funded a year of writing, while a Thesis Research Travel Grant provided the necessary funds to visit Kenyan archives—both funded by the University of Minnesota. In Kenya, my thanks go to the Department of History and Archeology at the University of Nairobi, and in particular then chair Dr. Ephraim Wahome, for providing me with an institutional home. Luise White generously agreed to read an early draft of the manuscript: I'm grateful for her extremely thoughtful comments as well as for her groundbreaking scholarship. My thanks also to the archivists and librarians at Rhodes House, University of Oxford, the Kenya National Archives, the

Jomo Kenyatta Library at the University of Nairobi, the British Library, and the British National Archives.

A huge thank you goes to Anna Clark, who has been endlessly supportive and an academic inspiration since I first read her work as an undergraduate student. I was tremendously lucky to work with her. Patricia Lorcin awes me with her ability to produce rich and important scholarship with seemingly effortless grace. Fun fact: she's also an extremely impressive Surrealist painter. M. J. Maynes, Helena Pohlandt-McCormick, Reg Kunzel, and Jigna Desai offered valuable feedback on the earliest iterations of this project; they continue to provide wonderful examples of how to produce insightful, rigorous scholarship. The opportunity to learn from a group of brilliant and fierce feminists is a blessing that everyone deserves and far too few of us get. I'm also deeply indebted to Jennifer Hall-Witt of Smith College; she introduced me to gender history, taught me to write and think like a historian, revised countless drafts of my senior thesis, and put up with a fair amount of crying with grace and patience.

At the University of Minnesota, I was blessed to build a queer family. The members of "Queer World" have been inviable allies in alternative world-making and have graciously played L-Word bingo at approximately six of my birthday parties. Karisa Butler-Wall is a brilliant feminist and an accomplished Zumba dancer. Watching her transition out of academia and build a life full of meaning, intentionality, and connection has left me proud and inspired. Angela Carter has taught me so much about disability studies and has supported my habit of breaking into song. Raechel Tiffe is creative and strong and brave and extremely enthusiastic about Catch-Phrase. Libby Sharrow is exceptional in everything they do and is one of the best storytellers I know. Eli Vitulli is smart and sensitive and very bad at responding to text messages, but we love him anyway. E. G. Nelson provided a much-needed connection to the world outside academia, and her bike race "Cirque de So Gay" remains the Minneapolis social event of the season. Jesús Estrada-Pérez was a brilliant scholar who felt deeply and lived loudly. I'm lucky to have known and loved him.

At Minnesota I was also blessed with a supportive community of peers. I benefited from the insights of several writing groups, the first with Mia Fischer, Katy Mohrman, and Jesús Estrada-Pérez, and the second with Melissa Hampton, Joanne Jahnke-Wegner, and Laura Luepke. Special thanks go to Adam Blacker, who has been enormously supportive and generous, and also forthcoming with facts about small German towns. Katie Lambright, Brooke Depenbusch, Wesley Lummus, Ketaki Jaywant, and Melissa Hampton helped me establish a small but highly defensible historian enclave in uptown Minneapolis. Ann Zimo, Jecca Namakkal, and Emily Bruce paved the way and never hesitated to offer advice and encouragement. Sophie House and Aubrey Menard made my stay in Oxford fun and saw me through a very tumultuous trans-Atlantic romance—I'm very grateful for their friendship. Lars Mackenzie and Sarah Records have cooked me countless dinners, shared their lovely pets, and welcomed me into their beautiful family with open arms. Anne Wolf has gotten me through the rough patches with commiseration, advice, and pictures of her charming kid. Meryl Lauer has been a steadfast and delightful friend, and an invaluable writing partner. Sami Pfeffer is a brilliant free spirit—I've learned so much from them about how to be brave and take risks.

I'm also very grateful for the folks that helped me publish this book. My editor at Duke, Liz Ault, was first a friend and fellow graduate student at Minnesota. Placing this project in the hands of someone I know, trust, and respect made the process so much easier—I'm grateful for her efforts and her unfailing belief in this project. The anonymous reviewers greatly improved this book with their thoughtful comments and trenchant critiques. I'm also grateful to the team at Duke, including Emily Estelle and Lisa Lawley, copyeditor Katherine Dhurandhar, and Brian Ostrander of Westchester Publishing Services for their work on the editing and production of this book.

The University of Massachusetts at Amherst provided me with my first job and introduced me to a number of wonderful colleagues. I stanned for Laura Briggs long before I met her, and she more than lived up to my expectations as a friend, neighbor, and mentor. Kiran Asher, Lezlie Frye, and Jina Kim made my short stay in Western Mass a great one. During that time, I also met the incomparable Jack Gieseking, who started as a significant other and—in the true spirit of queer kinship—remains a beloved friend. Jack's feedback and support have been crucial to the completion of this project, and he also taught me the correct way to pronounce GIS.

I was lucky enough to score a tenure-track job in the department of Gender and Women's Studies at the University of Kentucky. I really, really love my colleagues—they are smart and fierce and devoted to making change. Carol Mason deserves a special shoutout for being an outstanding friend and mentor. Patricia Ehrkamp adopted me as an honorary geographer—her friendship and guidance have been invaluable. I'm grateful to Anastasia Todd and Miles Feroli for their humor, their compassion, and their cat menagerie. Sharon Yam and Asher Finkel have shared many meals and dog training expeditions, and they let me sit around their house when I'm feeling lonely. As members of the LTT writing group, Sharon, Anastasia, and Karrieann Soto Vega have also provided generous feedback on parts of this book. Karrieann, her partner Jared Whear, and their dog Bizu the Sato have also provided much joy and friendship. Chelsea Ebin and Jack Vimo have offered countless vegan dinners and much-coveted queer companionship. Nikki Brown is a beacon of light and a trusted advisor on all things academic. Lindsey Chambers has taught me about philosophy and watched a lot of reality tv with me. My platonic life-partner Nari Senanayake is a priceless gem: calm, thoughtful, brilliant, and compassionate. She makes my life better in countless ways.

My sister, Olivia, remains my oldest and best ally. She has coached me through countless panic attacks, exposed me to the joys of *The Real Housewives of Atlanta,* and taught me several useful household spells. Her kids, Wes and Freddy, bring incalculable joy and endless poop jokes into my life. My honorary auntie Christine Longoria is one of the brightest spirits I've ever known—she's a continuous example of how to live a life that is full, bold, and brave. Rachael McMillan Coe, my first friend, is a wonderful bonus sister and an all-around mensch. Thanks to my parents, Reed and Martha Williams, who have always believed in and supported my academic aspirations. Reed has also taught me a lot about North American mammals, great meats of the world, and the importance of sharpening your kitchen knives. Last but certainly not least, a couple of nonhumans have brought immense joy into my life. My dearly departed cat, Miss Lady, started as a loan but became an essential companion and an endless source of love and tuna-scented breath. Rubin the Great Dane mix (named for Gayle Rubin—she's really into leather) causes me endless anxiety, drains my bank account, and hogs the couch. I love her very much.

Introduction

Primitive Normativity

The average native is simply an unmoral creature, and as
a general rule he becomes immoral only after contact with
certain forms of civilization, either Eastern or Western.
MEMO TO THE GOVERNOR'S OFFICE, COLONY OF KENYA

THIS PROJECT BEGAN with a puzzle. Early in my graduate program, I
was searching for a research topic that would allow me to examine discourses of race and sexuality in the British Empire. While looking for a
paper topic for a graduate seminar in African history, I started examining
primary sources from the Mau Mau rebellion. At first glance, these sources
seemed to validate all I had learned about imperialism and sexuality, as they
derided the Mau Mau as sexual deviants, supposedly involved in cannibalistic orgies that represented an atavistic return to savagery. Yet, these sources
also contained a more surprising discourse: the officials, settlers, and clergy
who penned these accounts consistently held up the supposedly deviant
practices of the Mau Mau rebels as evidence of their distance from *real*
Africans. Again and again, sources insisted that the Mau Mau could not
possibly represent the *authentic* African perspective precisely because of
the gendered and sexual aberrations of which they supposedly took part.

What was distinctive and disturbing about Mau Mau sexuality, both
settlers and officials agreed, was how intensely it contrasted with the sexual

normativity of the "uncontaminated" African population, who suppos-edly practiced a sexuality that was exclusively heterosexual, focused on reproduction, and absent of practices like rape, prostitution, pedophilia, and even masturbation. In fact, this notion that "authentic" Kenyan African sexuality was distinctly normative became an important facet of anti–Mau Mau propaganda: colonialists claimed that the Mau Mau rebels could not possibly represent the sentiments of the broader population since their excessive sexuality marked them as essentially un-African. Few of the histories of Mau Mau that I subsequently read seemed concerned with this discourse, and yet for me it seemed to beg a number of key questions. Why did the narratives about Mau Mau–era sexuality seem to differ so markedly from other histories of sexuality and imperialism? How far back did this narrative of African sexual normativity extend? And how did normativity—tied so closely to the bodies of those with power in other places and times—come to be ascribed to the most subaltern figures in Kenya? What could this shift tell us about the nature of normativity and deviance in race-making projects?

This book, *Primitive Normativity: Race, Sexuality, and Temporality in Colonial Kenya*, attempts to answer these questions by tracing narratives of African sexual normativity back to the very beginnings of Kenyan colonialism. I unpack a distinctive narrative about Kenyan African sexuality that emerged through the colonial encounter. Kenyan Africans, this narrative held, were unfettered by the moral restraints that more "civilized" Europeans placed on themselves. Yet, precisely because Africans never had to suppress their sexual drives, experts believed them to be incapable of developing the forms of sexual neurosis—including hysteria, homosexuality, and frigidity—that seemed to be plaguing European communities at the turn of the century. This primitive normativity meant that Africans were viewed as more sexually unpolluted than the more "deviant" populations who colonized them. Colonists were able to argue that Africans must be "protected" from forces like urbanization, Western-style education, and political participation that would expose them to forms of "civilized" sexual deviance. Not coincidentally, these were the very forces that tended to produce the most vocal and effective critics of colonial rule. Furthermore, this protection from "contamination" would be provided by more *abnormal* communities of settlers, settlers whose very distance from the natural, healthy sexual mores of the colonized signaled their more advanced civilizational status.

In providing a genealogy of primitive normativity, I'm suggesting that normativity and deviance are produced both *in relation* to each other and *through* other vectors of power, most notably race. I show that settlers' strategic claims to deviance were mobilized to gain and maintain access to power and to bolster the goals of the settler state. Normativity, meanwhile, functioned as an accusation that furthered and legitimated processes that targeted African populations for exclusion from the social body and even the human. In coining the term "primitive normativity," I am attempting to point to the degree to which ideas about African sexuality were tied to temporality, to an evolutionary narrative that placed African peoples in a prior moment in time. Their sexuality was thus deemed "normative" to the extent that it was supposedly absent of deviant practices, *but also* because it was understood to be suited to their particular stage of evolution.

Despite the ubiquity of sexual discourses in the archival record, sexuality has been relatively understudied in the history of colonial Kenya. Like much of African history, the historiography of colonial Kenya has been heavily weighted toward social histories. Since the late 1980s, however, several studies have adopted a more discursive approach to the history of colonial Kenya. Works by Brett Shadle, Dane Kennedy, David Anderson, Will Jackson, Paul Ocobock, Tabitha Kanogo, Lynn Thomas, and Carolyn Martin Shaw have greatly expanded our understanding of the operation of race, class, and gender in colonial Kenya.[1] Yet my project departs from these studies by incorporating insights from two fields that have not been consistently applied to African studies: settler colonial studies and queer theory. The next two sections expand on the concept of primitive normativity through its relationship to these literatures. First, I place the discourses surrounding Kenyan Africans within the context of settler colonialism and evolutionary time, via a brief cameo from your problematic fave.

The Temporality of Settler Colonial Sexuality

To understand how and why this discourse of primitive normativity emerged in colonial Kenya, we need to think of both colonialism and sexuality as temporal constructs. To illustrate this point, I shall briefly direct your attention to that doyenne of catchy pop music, Taylor Swift. In particular, I point you to the video for "Wildest Dreams" (2015), where Taylor appears decked out in 1950s safari gear and singing a song that, as far as I can tell, celebrates the joys of hooking up with a standardly attractive white man whilst being a normatively attractive white woman—in the great outdoors. We see the wildebeest on their migration, a giraffe standing by majestically, a lion roaring and shaking his mane while Swift vamps in a silk gown. A zebra wanders through the set of an Old Hollywood film, presumably searching for the craft services table. What we do not see in this tableau of African imperialism is any African *people*. The landscape is chock-full of exotic game animals—Teddy Roosevelt would have wet himself with excitement—but absolutely denuded of any nonwhite people. We don't even see the standard stock figure of a blank-faced servant in kanzu and fez, holding a tray of gin and tonics.

I bring up Taylor Swift not because she is fun to mock (although, let's be honest, there's that too), but because this video neatly encapsulates the temporal narrative that has been told and *continues* to be told about colonial Kenya since almost its beginning: Kenya is a place out of time, an Eden before the fall, a place where man and beast live in terrifying closeness, where the landscapes cleave dramatically and the sun beats down mercilessly, and where white people go to reconnect with their own primitive urges, their own wildest dreams. But in the real Kenya, this Edenic project was populated not just with charismatic animals but also with millions of Indigenous people farming, grazing their animals, and living on the land. In the temporal framework of colonialism, these people too were viewed as emblems of a lost time, as occupants of a past era that was both spatialized and racialized.

Already the clock is ticking a little queerly. The notion that time operates differently in different geographic spaces—that in fact large swaths of the globe exist *in the past*—is and was central to imperial projects. It has the distinction of being both completely illogical *and* accepted as a commonplace by the imperial powers of the "modern West" for much of the nineteenth and twentieth centuries. But what makes this temporality queer—not just strange, but *queer*—is that the temporal registers of colonial Kenya were, in key ways, demarcated and delineated by sexuality. Sexuality was, in fact, used consistently to *mark time* in colonial Kenya, a chronography that became a well-worn tool of both settlers and officials in their effort to establish and maintain white supremacy.

When I claim that sexuality is a temporal category, I don't mean to say that conceptions of sexuality change over time, although that is of course also true. Rather, I am pointing to how constructs of sexuality make a set of claims that link bodies, acts, desires, and orientations to particular temporal formations. I find the language of queer time to be helpful here not only in its ability to tie sexuality to the multiple timescapes of the settler colony but also to cue us in to how the settler colony disrupts and reshapes time through the language of sex. It's my contention that attending to the central temporal conflict of the settler colony—the idea that multiple time-scapes coexist in a single space—can help us understand how sexuality operates as an alibi of empire.

Let's unpack this temporal conflict. Colonial choreographies established two distinct times—the "here and now" of settlers and officials, and the "here and then" of both Africans and indeed *Africa* itself. (The colony's other racial groups—primarily Arabs and South Asians—were plotted into a third temporal regime that existed somewhere between now and then, a dynamic I'll discuss more in chapter 3.) While these temporalities were envisioned as distinct, the realities of settler colonialism meant that they slid against each other constantly, in precisely the kind of "frottage" that Keguro Macharia has suggested is constitutive of coloniality itself.[2]

This rubbing and chafing of settler "modernity" and Indigenous "primitivity" informed one of the central discursive preoccupations of the settler state—the problem of people sliding *in* and *out of* time. This dangerous temporal slip could occur in two separate registers and acquired two different names in colonial discourse. The first register was "detribalization," which represented the threat of an African who advanced too quickly into the time of "here and now." As Matthew Carotenuto writes, in Kenya, the establishment of Native Reserves, kipande pass laws, and the forced "repatriation" of poor or unemployed urban Africans all emanated from "a paternalistic state view that African colonial citizenship should be limited to the confines of rural life and carefully managed under the disciplinary oversight of static institutions of 'tradition' and gerontocracy."[3] In this imperial fantasy, "detribalization" occurred when Africans ceased to be under the control of these institutions and lost touch with the Indigenous norms that supposedly governed rural "tribal" life. The detribalized African was a central bogeyman of colonial discourse, blamed for urban crime, political discontent, and—importantly for this study—for all evidence of sexual "deviance" in African men and women. As the official E. B. Hosking stated in a report on the slums of Nairobi in 1930, "It is generally held that though the native in his own reserve is an estimable person of many virtues his detribalised cousin that haunts the towns is the scum of the Colony."[4] While Hosking felt that Nairobi might prove to be the exception to this rule, provided that adequate housing was made available for urban Africans, his description of settler attitudes toward African urbanization points to the ways in which the detribalization narrative annexed time to space—the rural was viewed as safe for Africans because it was the space of the "traditional" past, the urban as threatening because it was the space of the "modern" present.

For settlers and the colonial state, the solution to the dangerous detribalization of Africans lay in the preservation of "traditional" rural lifestyles: as historian Megan Vaughan writes, "the disruptive changes wrought by colonialism and capitalism could, so it was argued, be contained if only people obeyed their 'traditional' leaders and followed 'traditional' norms."[5] Detribalization presented a threat because it was believed that "primitive" Africans could learn bad behaviors through contact with "modernity." Even more importantly, the detribalization discourse stressed that to move *too quickly* from "primitivity" to modernity was to invite mental instability—the culmination of this discourse is clearly evidenced in the officially adopted explanation of the Mau Mau rebellion as a form of mass psychopathy among detribalized Gikuyu, which I'll discuss in the final chapter.[6] (The alternate spelling "Kikuyu" is also frequently used in both colonial-era and present-day histories of Kenya.) The detribalized native was depicted as essentially an African living out of time—a primitive person living in the space of modernity—and as I will show in this book, the key symptoms of this (fictional) social disorder were sexual and gendered in nature.

While detribalization represented a perilous forward move, its twin threat, degeneration, reversed the directionality. If detribalization implied a too rapid progression into the now, degeneration was the terminology for those "civilized" persons who slipped backward into the past. Again, the primary symptoms of degeneration were sexual. From the mid-nineteenth century, European powers worried about subjects who could no longer contribute to the growth and power of the nation. Those with impotence, neurosis, frigidity, homosexual tendencies, or fetishes threatened the health of the nation, both because their bodies were understood to be in physical decline and because their sexualities did not support the biopolitical goals of the state.[7] Those populations who appeared to be the most fecund—the poor—were also those marked as more "primitive" than the civilized middle class. Thus, especially in the post–World War I era, Western nations increasingly looked for ways to put middle-class men and women back in touch with their "primitive" roots. National parks, gymnasiums, and Boy Scout troops did this work, but so did more diffuse movements like jazz or modern art. All of these artistic and social movements sought to bring the "primitive" space of the colonized world to the metropole: if degeneration was a problem of excessive civilization, then these movements sought to incorporate the "primitive" into the daily life of Europeans.

As scholars like Will Jackson and Brett Shadle have shown, the potential "degeneration" of poor whites (often evidenced by a tendency to interact socially or sexually with Africans or Asians) was a concern of both colonial officials and settlers.[8] But in this book, I'm more interested in a different discourse, one that depicted Kenya as a reparative space where "overcivilized" Europeans might reconnect with their primitive sexual drives. Think back to Taylor Swift and the empty Eden that she evoked in "Wildest Dreams"—a name that in itself taps into Freudian ideas that the primitive "wild" self remains buried in the subconscious of "civilized" minds, making an occasional (but informative) appearance in our dreams. As I explore more in chapter 5, popular representations of Kenya conveyed the sense that this was a space where the subconscious could come to the fore, where frigid and dysfunctional Europeans could tap back into their sexual drives. In fact, this was viewed as absolutely necessary for the settler colonial state to thrive—new generations of settlers must be produced to ensure its continuation.

On its surface, the fear of detribalization/degeneration seems to bely the stated goals of twentieth-century imperialism: to usher colonized populations into modernity. Like most colonies in late-stage colonialism, Kenya was governed through the philosophy of trusteeship—the notion that the colonial power must hold land and resources in trust for a population that was not yet fit for self-rule. Trusteeship envisioned the colonized as wards of the state, recognizing the wards' right to inherit as soon as they should come of age. The premise that the wards would one day grow up and come into their inheritance proved to be a troublesome teleology since European states showed no intention of giving up their imperial holdings.

Here it's helpful to consider how this spatialization of time operated in the peculiar arena of the settler colony, and particularly in the African settler colony, where (unlike in Canada, Australia, or the United States) Indigenous populations were generally not targeted for elimination but rather preserved so as to provide labor for settler farms, mines, and businesses. In settler colonies, minority populations established claims to land, and even to indigeneity, and premised their lifestyles on the notion that they and their descendants were there to stay. Settler states had a clear biopolitical project—to produce more settlers—that belied the notion that land was merely being held "in trust" for a population that was not yet ready to inherit the state. Instead, settlers envisioned a future in which their descendants would continue to own disproportionate amounts of land and wield disproportionate influence in the colony.

Work by Mark Rifkin and Scott Lauria Morgensen has illustrated the need to consider settler colonial sexualities as distinct from those in other kinds of colonial spaces[9]—yet because their work assumes a North American model of settler colonialism, it is not adequate for understanding other kinds of settler colonial states. These include African settler colonies, where Indigenous populations tended to remain numerically superior throughout the colonial period. A recent study by T. J. Tallie brings a queer theoretical analysis to the study of settler colonialism in Natal, another space where settler colonialism was invested in the *preservation* of Indigenous populations (so as to ensure a consistent labor supply) rather than in their elimination. Tallie's study insightfully considers how Nguni peoples were rendered "queer" through the colonial process. "If settler colonialism itself is presented as a form of orientation," Tallie notes, "of making a recognizable and inhabitable home space for European arrivals on indigenous land, then native peoples and their continued resistance can serve to 'queer' these attempted forms of order. In such circumstances, the customs, practices, and potentially the very bodies of indigenous peoples can become queer despite remaining ostensibly heterosexual in their orientation and practice, as their existence constantly undermines the desired order of an emergent settler state."[10]

This project builds on this scholarship, answering the demand to produce studies of sexuality that attend to the specific dynamics of the settler state. However, my research reverses the directionality of these arguments, outlining a case study in which queerness became annexed to the colonizer while a narrative of sexual normativity was ascribed to colonized people. Zakiyyah Iman Jackson has talked about the plasticity of Blackness as a racial construct, its ability to take on any form that will ensure the continuation of white supremacy.[11] While representing a dramatic reversal of the standard narrative of African sexual pathology, the discourse of primitive normativity served the same ends—maintaining the power of the white supremacist state.

What's So Queer about Primitive Normativity?

What does it mean to apply queerness as an analytic to forms of sexuality marked as normative? In other words, how am I deploying the terms normative and queer in this text? I use queerness not to characterize acts or desires or orientations but rather to outline the epistemic regimes that informed the colonial discourses and, in turn, policies that produced racial categories in Kenya. I use queerness not as a device to uncover the "truth" of colonial sexual practices but rather to illustrate how race and sexuality were constructed in relation to each other and in relation to notions of temporality. African sexuality was marked as "normative" to the extent that it was envisioned as appropriate to the evolutionary stage of "primitive" peoples. The behaviors and desires that supposedly characterized African sexuality were also deemed normative in that they were viewed as exclusively heterosexual, reproductively oriented, and absent of "deviant" sexual practices such as homosexuality, prostitution, and rape. However, it was precisely this normativity, this lingering in an earlier stage of (sexual) evolution, that fundamentally marked Africans as Other—as people (to borrow from Rahul Rao's framework) who existed out of time.[12] While the sexual behaviors, desires, and orientations were normative, it was the timescape of African sexuality that was fundamentally queer.

We can make more sense of this seeming contradiction by looking closely at the work of some other folks who have explained how discourses of the queer and normative interweave in surprising ways with the construction of race. We are used to thinking about normativity—and, more specifically, heterosexuality—as the opposite of queerness. At least in academic circles, we also tend to think of queerness as positive, as antiestablishment, even as emancipatory. But when we put race and queerness into conversation, we frequently find that queerness often operates otherwise—as Macharia writes provocatively, "I do not think black and queer play well together."[13] Cathy Cohen's now classic essay "Punks, Bulldaggers, and Welfare Queens" is a case in point. In this piece, Cohen critiques how "queer politics has served to reinforce simple dichotomies between heterosexuality and everything 'queer'" without seeking to understand "the ways in which power informs and constitutes privileged and marginalized subjects on both sides of this dichotomy."[14] In particular, Cohen draws our attention to the way that certain racialized figures become marked as queer despite or even because of their heterosexuality, such as the "welfare queen," a figure "who may fit into the category of heterosexual, but whose sexual choices are not perceived as normal, moral, or worthy of state support."[15] This is an ostensibly straight figure who is nevertheless rendered queer by virtue of the intersections of race, class, and gender. In fact, it's her heterosexuality—her ability to reproduce through heterosexual sex—as read through her race that marks her out as fundamentally queer. Cohen's elaboration of "heterosexuals on the (out) side of heteronormativity"[16] is useful for this study in that it shows how race can fundamentally reshape how sexualities are oriented toward normativity.

In using queer theory to rethink the relationship between normativity and power, I also build on work by a burgeoning group of Africanist scholars who have theorized queerness as a colonial formation. Marc Epprecht has historicized the emergence of the idea that Africans are exclusively heterosexual, tying it to colonial regimes of power and trends in sexology and anthropology.[17] Specifically, he contests the common narrative (articulated by a number of modern African politicians and religious leaders) that homosexuality was introduced to Africa through imperialism, arguing instead that *homophobia* was a colonial import. Taking a different tack, Neville Hoad has considered how Africans were rendered "queer" through colonial processes. Like Epprecht, he considers the intellectual trends that tied African sexuality to temporal regimes, but he resists the tendency to identify colonial and precolonial African sexual practices as "homosexual," since the use of this language "precisely reproduces the terms of the debate it wishes to end in a landscape of assertion and counterassertion where finding practices that look 'homosexual' to a Western eye has little intellectual or political capital."[18] Instead, he focuses less on identities and more on representations, drawing particular attention to the ways in which nineteenth- and early twentieth-century discourses related the sexuality of "primitive" peoples to "deviant" Westerners. "What the decadent/degenerate shares with the primitive," he writes, "is a position on the fringes of the normative evolutionary narrative."[19]

While I draw heavily on the work of these two scholars, particularly on their attention to the temporal dimensions of the discourses surrounding African sexuality, I diverge in a few key respects. Most obviously, the scholarship that applies queer theory to African studies is heavily focused on southern Africa; by extending our analysis to other parts of the continent, we can develop a broader and deeper understanding of colonial sexual formations. I also expand my examination to consider not only hetero-/homosexuality but also other sexual practices and desires that drew the attention of colonial officials and settlers. As Keguro Macharia notes, "Focusing on the acceptability of homosexual acts and identities leaves unexplored other histories of intimate dissidence and policing."[20] By extending our analysis to claims about not only same-sex desire but also rape, sex for pay, intergenerational sex, solo sex, and other practices outside of the "charmed circle" of sexuality,[21] I am able to accomplish my second goal: accounting for the prevalence of a discourse that tied Kenyan

African sexuality to *both* evolutionary backwardness and normativity. Ann Laura Stoler and Macharia have both observed that the Foucauldian quartet of "the homosexual, the masturbating child, the hysterical woman, and the Malthusian couple" was shaped in relation to a fifth category: the colonized, "primitive" subject.[22] This book explores this relationship, mapping the dialectic relationship between anxieties about degeneration among the most "civilized" populations and fears about the contaminating effect of modernity on colonized peoples.

In his study of queerness in the African diaspora, Keguro Macharia offers another provocation. He asks how the thingification of African peoples impacted their relationship to queerness and normativity, and how it should shape our scholarly approaches to the study of sexuality in African contexts. While queer studies has been primarily interested in sexuality as "the place of subjectification," queer Black studies calls instead for a study that names "theft and commodification, thing-making and gender-undifferentiation. The queerness of the black diaspora," he continues, "would stem from an effort to describe this figuration, which is unaccounted for in sexology's archives: the thing 'severed' from its 'active desire.'"[23] In other words, the desire to find sexual subjects or subjectivities can problematically redirect us from the work of locating and describing racial regimes and how they produced Africans and their diasporic descendants as populations, as generalities, as resources and commodities. As the next section describes, my archival approach largely eschews questions of sexuality subjectivity, focusing instead on uncovering the processes that ascribed a single, shared sexuality to all Kenyan Africans, and showing how it was used to dispossess them.

Method and Archives

This project is rooted in archival research. I conducted research in three key locations: the British National Archives in London, the Rhodes House Archive in Oxford, and the Kenyan National Archives in Nairobi. I also made rather promiscuous use of published primary sources, from ethnographies to memoirs to romance novels. It's worth saying a bit about what these archives are and are not capable of doing, as well as how I utilized them with these limitations in mind.

I approached the archive as a space where I might reconstruct discourses surrounding gender and sexuality as they related to race and power. As

Regina Kunzel puts it, archives are "less depositories of documents than themselves historical agents, organized around unwritten logics of inclusion and exclusion, with the power to exalt certain stories, experiences, and events and to bury others."[24] Colonial archives are great places to find discourses about sexuality. They are often less able to offer information about people's actual sexual desires, practices, and orientations. This is because, as Foucault pointed out, people are likely to enter the archive only at the moment they become infamous, at the moment when their lives brush up against power in exceptional ways.[25] It's also because the people who compiled the archive tend not to be the same people that the archive is discussing and representing. But perhaps most importantly, it's because colonial archives were compiled with an agenda, and that agenda was the maintenance of the colonial state. In short, we're just not likely to get an unmediated, accurate look at the sex lives of African people in a written archive.

There are a number of strategies that I could have used to try to search for data about the sexual subjectivity of Kenyan Africans. For instance, a number of folks have asked me why I did not conduct oral histories for this project. The most basic answer is that the people who experienced the events discussed in most of this book are no longer alive. It would probably have been possible for me to locate folks who were alive during the Mau Mau rebellion, but as a white queer American woman, I did not feel that it was appropriate for me to ask elderly Kenyans about sex and sexuality. (Interestingly, and I think quite problematically, a number of folks along the way have suggested that I could interview present-day Kenyans to gain data about, for instance, anti-Asian sentiments in the 1920s. This seems to me to indicate some of the most egregious ways that the idea of Africa and Africans as unchanging and essential has filtered into the academic consciousness.)

But most importantly, I didn't ask these kinds of questions because part of my argument is that any time we associate *this kind of people* with *this kind of sex* we create the potential to do a certain kind of violence. I'm not interested in telling you what kinds of sex African people *actually had* because I think this is a question that reinforces the racial epistemes that I'm trying to critique. It recirculates the notion of essential racial difference that was introduced by colonists. It also trucks in the same logic that has led several African leaders to proclaim that certain sexual practices (notably homosexuality) are foreign to Africa, and hence cannot be tolerated. Of course, it's possible to talk about the messages that Africans received about sexuality from their cultures, or about sexual practices or orientations that are important and meaningful to specific cultures.[26] But the discourses that I trace in this book asserted that Africans engaged in a particular set of sexual practices, and eschewed a number of other kinds of sex, and that these preferences were a result not of cultural norms or local histories, but of the essential racial difference of African people. To investigate whether such representations were "true" or "untrue" seems to me to offer this narrative a degree of legitimacy that it does not deserve.

So if I did not approach the archive looking for the "truth" of African sexuality, how did I approach it? My method follows two scholars who have viewed the archive not as a space of absence and incompletion but rather as a subject in its own right, a space of imperfect abundance. I was greatly influenced by Ann Laura Stoler's invocation to examine sources "along the archival grain."[27] This approach is a rejoinder to the social historian's imperative to read "against the grain" of the archive, to read the archive for what is unsaid, for what is left out, and especially for who is silenced. The latter is a valuable and essential reading method that has enabled social histories. But it leaves us in the position of treating the colonial archive as a potential source of "truth." Not only might this truth not be available in archives produced by and for those exerting colonial power, but the search for this truth itself might problematically reiterate some of the empiricist modes of colonialism itself.

Reading *along* the archival grain, meanwhile, is primarily invested in determining how the structure of the archive, its internal logics and overarching frameworks, determine the kinds of evidence that can be found therein. When we read along the archival grain, we approach the colonial archive as a genre, and are attentive to how the rules and norms of that genre shape the kinds of information that are included, as well as those that are left out. As Stoler puts it, there is benefit in "attending not only to colonialism's archival content, but to the principles and practices of governance lodged in particular archival forms."[28] Through the multiyear process of reading this archive, I gradually learned these principles, from how to interpret the annoyed marginalia of a colonial official on a memorandum, to the right way to sign off a letter to the editor of the *East African Standard*, to the fifteen or so words of Kiswahili to insert into your memoir for authenticity's sake. Unlike in Stoler's work, the archive is not the subject of this book; nevertheless, the process of reading along the grain has helped me understand how colonial discourse operated.

I'm also compelled by Anjali Arondekar's work on the colonial archive, which asks "Why does sexuality (still) seek its truth in the historical archive?"[29] I read her as resisting the tendency to look for a better, fuller, more expansive archive, one that will answer all our questions and offer us the "truth" about the past. Instead, Arondekar is interested in what the elisions and absences of the archive can tell us. She resists the urge to find sexual subjectivity and thinks instead about how the archive assembles a narrative around sexuality that does not necessarily cohere around an individual. Her method "redirects attention from the frenzied 'finding' of new archival sources to an understanding of the processes of subjectification made possible (and desirable) through the very idiom of the archive."[30] She argues that "the critical task lies in crafting an archival approach that articulates against the guarantee of recovery."[31] In thinking about archival research as a project of recovery, we lose the opportunity to meet the archive on its own terms, to adopt a certain critical view of the archive that refuses the premise/promise of complete knowledge or mastery—themselves imperial and empiricist ways of approaching information. Instead, my method embraces the fact that I am telling a partial story, in both senses of the word: the story is incomplete, and it also reflects the topics that I am partial to. Thus, this project retains a certain degree of faithfulness to the archive, even while critical of its forms and limitations.

In the final section of this introduction, I offer a brief overview of the history of colonial Kenya. Readers who are familiar with this history may wish to skip to the next chapter. As I'll show, Kenya's status as a rather strange settler state helped heighten and sharpen the discourse of primitive normativity as white settlers sought a way to present themselves as protectors of African populations even while divesting them of land and liberty.

Kenya: A Strange Settler State

The Kenyan settler state was both typical of settler colonies, in that the state consistently favored the interests and well-being of white settlers over all other populations, and distinctive in that, unlike other Anglophone African settler colonies like Rhodesia or South Africa, Kenya was governed from the Colonial Office in London, where the demands of the settlers had to be balanced against the state's duties as "trustees" of colonized peoples. This is why Kenya was, in the words of the historian John Lonsdale, Britain's "most troublesome African colony."[32]

In 1888, the Imperial British East African Company received its royal charter. The company quickly floundered, thwarted by the lack of transport, the dearth of mineral resources, and the lack of interest in their products expressed by the local population.[33] In 1895, the British government stepped in, establishing the East African Protectorate (EAP) and taking over the proposed railway project that would stretch from the coast to Uganda. Unable to induce local African populations to provide labor, the government imported indentured laborers from India to build the railroad.[34] By the time the Uganda Railroad was completed in 1901, just under thirty-two thousand Indians had been imported as laborers.[35] After the railway's completion in 1901, roughly seven thousand Indians remained in the protectorate, most becoming traders, artisans, owners of small shops (dukas), and clerks.[36] In this capacity, Kenyan Indians became extremely important to the colonial economy; Desh Gupta estimates that by 1903, 80 percent of the protectorate's capital was in Indian hands.[37] The importation of railway laborers was not, however, the only period of Indian migration; as Sana Aiyar points out, Indians in Kenya retained a connection to their homeland, participating in circular migratory patterns that sent them back and forth across the Indian Ocean.[38] The Indian population continued to grow throughout the colonial period, always outnumbering the other significant immigrant population—the Europeans.

In the earliest years of the protectorate, European migrants came primarily from the South. The first decade of the twentieth century saw a small wave of migration of South Africans (chiefly British South Africans) to East Africa, which M. P. K. Sorrenson accounts for as "a minor repercussion of the Anglo-Boer War and the post-war depression caused by the withdrawal of troops, a shortage of labour in the mines and the slow recovery of the war-torn economies."[39] A smaller migration of Boers occurred in 1907; these migrants tended to settle in the Uasin Gishu plateau, away from the administrative centers of the colony (first Mombasa, and after 1907, Nairobi). Colonists also arrived from Britain; in fact, the most vocal and politically influential Europeans in the colony, including Lord Delamere, Berkeley and Gailbraith Cole, Colonel Ewart Grogan, Lord Cranworth, and Lord Hindlip, emigrated from Britain. Regardless of national origin—whether from Britain, South Africa, or even America—white settlers in Kenya were known as "Europeans," a racial rather than geographic classification.

Kenyan Europeans had a vested interest in presenting a united front. Although there were real differences in social class and national origin within the white settler population, Kennedy notes, "colonists showed great reluctance to demonstrate their disagreements in public debate, preferring instead to resolve such matters through private negotiations between the government and special interest groups such as farmer and other occupational associations."[40] Furthermore, because the white settler population was so small, class divisions were not as rigorously enforced in social spaces like Nairobi's Muthaiga Club as they would have been in the metropole—a tendency that Kennedy characterizes as "a deliberate rejection of European social values."[41] Thus, he concludes, "If the claim of a homogenous white society was little more than a myth, then, it nevertheless proved an exceedingly potent one" because "by obscuring the genuine divisions between colonists, the myth of homogeneity, even classlessness, eased the social schizophrenia that troubled European immigrants" and provided a sense of racial solidarity.[42]

But what were the divisions between colonists that were papered over through this myth of homogeneity? The first key division was based on social class. While, as Kennedy notes, class divisions were less rigid in the context of the colony, there was nevertheless a consistent fear expressed by both settlers and the colonial government about the growth of a class of "poor whites." In fact, the colonial government actively discouraged the growth of such a group by creating financial obstacles to white settlement in Kenya. The Kenyan government did not offer assisted passage and set minimal capital requirements for settlement in desirable farming areas.[43] Because Kenyan Indians had an established presence as tradespeople, shop owners, and clerks, Kenya offered few employment opportunities for poor whites.[44] Even the major government-sponsored emigration program, the Soldier Settlement Scheme adopted after World War I, was designed to accommodate only the "better class" of migrants.[45] Although the scheme allowed 250 small farms to be distributed to veterans without a capital qualification, the majority of plots were sold to ex-soldiers who met a capital requirement of £500—a requirement that was almost immediately raised to £5000 by Governor Northey.[46] Such restrictions guaranteed that the scheme would recruit a population of "Young Officers and Old Public School Boys"—the target specified in a pamphlet promoting the Soldier Settlement Scheme.[47] Kenya also saw significant immigration by retired civil servants/officers from India and other African colonies: as Kennedy puts it, "The rising rate and progressive bent of income taxes and death duties, the declining number and increasing expense of servants, the spreading influence of technocratic and meritocratic values, the growing power of the working class" in Britain made former officers hesitant to return home.[48] By retiring to Kenya, ex-officers were able to maintain a lifestyle that was increasingly impossible at home.

In Kenya, the small population of poor whites became a matter of public concern far beyond their actual numbers or influence. As I will discuss more in chapter 4, poor whites were viewed as the most likely to reduce white "prestige" by behaving with either too much "familiarity" or too much cruelty toward non-white populations. As Brett Shadle notes, there was particular concern about poor white men "going native"—taking African wives and bearing multiracial children.[49] There was an ethnic dimension to this division as well: South Africans—especially but not exclusively those of Boer origins—were considered particularly prone to such misbehavior. Many of the earliest European migrants to the colony came from South Africa. Despite the fact that most of these migrants were British South Africans, they tended to be to be lumped in with Boers. Dane Kennedy quotes a colonial administrator's summary of the situation: "English people think that the majority of the lower class Afrikanders [here meaning British South Africans] have all the vices of the Dutch without any of their redeeming qualities."[50] As the administrator's statement indicates, South African origin was frequently conflated with lower class status.[51] In fact, most South African immigrants *were* poorer than British-born immigrants, at least in part because they were able to enter the colony by walking through the borders. Potential immigrants from Britain, meanwhile, had to satisfy a capital qualification as well as pay for their transportation to the colony. Kenyan South Africans tended to congregate together and were not politically influential; only a few families, like the Cloetes, became important figures in the Kenyan political scene. Afrikaners who did not own property and instead worked as farm laborers were deemed particularly suspect.[52] Kenyan South Africans were also associated with the troubled racial dynamics of their home country, an example that Kenyan officials were determined to avoid. The existence of a population of poor whites in South Africa was viewed as causing a number of problems and was to be avoided at all costs. In fact, Europeans who threatened to become dependent on the state were classified as "Distressed British Subjects" and deported from the colony.[53] These measures were largely successful in preventing the growth of a substantial class of poor whites. Yet the specter of poor whites played a disproportionate role in colonial rhetoric.

The other major divergence within the European population was that between settlers and officials. As will be discussed further in chapter 3, Kenya adopted a policy of "Native Paramountcy" in 1923, which declared that the interests of the African majority must be prioritized in colonial policy. The Colonial Office proved a thorn in the side of settler interests, checking some of their more draconian aspirations and maintaining—at least in theory—an interest in the welfare of its African subjects. Yet this distinction can be easily overstated—many officials were sympathetic to settler interests, and, as noted previously, many of them became settlers themselves on retirement. Settlers also proved adept at advocating for their own interests. Almost as soon as European settlement began, settlers joined together to create organizations that would advocate for their own interests—the most influential being the Convention of Associations, formed in 1910.[54] While settlers consistently pressed for policies that decreased African geographic mobility, robbed Africans of ancestral homelands, and impressed Africans into labor, they claimed to do so in the service of Africans. As Shadle puts it, "paternalism would become one of the defining features of settler thinking: it was both a duty to civilize Africans and emotionally and psychologically pleasurable to do so."[55] Thus, Kenyan settlers presented themselves as trustees of African welfare, even while advocating for policies that actively harmed African people.

What were these policies? First, whites enjoyed disproportionate political power in the colony. Europeans dominated representation in the colony's Legislative Council (or LegCo); in 1919, Europeans elected eleven members to the LegCo, while Asians elected just two members, and Arabs and Africans were represented by a (white) nominated member. While the LegCo members only had the ability to advise the governor on policy decisions, their perspectives were taken quite seriously. There was even the occasional threat of white rebellion, as discussed in relation to the Indian Crisis in chapter 3.

Additionally, a number of discriminatory policies limited African access to land, coerced Africans into working as laborers on white-owned farms, and required Africans to perform communal labor for projects that chiefly benefited white settlers. The Crown Lands Ordinance of 1903 set the stage for an appropriation of African lands by white settlers, allowing Crown lands to be leased to European settlers for a period of ninety-nine years and defining African land rights in terms of occupation.[56] At the time, Indigenous African peoples were recovering from a famine, smallpox, and an outbreak of rinderpest that killed large numbers of cattle; Luise White estimates that these forces killed as much as 70 percent of the population of central Kenya.[57] The decimated population of both people and livestock meant that many areas of grazing land that had historically been used by central Kenyans were unoccupied and, hence, deemed to be up for grabs by the colonial government. Beginning in 1904, the government began moving Africans into "Native Reserves," areas of (usually substandard) land set aside for the use of Africans. Reserves also segregated

Africans into "tribal" populations, solidifying ethnic divisions that were considerably more fluid prior to colonization.[58]

With Africans funneled into Native Reserves, their former homelands were opened for European occupation. Another Crown Lands Ordinance in 1915 defined the reserves as Crown land and prevented Africans from selling this land. This ordinance also gave the governor the power to veto the sale or lease of land in the highlands to nonwhites.[59] Thus, well before the East African Protectorate became the colony of Kenya in 1920, the practice of segregated land ownership had been established in Kenya.[60]

Having established farms in the White Highlands, white settlers needed laborers to work on them. However, both the government and the settlers opposed the South African style of sharecropping (known as "Kaffir farming") on the basis that it would establish a landlord–tenant relationship between white landowners and African laborers. Such a relationship would allow Africans to develop tenant rights to the land. Instead, white farms in Kenya employed "squatted labor": African men and their families were allowed to live on white-owned farms and cultivate their own crops there in exchange for performing a set amount of labor (originally 180 days per annum but expanded to up to 270 days in 1937)[61] on the farmer's land. The practice of "Kaffir farming" was officially banned by the Resident Native (Squatters) Ordinance of 1918, thereby establishing a labor system that Ghai and McAuslan characterize as "involving elements of involuntary servitude."[62] Although a variety of ethnic groups performed waged labor for the European settlers, the farms of the highlands tended to be dominated by the Gikuyu, Nandi, and Kipsigis, with the majority of squatted labor being Gikuyu.[63] By 1930, more than 150,000 Gikuyu were squatting on white-owned farms.[64]

The Kenyan government bowed to settler pressure by establishing a number of measures to control and coerce labor. The "Hut Tax" (first levied in 1901) required African men over the age of sixteen to pay a set tax for each hut they occupied;[65] the tax thereby had the effect of forcing men to leave the reserves and enter into waged labor to pay the tax.[66] A number of Masters and Servants ordinances (imposed in 1906, 1910, and 1916) fined laborers who "deserted" their place of employment before the end of their contracts.[67] As David Anderson points out, the punitive element of Masters and Servants legislation had been eliminated in Britain by the Employers and Workmen Act of 1875: the introduction of Masters and Servants laws in East Africa thus "arose from a deliberate decision to impose a type of legislation that was by then already considered outmoded in the metropole."[68] The enforcement of the Masters and Servants legislation was enabled by another piece of legislation, the Registration of Natives Ordinance, passed in 1915 but not enforced until after the end of World War I. This ordinance required every African man over the age of fifteen to carry a pass containing identification and an employment record.[69] The pass was known as a kipande, meaning "a piece" in Kiswahili, for the small metal container in which it was carried (usually hung about the neck). Employers signed the laborer's kipande at the end of their contract; if an employee did not receive this signature at the end of his contract, the worker could not obtain work elsewhere.[70] Settlers could take advantage of this fact to silence disputes with their laborers: as Anderson notes, "By failing to sign a kipande, or by noting derogatory remarks on the document, an employer might entrap the worker or prevent him from moving to new employment."[71]

The colonial government also resorted to more direct methods of forcing Africans into waged labor. Most infamously, the Kenyan government required African men to do twenty-four days of unpaid "compulsory labor" each year, based on the belief that such labor had been "traditionally" exhorted by Indigenous leaders; importantly, any African man who had worked for wages during three months of the previous year was exempt.[72] This communal labor was generally used for public works projects such as building roads and bridges. However, in 1919, the Chief Native Commissioner John Ainsworth (acting on the orders of the governor) responded to settler pressure with a circular explicitly exhorting government officials and "Native Chiefs and Elders" to "exercise every possible lawful influence to induce able-bodied male natives to go into the labour field" working for white farmers.[73] Women and children were also to be encouraged to pitch in.

In a multitude of ways, then, the colonial state was set up to benefit white settlers and to control the mobility of Africans, forcing them into coercive forms of labor and denying them access to arable land. Yet, despite all of these advantages, settlers in Kenya still perceived themselves as disadvantaged because they remained under the restraining influence of the Colonial Office. While I don't think that primitive normativity is a discourse exclusive to Kenya, I do suspect that Kenya's peculiar status as a strange settler colony caused primitive normativity to become an especially prominent colonial narrative. Because the Colonial Office maintained that their primary duty was to protect the welfare and interests of Africans (the so-called "Doctrine of Native Paramountcy"), Kenyan settlers tried to present their claims to authority and power as *beneficial* to colonized populations. They did so in part, I argue, by positioning themselves as trustees of African sexual morality. Settlers presented the rural Native Reserves and white-owned farms as safe spaces where Africans would not be exposed to "civilized vice." They stressed, however, that urbanization, mission education, or political activity inevitably led to detribalization. Not coincidentally, African morals were deemed "safest" in those spaces where Africans served white settler interests most effectively. Keguro Macharia summarizes this dynamic neatly: "The myth of the vice-free, indigenous African became central to colonial governmentality. If contact with the wrong kinds of spaces and foreigners corrupted Africans, the argument went, then colonial powers had an obligation to safeguard Africans by policing their interactions and their movements."[74]

Ironically, then, Kenyan colonialism ascribed sexual normativity to the populations deemed least capable of self-rule, the groups with the least access to power. The groups with the most power, meanwhile, were those whose cultures were deemed most likely to contaminate and damage African sexual normativity. Kenyan discourses thus reversed the usual pairings of normativity/power and deviance/subjugation, but they did so in ways that not only reinforced but actually enabled white supremacy. How can we make sense of this seeming contradiction?

To sort out this puzzle, we need to account for and understand the role played by the notion of evolutionary time in imperial discourses of sexuality. The next chapter, "The Intellectual Roots of Primitive Normativity," provides some background on the intellectual history that allowed the narrative of primitive normativity to develop. In particular, I show how two fields, anthropology and sexology, both revised their notions of the "primitive" in the late nineteenth and early twentieth centuries. This reevaluation set the stage for the discourse of primitive normativity by tying sexual health to the "natural," "unrepressed" sexuality of "primitive" peoples. I also outline the response by one very prominent anthropologist, Jomo Kenyatta, a mission-educated African leader who would one day become the first president of independent Kenya.

Chapter 2, "Sleeping Dictionaries and Mobile Metropoles: Female (A) Sexuality in the Silberrad Scandal of 1908," tells the story of Hubert Silberrad, a colonial administrator who sparked a major controversy in Britain by taking three adolescent African girls as mistresses. Silberrad offered an interesting defense: he argued that he had not acted immorally, since he had followed local protocol by "purchasing" the girls from prominent

African men. Silberrad's defense points to an important feature of colonial discourse: while scholars of race and sexuality have shown that women of African descent have often been (and continue to be) depicted as hypersexual, in Kenya, colonial authorities argued that Africans viewed women as mere "chattel," and that as such they had no sexual agency at all. Riffing off the work of Hortense Spillers, I interrogate how African women were unsexualized through the rhetoric of "traditional" attitudes toward women.

From its birth at the turn of the twentieth century, Kenya was a colony with two competing groups of settlers. European settlers possessed the most land and power, but settlers from India arrived earlier and maintained much larger numbers throughout the colonial era. Chapter 3, "'Stoop Low to Conquer': Primitive Normativity and Trusteeship in the Kenyan 'Indian Crisis' of 1923," shows how Kenyan politics triangulated discourses of race and sexuality through the colony's major populations: white, African, and Indian. The chapter focuses on a political crisis that occurred in the early 1920s, when Kenyan Indians' demands for political equality with whites came to a head. The notion that Indians practiced deviant sexual behaviors that made them morally unfit to be colonial mentors to Africans formed a central tenet of the white response. Perhaps more surprisingly, Indians responded in kind, not only asserting their suitability to colonize a more "primitive" African race but also maintaining that it was white women, not Indians, who were morally and sexually depraved. As both Indians and white settlers framed their demands within the language of trusteeship, Africans were racialized by proxy as sexually normative, and therefore unready for political participation.

The next chapter, "White Peril: Rape, Race, and Contamination," examines cases of alleged interracial rape in the interwar period. In the 1920s, an official government commission was appointed to investigate the problem of "Black Peril," a term used across colonial spaces to refer to sexual assaults allegedly committed by Black or brown men on white women and children. The commission was prompted by several well-publicized cases where adult male African domestic servants were accused of assaulting white or Indian children. Scholars have long shown how such scares were used as a tool of white supremacy and have stressed that actual incidences of rape were not correlated to the outbreak of Black Perils. However, the Kenyan committee came to a surprising conclusion: not only was Black Peril deemed a rare occurrence in the colony, but in those cases where it *had* occurred, the commission thought white mothers were to blame. Both settlers and colonial officials advanced a narrative that I term "White Peril,"[75] which accused white women of teaching African men to desire deviant sexual acts by behaving with excessive familiarity toward their domestic servants.

A series of romance novels form the basis of chapter 5, "Queering Settler Romance: The Reparative Eugenic Landscape in Nora Strange's Kenyan Novels." Over the course of her lengthy career, Strange wrote more than fifty romance novels, almost half of which take place in Kenya. This chapter moves the geographic focus away from Kenya to consider how ideas about Kenya as a prelapsarian space traveled to the metropole and beyond. I argue that Strange's novels presented readers with an image of Kenya as a "eugenic landscape," a space that separated fit settlers from those who were not suited to carry on the colonial mission. The vibrant, "primitive" landscape of Kenya reinvigorated "overcivilized" settlers who had lost touch with their primitive sexual drives. Those settlers who were eugenically unfit, however, were eliminated through their interactions with the flora and fauna of Kenya. Strange thus funneled concerns about the "degeneration" of Europeans through narratives of the colony as a reparative space.

The final chapter of the book, "Eating the Other: Erotic Consumption in Anti–Mau Mau Discourse," brings us full circle. Having established that primitive normativity was viewed as an essential feature of "authentic" African life, the chapter shows how this discourse worked to discredit the Mau Mau rebels of the 1950s. In short, contemporaries argued that the deviant sexual practices that supposedly accompanied Mau Mau oathing rituals proved that they were not legitimate Africans. As such, their demands for land and freedom could be ignored.

Together, these chapters illustrate the discursive terrains in which primitive normativity was outlined as well as the ways in which this discourse served the goals of the settler state. By bringing the concept of evolutionary time into examinations of race, gender, and sexuality, we can understand how the normativity could function as a disenfranchising accusation, rather than an empowering affirmation.

ONE

The Intellectual Roots of Primitive Normativity

IN HER STUDY *Gone Primitive*, Marianna Torgovnick observes that "The primitive does what we ask it to do. Voiceless, it lets us speak for it. It is our ventriloquist's dummy—or so we like to think."[1] Her statement points to the plasticity of the notion of the "primitive"—which (like Blackness) can be molded and shaped to meet the needs of a particular time and place. In this chapter, I discuss the concept of the primitive and its evolution in the related fields of anthropology and sexology. In particular, I show how the concept of primitivity, as deployed in this field, is key to understanding sexuality as a temporal category. In short, around the turn of the twentieth century, primitivity came to be understood as a universal stage of human (sexual) development that all peoples must pass through on the way to "civilization." Primitive sexuality was no longer conceptualized as simply deviant, but instead came to represent a pure, unrepressed sexuality that survived in the subconscious of even the most "advanced" peoples.

The stakes of this conceptualization were different for different groups of people. For Europeans, the situation seemed to call for the shedding of "overcivilized" sexuality through a reconnection with the "primitive." For colonized peoples, however, the narrative emphasized the threat of contamination posed by more "civilized"—and hence more repressed—groups. Such concerns about the dangers of contamination were particularly useful in the space of the settler colony, where the language of "detribalization" was deployed to capture the threat that too-rapid "civilization" posed to African sexual and moral well-being.

Presenting African societies as vulnerable to contamination from "immigrant" cultures allowed settlers to position themselves as benevolent guardians of African welfare even while opposing the mandate to "civilize" African peoples. The notion that African societies must remain pristine and untouched challenged the teleology of colonialism; while the civilizing mission implied that colonized peoples would eventually be ready for self-rule, this valorization of untouched "primitive" cultures supported settlers' demand for minority rule over a permanently "backward" population. However, the discourse of African primitive normativity created the possibility for an alternative reading. In the final part of this chapter, I examine the work of the Kenyan ethnographer Jomo Kenyatta. By presenting Gikuyu sexuality as superior to that of Westerners, Kenyatta turned the discourse of African primitive normativity on its head, using it to support a Gikuyu nationalist agenda.

"Primitive Normativity" in Sexology and Anthropology

The discourse that I'm calling "primitive normativity" was the product of nineteenth-century evolutionary racism, a discourse that suffused many areas of colonial rhetoric but was especially prominent in anthropology. Importantly, the language of sex, gender, and sexuality was deeply imbricated in defining and delineating the "races." In fact, evolutionary theory held that one of the characteristics of a "primitive" people was a sexuality characterized by consistent access to sex and an absence of shame. What was also absent, however, were practices associated with "civilized" vice; prostitution, homosexuality, adultery, rape, and incest were all considered to be foreign to the most "primitive" societies. As Marc Epprecht explains, because Africans were viewed as being close to nature, "by definition this meant that they could neither be decadent nor exhibit social traits and behaviors that were assumed to come with a sophisticated level of culture."[2] African sexuality (as constructed by outsiders) was thus normative to the extent that it was deemed *appropriate to their stage of evolutionary development* and *absent of sexual neurosis*. Because, however, this normativity was explicitly tied to evolutionary "backwardness," it actually *reinforced* claims that "primitive" peoples needed to be colonized and controlled.

We can understand this better if we place the discourse of primitive normativity within the broader context of anthropological and sexological discourses. Over the course of the nineteenth and twentieth centuries, the notion that "primitive" populations ought to be preserved and protected emerged in several fields. First, by the mid-nineteenth century, British imperial policy had begun to move away from the rhetoric of a colonial "civilizing mission." While earlier imperialists had viewed colonized cultures as backward and in need of reform, the new philosophy of indirect rule used Indigenous institutions and leaders as instruments of imperial governments. Because of its reliance on Indigenous social structures, the philosophy of indirect rule sought to preserve rather than reform "native" cultures. Indirect rule developed in tandem with the notion of trusteeship, which envisioned colonized peoples as wards in the care of benevolent colonial guardians. As trustees of "native welfare," colonial powers had a responsibility to both protect Indigenous societies and prepare them for eventual self-rule.

These new approaches to imperialism were in turn tied to the development of anthropological thought over the course of the nineteenth and twentieth centuries. The idea that "primitive" peoples occupied an earlier stage of development than their European peers was particularly associated with the evolutionist school of anthropology. The evolutionists, led by Sir Edward Tylor, believed that all human societies progressed through various stages of development until they arrived at the civilized ideal.[3] The evolutionists favored the comparative method, which held that since all societies passed through the same stages in the same order, data gathered from "primitive" peoples in the present day could be used to reconstruct the past of more "civilized" peoples. As Celia Brickman explains, for evolutionists, "Human life was seen as evolving through time (if it was not to be weeded out by extinction) toward its evolutionary telos, the European masculine subject; the implication, so important for developments in anthropological and social theory, was that deviations from this normative end were represented as prior in evolutionary time."[4] The comparative method contained a built-in motivation for the preservation of "primitive societies"; to be useful as data, they needed to remain uncontaminated by more "advanced" cultures.

Around the turn of the century, anthropologists began to turn away from evolutionist narratives and question the notion that "mankind" was inevitably marching toward progress and perfection. This next generation of anthropologists grew up in a culture that was deeply concerned about the degeneration of the European population.[5] As Andrew and Harriet Lyons put it, at the turn of the century, "A current of pessimism about urbanization, industrialism, and social instability was reflected in the belief that modern society could unwittingly defeat the forces of natural selection and allow the undesirable elements that flourished in its unhealthy cities to reverse the tide of progress."[6]

World War I brought this pessimism to a head, as Europe's young men returned home physically and psychologically broken.[7] As the historian Henrika Kuklick writes, "The generation who lived through these changes regarded human nature as fundamentally irrational, and considered individual and social degeneration as just as natural as progress."[8]

This period also saw a drastic revision in anthropological visions of sexuality. For most of the nineteenth century, anthropologists had argued that the sexuality of "primitive" peoples was characterized by "primitive promiscuity," characterized by a lack of restrictions on sexual behavior and, hence, a hypersexual and excessive sexual culture.[9] However, at the turn of the century, a new vision of "primitive sexuality" emerged that evinced "a tendency to replace fictive images of lascivious savages with representations of primitives as either less highly sexed than civilized men and women, less imaginative in their exercise of the sexual function, or blocked by taboo or environmental restraints from the full exercise of their libidos."[10] Andrew and Harriet Lyons highlight the role of three thinkers, the British sexologist Havelock Ellis, the Finnish sociologist Edward Westermarck, and the English anthropologist Ernest Crawley, in this turn—indicating that the consensus was shifting across various social sciences. Westermarck maintained that the notion of primitive promiscuity was based on faulty evidence collected by missionaries and travelers rather than trained scholars. When promiscuous behaviors *did* appear in "primitive" societies, he hypothesized that it was the result of contact with "civilization" in the forms of slavery and colonization. Furthermore, Westermarck argued that because Europeans married later than their "primitive" peers, *they* were more likely to become promiscuous: "Irregular connexions between the sexes," he wrote, "have on the whole established a tendency to increase along with the progress of civilization."[11] Ellis and Crawley both read Westermarck's work and produced studies that emphasized sexual restraint in "primitive" societies rather than excess. This rejection of the "primitive promiscuity" hypothesis did not, however, undercut claims to European superiority. Counterintuitively, while "primitive" peoples might have a healthier sexuality than Europeans, the association of deviance and degeneration with civilization actually meant that the "natural" sexuality of primitive peoples was offered as evidence of their backwardness.[12]

The work of these thinkers, especially Ellis, was deeply influential on one of the most important anthropologists of the twentieth century. Bronisław Malinowski was one of the leading figures of the functionalist school of anthropology, which tended to account for differences between peoples in terms of culture rather than race. Lyons and Lyons have noted certain commonalities between the writings of Malinowksi and Ellis: in the work of both, "Savage sexuality is free, healthy, and somewhat monotonous. Civilization, affecting the pliant individual in many ways, has brought with it better maternal care, more variation, and more passion, but this sophistication has clearly exacted a toll in the form of unsuccessful and unhappy experiments."[13]

The idea of a "monotonous" sexuality underscored the belief that certain kinds of deviant sexual acts did not occur among the most "primitive" peoples: the sex lives of "primitive" peoples were thus restricted to procreative sex between opposite-sex partners. Yet Malinowski believed that the peoples he studied enjoyed greater sexual freedom in that they were able to engage in (heterosexual) sex from an earlier age and had greater knowledge of sexuality than their European peers—this freedom, he believed, accounted for the rarity of homosexuality among the Trobrianders. Thus, Malinowksi agreed with Ellis that it was possible to "learn a great deal of healthy stuff from savages."[14] In fact, as Marianna Torgovnick argues, Malinowksi, Ellis, and Freud "sought the universal truth about human nature and conceived of primitive societies as the testing ground, the laboratory, the key to that universal truth."[15]

Not surprisingly, then, Malinowksi also echoed discourses of the danger of "detribalization," seeing it as a threat to the sexual health of "primitive" peoples. He advocated for the preservation of "traditional" societies and was particularly opposed to missionaries' attempts to reform the sexual practices of colonized peoples.[16] He suggested, for instance, that the segregation of boys and girls in Melanesian missionary schools had the effect of promoting homosexuality; interference with Indigenous sexual and gendered norms might have the unfortunate effect of introducing previously unknown forms of deviance.[17] As George Stocking notes, Malinowski believed that "the passage from savagery to civilization was also a passage away from a relatively easy and harmonious genital sexuality."[18]

Two elements of these discourses are key. First, anthropologists, sexologists, and sociologists increasingly believed that "primitive" sexuality eliminated (or at least dramatically minimized) the tendency toward "deviant" sexual practices, signified especially by same-sex sexuality. The second is that these experts argued that interference with "primitive" cultures was likely to introduce previously unknown sexual foibles into colonized communities.

This academic discourse in turn shaped approaches to colonial administration, particularly since many academics argued that their work was relevant and important precisely because it would guarantee the effective administration of colonial possessions. Thus, while Malinowski believed that the study of "savages" could yield dividends for European sexual health, he did not reject colonialism. On the contrary, he argued that anthropological research was necessary for the proper execution of indirect rule. Although officials in the Colonial Office and leading missionaries like J. H. Oldham tended to embrace the functionalist point of view, the staff on the ground in British Africa "developed a distinctive variant of Evolutionist anthropology to rationalize and guide their consistent managerial practices."[19] In part, this was because of its utility: as Kuklick writes, "Colonial officials were able to use evolutionist arguments to resist whatever innovations they saw as threatening to their authority; primitive peoples would suffer cultural degeneration unless their progress was negotiated very gradually."[20] Colonial authorities thus used anthropology to present "detribalization" as a threat to the well-being of "native" peoples. Indeed, Seligman went so far as to suggest that attempts to "raise them [primitive peoples] to a higher cultural level . . . have generally led to their disappearance."[21] Thus, the reevaluation of "primitive" societies as in need of protection and preservation neatly aligned with concerns about the potential dangers of detribalization.

Simultaneously, experts increasingly stressed the potential that "civilization" might be damaging to the health, well-being, and even morality of *European* peoples: indeed, in 1935 the anthropologist R. R. Marett raised the question of "whether it is possible to be both civilized and good."[22] The parallels between new anthropological visions of "primitive" sexuality and anxieties about European degeneration were not coincidental—rather, they worked in tandem.

In his study *Faces of Degeneration*, Daniel Pick explores the "interlocking languages of progress and degeneration" that characterized medical and biological discourses during the nineteenth century.[23] Increasingly concerned with the eugenic consequences of urbanization and poverty, "Evolutionary scientists, criminal anthropologists and medical psychiatrists confronted themselves with the apparent paradox that civilisation, science and economic progress might be the catalyst of, as much as the defence against, physical and social pathology."[24] Nowhere was this paradox illustrated more clearly than in Freudian psychoanalysis. Freud echoed the preoccupation of anthropologists and administrators with the nature and value of "primitive" societies. In turn, during the 1910s and particularly the 1920s, anthropologists of a variety of schools (including Malinowski) applied psychoanalytic theory to their work. The connections between Freud's vision of sexual development and evolutionist notions of cultural development are crucial to understanding the concept of "primitive normativity." By analyzing Freud's ambivalent view of civilization, we begin to see how colonial discourses could present "primitive" sexuality as simultaneously aberrant and ideal.

As several studies have pointed out, evolutionist anthropology provided the foundation on which Freud built his theories of human sexuality.[25] In particular, there was a strong parallel between Freud's idea that individuals transitioned through a prescribed series of sexual stages on their way to maturity and the evolutionist narrative of a universal progression through civilizational stages. Freud borrowed ideas from several major nineteenth-century evolutionist and eugenicist thinkers, notably Sir Edward Burnett Tylor, Herbert Spencer, Jean-Baptiste Lamarck, and Ernst Haeckel. From Tylor, he adopted the comparative method and the doctrine of survivals. As discussed earlier, the comparative method proposed that, since all human societies progressed through the same civilizational stages in the same order, observations about the lives of "primitive" peoples in the modern era could be extrapolated back to the history of "civilized peoples." Data about twentieth-century Africans, for example, could tell anthropologists about how pre-Roman Britons lived. The comparative hypothesis informed Freud's belief that the psyche of the "modern" adult European subject represented a more advanced evolutionary stage than that of a "primitive" subject, either in the European past or the non-European present.

The second concept Freud borrowed from Tylor, the doctrine of survivals, suggests that even when a society progressed out of a lower stage of development, some of the remnants of the earlier stage lived on in their culture. Tylor cited the presence of superstitions in modern cultures as "survivals" from an earlier era; superstitions indicated that "the civilization of the people they have been observed among must have derived from an earlier state, in which the proper home and meaning of these things are to be found."[26] Freud applied this doctrine of survivals to his conception of the subconscious, arguing that under certain conditions a subject stepped back into a more primitive mode of being that lingered in the subconscious. Regression was thus a historical action, one that moved the subject back in evolutionary time.

Building on both Spencer and Lamarck, the zoologist Ernst Haeckel outlined a concept that would prove essential to Freudian psychoanalysis: the recapitulation hypothesis. In his study *Generelle Morphologie*, first published in 1866, Haeckel proposed that the embryo of an individual organism repeated the history of its species during its development. The gills present in a human embryo, therefore, were not only fishlike but in fact indicated that the embryo was passing through the fish stage of human evolution. In keeping with the idea of the heritability of acquired traits, Haeckel suggested that "each newly acquired characteristic would be added on to, and henceforth preserved in, the ontological development of the next generation."[27] Embryos thus possessed the cumulative intellectual heritage of their species.

The recapitulation hypothesis is key to understanding how Freud tied the "primitive" to infant sexuality. As a child passed through the stages of sexual development, he/she reenacted the sexual development of their culture, thereby recapitulating the past. Provided that the individual progressed successfully through the oral, anal, phallic, and latent stages of sexual development, the individual would finally arrive at mature genital sexuality. As the child passed through these sexual stages, he/she was simultaneously passing from a primitive to a civilized worldview; Freud maintained that the psychic arrangement of a "primitive" adult was analogous to that of a European child. In some cases, a subject regressed to an earlier stage of sexual (and therefore civilizational) development, becoming neurotic. Applying anthropological theories to sexual development, Freud developed his own comparative hypothesis: as Brickman writes, "Once it could be taken as established that neurotics = children = primitives, taboo and other cultural expressions of so-called primitive societies could be explained with recourse to data from neurotic patients and children and vice versa, so that anthropological data concerning children and neurotics could each provide solutions to the questions posed by the other."[28]

Importantly, although an oral fixation, for instance, would be a sign of regression and psychic ill health in a European adult, an oral fixation was entirely appropriate for an infant; in fact, the oral fixation was necessary not only for the child's survival (since it needed to focus its energies on breastfeeding) but also for its sexual development. A sexual practice, therefore, was rarely objectionable in itself; it only became problematic when the practice was engaged in at a stage when the subject should have progressed beyond it.

Thus, while Freud clearly believed that "primitive" peoples possessed a less advanced sexual personality, he did not necessarily see this as problematic. For this reason, I would contest Brickman's statement that, in Freudian thought, "because pathology and perversion, too, were defined as regressions to or arrests at earlier stages on the developmental scale, racial/cultural difference could become psychoanalytically legible *only* as perversion or pathology."[29] I make this point not to minimize the racial implications of Freudian thought; clearly Freud believed deeply in the superiority of European cultures to those of non-Western peoples. But I would argue that Freud understood race as an essentially temporal category, a starting point from which European subjects would depart and progress. Ultimately, he was simply not very interested in racialized people *except* in their capacity to theorize European psychic and sexual development. Europeans could be deviant and perverse and pathological; racialized populations could only ever be "primitive."

Freud was also prominent among the thinkers who worried about the effect of "civilization" on the sexual health of his patients. In fact, Freudian thought revolved around a central tension: the suppression of the sex drive was both essential and potentially dangerous for the European subject. Freud believed that "progress" was only possible when subjects redirected their sex drive to cultural production—what Freud called sublimation: he explained that "The forces that can be employed for cultural activities are thus to a great extent obtained through the suppression of what are known as the *perverse* elements of sexual excitation."[30] However, sublimation created the potential for perversion or neurosis. Perversion occurred when a subject failed to pass through the stages of sexual development, becoming stuck in an earlier stage. Interestingly, Freud distinguished between perverts and inverts (homosexuals), even suggesting that "The constitution of people suffering from inversion—the homosexuals—is, indeed, often distinguished by their sexual instinct's possessing a special aptitude for cultural sublimation."[31] In other words, inverts were uniquely skilled at redirecting their sexual energies toward cultural production—making them, perhaps, uniquely civilized. Freud blamed civilization for "the harmful suppression of the sexual life of civilized peoples (or classes) through the 'civilized' sexual morality prevalent in them."[32]

In particular, Freud worried about the impact of the moral standard that demanded sexual abstinence outside of marriage. While he admitted that "for a few specially favourably organized natures," the efforts to remain abstinent might "'steel' the character," Freud maintained that in general abstinence tended "to produce well-behaved weaklings who later become lost in the great mass of people that tends to follow, unwillingly, the leads given by strong individuals."[33] Paralleling the fear of "detribalization" in African societies, Freud believed neurosis was particularly likely to occur in cases where the subject was too rapidly exposed to civilization: "the physician finds food for thought," he wrote, "in observing that those who succumb to nervous illness are precisely the offspring of fathers who, having been born of rough but vigorous families, living in simple, healthy, country conditions, had successfully established themselves in the metropolis, and in a short space of time had brought their children to a high level of culture."[34]

Freud was not alone in this belief about civilization's negative effect on sexual health. The historian Marc Epprecht has discussed the larger context of this narrative in his study *Heterosexual Africa?*[35] Both Carl Jung and Marie Bonaparte believed that the study of "primitive" peoples could be used to cure the sexual dysfunctions of Europeans. As Epprecht puts it, Bonaparte believed that psychoanalysts could "reveal the innate human sexual instinct unencumbered by the niceties of etiquette, guilt, or repression" by studying "primitive" peoples, thereby helping "to make civilized people happier and more fulfilled in their sex and emotional lives."[36] In fact, as Bodil Folke Frederiksen has shown, she applied this theory to herself in a rather extreme fashion. Bonaparte, who had been a patient of Freud's in the 1920s, believed herself to be a sexually dysfunctional and "masculine" woman, unable to achieve the mature vaginal orgasm.[37] (The fact that her husband, Prince George of Greece and Denmark, was gay probably didn't help matters.)[38] In 1935, Malinowski (who had taught Bonaparte's son Peter) arranged a meeting between Bonaparte and his student Jomo (Johnstone)[39] Kenyatta, a leading defender of the practice of clitoridectomy among the Gikuyu. Bonaparte was intrigued by clitoridectomy, but not for the nationalist reasons that inspired Kenyatta. Rather, she theorized "that because of African free sexuality and possibly because of the prevalence of clitoridectomy, African women might be better 'vaginalized', as she expressed it, and thus more feminine than European women."[40] Bonaparte subsequently underwent several operations to move her clitoris closer to her vaginal canal in an effort to cure her supposed sexual dysfunction, before ultimately deciding that psychoanalysis was a more effective treatment.[41]

As the case of Marie Bonaparte shows, the discourse of primitive normativity was so compelling that "primitive" sexual practices could be envisioned as a cure for modern sexual disorders. It is particularly striking that Bonaparte embraced clitoridectomy, a practice targeted by missionaries as emblematic of the "barbarity" of East African cultures. The focus of psychoanalysis on the potentially damaging effect of "civilization" on sexual health created room for the possibility that "primitive" sexuality might be healthier and more "natural" than that of evolutionarily "advanced" peoples. Yet, because this idea of African primitive normativity was firmly lodged in an intellectual tradition of evolutionary racial thought, the association with normativity did not enable Africans to access power. Quite the contrary: because sexual deviance was seen as a product of civilization, the complete lack of deviance that supposedly characterized African sexualities also signaled their political immaturity. It was thus possible for African sexualities to be conceptualized as both backward and normative. Visions of African sexuality were never based on careful empirical data on the actual sexual practices of African people or the place of sexuality in their worldviews. Rather, this was a vision crafted in European minds to meet European needs. In the nineteenth century, the image of a pathological, hypersexual African Other had proved useful in legitimizing the slave trade and the extension of imperialism. In the twentieth century, a vision of an instinctual, natural African sexuality proved equally useful to the maintenance of African empires.

To what extent, though, did these anthropological discourses filter down to Kenyan settlers and officials? Primitivism as a movement—in art, music, and literature—presented the new vision of "primitive man" to a broad population. As Marianna Torgovnick has shown, a preoccupation with the "primitive" appeared in a variety of formats, from the paintings of Picasso and Gauguin to the explosion of jazz to the popular Tarzan novels.[42] These genres solidified the "primitive" as an object of interest and exposed a broad audience to the new vision of the "primitive" as a source of health and vibrancy. Katherine Luongo has also described the development of an "anthro-administrative complex," whereby colonial officials created amateur anthropological studies of the peoples they governed.[43] Anthropological discourses were created not only in the metropole but also on the ground in Kenya—and this brand of anthropology was explicitly geared toward producing knowledge about colonized peoples so as to better control them.

The language of psychoanalysis shows up to a surprising degree in colonial sources—the language of repression, complexes, and sublimation appears with some frequency. But the most common way that this anthropological discourse filtered down to the average Kenyan European was through the language of detribalization, broadly used by settlers, officials, missionaries, and commentators on virtually all points of the political spectrum. With its contention that too-rapid progress presented a threat to the moral well-being of Africans, the discourse of detribalization neatly encapsulated the notion that sexuality was temporally and spatially bound. Deeply indebted to the psychological and anthropological narratives described previously in this chapter, the language of detribalization proved an enduring and accessible discourse in Kenyan colonial history. It allowed Kenyan whites to argue that any African who left the space of the Native Reserve or white-owned farms could be exposed to elements of "civilization" that they were psychologically unprepared to deal with. The result would be their moral contamination and degradation. As I will discuss further in chapter 6, this discourse reached its apogee in the Corfield Report, the official explanation for the Mau Mau rebellion, which argued that the rebels suffered from a psychological disorder brought on by detribalization. Far from being a new innovation, the Corfield Report was in many ways the logical conclusion of the discourse of detribalization that had flourished throughout the colonial period.

However, this was not the only possible use of these discourses. The next section examines the work of Kenya's most famous ethnographer, Jomo Kenyatta, showing how he molded the language of primitive normativity to serve a different set of goals. Rather than using the language of detribalization to support white supremacy, Kenyatta deployed it to support Gikuyu nationalism. However, his approach was still deeply conservative—Kenyatta's use of the discourse of primitive normativity was fundamentally concerned with keeping wayward Gikuyu (especially women) in their place. Kenyatta's repurposing of the discourse of primitive normativity is thus an early example of a discourse surrounding gender and sexuality that has come to predominate in postcolonial Kenya, one that polices the behaviors, movement, and liberty of women and sexual minorities in the service of upholding "traditional" African values.

Primitive Normativity Revised

Jomo Kenyatta, who would eventually become the first president of independent Kenya, was one of several famous students of Bronisław Malinowski. Both the author Elspeth Huxley and the Africanist scholar

Margery Perham also took Malinowski's seminars and went on to produce important texts.[44] Kenyatta was a mission-educated Kenyan African who would become a prominent Gikuyu nationalist. He was also the first African to write an ethnography of his own people, *Facing Mount Kenya* (1938). As Bruce Berman notes, in *Facing Mount Kenya*, Kenyatta "invented a homogenous Kikuyu society that spoke with one voice."[45] Kenyatta adopted the position as spokesman and defender of Gikuyu culture. What has not been previously recognized is the degree to which Kenyatta was invested in presenting the Gikuyu as having an exemplarily *normative* sexual culture. Kenyatta's training as an anthropologist allowed him to build the case for Gikuyu sexual normativity using a discursive framework familiar to colonial Kenya, but his political mandate was much different: Kenyatta asserted the inherent worthiness—indeed, superiority—of Gikuyu culture through the medium of sexuality and used this narrative to promote a particular vision of Gikuyu independence.

Kenyatta was far from alone in embracing sexual and gendered conservatism. As John Lonsdale has shown, he was part of a broader group of mission-educated elites who viewed unruly women as a sign of the times. Urban women and prostitutes (often viewed as one and the same) were seen as a particular threat to the health and well-being of the incipient Gikuyu nation. Leaders in the Kikuyu Central Association and contributors to Kenyatta's paper *Muigwithania* echoed colonial concerns about the danger of urban space and detribalization when they warned that "women who went to school, stayed overnight in rural trading centres, or worst of all, sold vegetables in Nairobi" were at risk of becoming prostitutes.[46] Gender normativity, in the form of polygynous marriage and female subordination, was deemed key to the health of the Gikuyu people.[47] What Kenyatta added to this rhetoric was the use of functionalist anthropology to make his case in a language that the colonizer might be compelled to understand.

Kenyatta and Malinowski first met in 1934 when Kenyatta was in London serving as a representative of the anticolonial Kikuyu Central Association; a year later, Kenyatta matriculated at the London School of Economics.[48] Several scholars have described how Kenyatta deployed his anthropological training to advance a particular set of interests. Kenyatta viewed functionalist anthropology as an effective method to defend Indigenous culture; as Stocking puts it, "Kenyatta was able to find in functionalism a justification for the value of traditional cultural practices that Europeans deemed 'savage and barbaric, worthy only of heathens who live in perpetual sin,'" especially the practice of clitoridectomy.[49] As

Bruce Berman argues, *Facing Mount Kenya* was an explicitly political text (despite Malinowski's contention that the "definite political bias" that characterized Kenyatta's early work had been almost "entirely eradicated by the constant impact of detached scientific method on his mental processes").[50] Berman focuses especially on Kenyatta's representation of Gikuyu land ownership, his construction of the Gikuyu as a homogenous, united people, and his presentation of himself as the appropriate representative of the Gikuyu community.[51] As Simon Gikandi puts it, "If the institutions of colonial knowledge were busy inventing tradition for the colonized, members of the African elite could not be blamed for wanting to become agents of this invention."[52] As I will show here, the traditions that Kenyatta was invested in were deeply imbricated in the discourse of African sexual normativity. Kenyatta's discussions of sexuality, specifically clitoridectomy, premarital sexual practices, masturbation, hetero-/homosexuality, and polygyny, were all focused on proving the superior sexual normativity of the Gikuyu people.

In *Facing Mount Kenya*, Kenyatta also devoted considerable energy to a defense of clitoridectomy (and irua—the coming of age ceremony during which both boys and girls were circumcised), arguing that the practice was central to the "tribal psychology" of the Gikuyu, "the very essence of an institution which has enormous educational, social, moral, and religious implications."[53] Here Kenyatta "defended the positive function of initiation rites, particularly clitoridectomy, in direct response to missionary attacks on their supposed barbarity and encouragement of sexual promiscuity by claiming instead that they actually turned children into socially and sexually responsible and disciplined adults."[54]

While missionaries suggested that circumcision (and the rituals surrounding it) was an immoral practice that promoted promiscuity, Kenyatta's chapter "Sex Life among Young People" argued that irua was the time when young people learned "the matters relating to rules and regulations governing sexual indulgence."[55] In particular, initiates learned an intimate practice that protected their sexual and mental health: "In order not to suppress entirely the normal sex instinct, the boys and girls are told that in order to keep good health they must acquire the technique of practicing a certain restricted form of intercourse, called ombani na ngweko (platonic love and fondling). This form of intimate contact between young people is considered right and proper and the very foundation stone upon which to build a race morally, physically and mentally sound. For it safeguards the youth from nervous and psychic maladjustments."[56]

Ngweko became a central pillar in Kenyatta's depiction of Gikuyu sexual normativity. As Keguro Macharia has pointed out, Kenyatta produced a form of "counter-discourse" that "indicts Europe's degeneration, all the while praising unassailable black sexual propriety."[57] The influence of psychoanalytic theory is clear in Kenyatta's description of ngweko as a practice that prevents "psychic maladjustments" by providing an outlet for sexual instincts.[58] More to the point, ngweko is presented as a practice central to the continuation of the Gikuyu, as both a metaphorical reproduction of Gikuyu culture and a modality facilitating the literal reproduction of the Gikuyu people. Quoting Macharia again, "as a heteronormative practice that is not immediately hetero-reproductive, ombani na ngweko binds the very concept of futurity to the promise of reproduction, and in so doing produces ethnicity as a hetero-promise. One becomes and retains full ethnicity in fulfilling this hetero-promise to reproduce."[59]

Importantly, Kenyatta also presented self-control as key to the practice of ngweko. He noted that many missionaries viewed ngweko as sinful due to their mistaken belief that it must involve sexual intercourse. Non-Christianized Gikuyu, however, "find it difficult to understand this sort of European puritanism, for a Gikuyu man has been taught from childhood to develop the technique of self-control in the matter of sex, which enables him to sleep in the same bed with a girl without necessarily having sexual intercourse."[60] "Since a white man would not be able to restrain himself under similar circumstances," he continued, they falsely assumed that Africans could not either.[61] Here Kenyatta presented Gikuyu men as possessing that quintessential characteristic of "civilization"—self-control—and possessing it in greater measure than their European peers.

In keeping with Freudian stadial sexuality, Kenyatta described Gikuyu sexual development as the stately progression through a number of stages, culminating in a universal reproductive heterosexuality. In his discussion of masturbation, for instance, he emphasized that it was acceptable only during a specific stage of development. While he noted that "before initiation it is considered right and proper for boys to practice masturbation as a preparation for their future sexual activities," after irua, masturbation was taboo.[62] A boy who continued masturbating after initiation "would be looked upon as clinging to a babyish habit, and be laughed at, because owing to the free sex-play which is permitted among young people, there is now no need to indulge in it."[63] Kenyatta described masturbation as "preparation" for heterosexual reproductive intercourse, a practice that was helpful and healthy at a particular stage of sexual development. Yet once a new form of sexual play (ngweko) is opened up, any boy "clinging to a baby-ish habit" would be mocked. Again, Kenyatta stressed the ways in which Gikuyu sexual culture facilitated the progression through sexual stages and prevented regression to an earlier stage not only through social disapproval but also by offering another outlet for sexual energies. While the European passed through a latency stage, repressing sexual instincts with potentially disastrous results, the Gikuyu male attained heterosexual maturity by pro-gressing through a series of culturally sanctioned sexual outlets.[64]

Importantly, Kenyatta specified a male subject in his discussion of mas-turbation: he noted, in fact, that the Gikuyu frowned on masturbation by girls, and even suggested that one motive of "trimming the clitoris [is] to prevent girls from developing sexual feelings around that point."[65] Like Bonaparte, Kenyatta suggested that clitoridectomy prevented female fri-gidity by restricting sexual pleasure to the vagina rather than the clitoris; however, while Freudians like Bonaparte would see clitoral orgasm as a precursor to vaginal maturity, Kenyatta suggested that clitoridectomy pre-vented the development of clitoral sexuality at all.[66]

When Gikuyu men and women did reach the stage of life in which sex-ual intercourse was permissible, Kenyatta maintained that they practiced a sexuality that was strictly heterosexual and geared toward reproduction. As Marc Epprecht points out, Kenyatta "categorically denies the existence of same-sex sexuality in Gikuyu tradition."[67] But in fact, Kenyatta went much further, emphatically maintaining that "In the Gikuyu community any form of sexual intercourse other than *the natural form*, between men and women *acting in the normal way*, is out of the question. It is consid-ered taboo even to have sexual intercourse with a woman in any position except *the regular one*, face to face."[68]

Epprecht is right to note that Kenyatta described Gikuyu sexuality as strictly heterosexual: Kenyatta claimed that "the practice of homosexuality is unknown among the Gikuyu" because "the freedom of intercourse al-lowed between young people of opposite sex makes it unnecessary, and encourages them to acquire experience which will be useful in married life."[69] Like Kenyan white settlers and administrators, Kenyatta suggested that there was no need for homosexuality in an environment where the sex drive was not repressed. Yet Kenyatta also asserted a broader Gikuyu sexual normativity even within heterosexual practice; his insistence on the *normal, natural, regular* nature of sexual intercourse (to the extent that he claimed Gikuyu only had sex in the missionary position) echoed the broader narrative of primitive normativity.

Kenyatta also responded to missionaries' criticism of the practice of polygyny in Gikuyu culture, presenting it as a way of ensuring reproduction and protecting women. While he maintained that the purpose of Gikuyu courtship was to foster "mutual love and gratification of sexual instinct between two individuals," after marriage, "it becomes a duty to produce children, and sexual intercourse is looked upon as an act of production and not merely as a gratification of a bodily desire."[70] Polygyny allowed men to have more children, another nod to his claim that Gikuyu sexuality was purely reproductive. He also countered the missionaries' belief that "African women are regarded as mere chattels of the men" who were purchased by their future husbands with a detailed description of Gikuyu courtship, emphasizing the fact that girls had to consent to be married.[71]

Contradictorily, however, Kenyatta also advocated polygyny as a method of social control over women's bodies and desires, using it as evidence of the value of Gikuyu culture. Because polygyny "provide[d] that all women must be under the protection of men," it prevented the problem of surplus women; "there is no term in the Gikuyu language," he wrote, "for 'unmarried' or 'old maids.'"[72] Early marriage had an additional advantage: he claimed that "in order to avoid prostitution (no word exists for 'prostitution' in the Gikuyu language) all women must be married in their 'teens, i.e. fifteen to twenty."[73] Interestingly, the claim that no word for prostitution existed in various Kenyan African languages was also consistently circulated by settlers and administrators. Linguistic absence thus served as evidence of sexual normativity.

Kenyatta's work has been primarily understood as a defense of Gikuyu cultural norms and, hence, as a challenge to colonial hierarchies. What has not been recognized is the degree to which Kenyatta conducted this defense according to the terms already laid out by the discourse of primitive normativity. We can see this most directly in his references to the dangers of "detribalization,"[74] in his assertion of the absence of "deviant" sexual practices in "traditional" Gikuyu societies, and his reliance on a stadial model of sexual development borrowed directly from Freud (and, by extension, from evolutionary anthropology with its attendant correlation of race to sexual habit). Kenyatta thereby crafted a definition of Gikuyu identity that tied cultural authenticity to adherence to a set of sexual norms.

Finally, Kenyatta's description of Gikuyu sexual practices expressed a brand of cultural conservatism that echoes more recent African denunciations of "deviant" sexual practices as essentially un-African. By joining cultural authenticity to sexual normativity, Kenyatta anticipated current statements by some African leaders that exclude sexual "deviants" from the imagined community. As Sylvia Tamale notes, "The sad, tired but widely accepted myth that homosexuality is un-African has been valorized and erected on the altar of falsehood time after time."[75] Because the discourse of primitive normativity defined the worth and value of Indigenous societies in relation to a set of sexual practices, even an explicitly anticolonial text like *Facing Mount Kenya* ultimately fails to extricate African "authenticity" from a Western rubric.

While primitive normativity was a discourse developed by colonizing groups, Kenyatta's work emphasizes how African subjects were both influenced by and folded into the predominant discursive regimes of colonial Kenya. The next chapter moves back in time to the earliest stages of white settlement, exploring a colonial sex scandal that resulted in major policy changes. In particular, I explore how African women's supposed status as "chattel" was used to erase their agency in matters of sexuality.

TWO

Sleeping Dictionaries and Mobile Metropoles

Female (A)Sexuality in the Silberrad Scandal of 1908

IN DECEMBER OF 1908, *The Times* of London printed a letter from an outraged resident of the East African Protectorate (EAP):[1] "I have for long felt," he wrote, "that the interests of this country were suffering from the demoralization of native women by British officials, and the misuse of their position under the Government for this purpose."[2] W. Scoresby Routledge and his wife Katherine had learned of one such case involving the Assistant District Commissioner (ADC) at Nyeri, in the central highlands of Kenya. The ADC, Mr. Hubert Silberrad, had taken several young African girls as mistresses, one of whom was already married to an African askari (soldier) under Silberrad's command. When the askari, Mgulla,[3] complained about Silberrad's involvement with his wife, he was jailed for insubordination. In his letter, Routledge explained that he had refrained from publicizing the issue in the hope that the colonial government would act decisively to end such abuses of power. However, he decided to report the incident to *The Times* after learning the terms of Silberrad's punishment: namely, that he would lose a year of seniority and not be put in charge of a district for two years.

Declaring this punishment to be "utterly insufficient," Routledge asked his readers to consider the larger implications of Silberrad's actions: "The question at issue" he wrote, "is whether the representatives of the Crown are to be allowed to withdraw ignorant girls committed to their charge from the well-defined lines of tribal life, and to lead them into courses of which the inevitable tendency is to end on the streets of Nairobi."[4] Routledge raised the twin specters of urbanization and prostitution—key markers of detribalization—as the inevitable result of Silberrad's seduction. The letter implicitly mobilized the discourse of "primitive normativity" to present Silberrad's actions as a violation of the principle of trusteeship; rather than protecting vulnerable Africans, and preserving their cultures, Silberrad had corrupted innocent girls and destroyed their "traditional" sexual morality.

Although many contemporary observers joined Routledge in his outrage, another cohort suggested that Silberrad's behavior was neither particularly unique nor especially detrimental. During a discussion of the scandal in the House of Commons, for instance, Scottish Member of Parliament (MP) Cathcart Wason offered a sort of warped cultural relativism: "African morals are not ours," he stated. "In some respects they may be better than ours, in other respects, worse; at any rate, they are not the same. What would be deplorable in any country is not in Africa the very serious offence it has been made out to be."[5] In fact, Silberrad's primary defense lay in his assertion that he had followed African moral standards by "purchasing" the girls from their male guardians—just as an African man looking for a wife would supposedly do. Applying the principles of indirect rule to the sexual realm, Silberrad attempted to legitimize his relationships with the three girls by arguing that he had tapped into Indigenous networks of authority and followed local protocol.

This chapter uses the Silberrad sex scandal as a lens through which to examine colonial understandings of female sexuality during the earliest stages of Kenyan colonization. As Brett Shadle has noted, "While whites in other times and places often portrayed Black women as hypersexualized, white stereotypes of African women in Kenya focused more on their exploitation by African men."[6] Far from being depicted as hypersexual, women in East African societies were considered to be essentially *asexual*, so oppressed that their sexual desires became moot. *Precisely because* African girls/women were presented as property owned and exchanged between men, their own sexual desires (or lack thereof) were viewed as entirely irrelevant; they were simply passive receptacles of male sexual desire.

The discourse of primitive normativity thus evacuated the issue of female sexual desire from racializations of African women.

This dynamic is particularly clear in the responses to the Silberrad scandal. While his supporters argued that Silberrad had committed no offense since he had followed local protocol in "purchasing" the girls, his opponents argued that no African woman was capable of consenting to sex with a powerful white official. In the process, both sides dismissed the possibility of African women's sexual agency, viewing them instead as either wards of their male family members or of the colonial state.

Hortense Spillers has described how the racial formations of the United States ungendered Black women.[7] Subjected to the same forms of hard labor as men, denied the ability to mother their children, and exposed to sexual abuse and violence, Black women were denied the status of femininity granted to their white peers. While the main thrust of the feminist movement in the 1980s was to disrupt gender binaries and contest gender as a category, Spillers suggests that this project doesn't work for Black folks; instead, she argues, Black women are actually still struggling to gain gender differentiation. She poses a poignant question: Does sexuality exist under slavery?[8] This chapter follows Spillers' insights, with a twist. In Kenya, I argue that a different racial formation emerged that characterized African women as lacking the agency to have any sexuality at all. The discourse of African women as chattel property thus resulted in the unsexing of East African women.

The Silberrad case also reveals an interesting parallel between depictions of white women and African women in the settler state. Both were portrayed at various times as the necessary lubricant for the smooth running of the colony. While African women were sometimes depicted as "sleeping dictionaries," whose sexual labor was intertwined with their value as instructors of language and culture,[9] European women were depicted as mobile metropoles who would ensure that British cultural values were maintained in the distant spaces of the empire.

To be clear, white Kenyan women were certainly granted significantly more agency than African women and treated with a great deal more respect. Nevertheless, there are key resemblances between colonial discourses about the role and function of white and African women. Both were viewed as the embodied bearers of culture: African women were constructed as the ultimate guardians of rural African traditions and norms, while white women's presence supposedly prevented officials from "going native" by personifying British cultural standards. In the case of both white and African women, women's value was defined through their ability to help men function in colonial spaces, especially through physical, cultural, and sexual labor. African women were consistently described as "drudges" whose agricultural work held together African villages. As concubines, they supposedly aided cross-cultural interactions between colonizer and colonized. White women, meanwhile, were viewed as a necessary conduit to redirect white men's desires and guard their morality: as we will see, in the wake of the Silberrad scandal, many authorities advocated for the introduction of white women into the colonies with the explicit intention of preventing interracial sex. Such discourses simultaneously constructed British men as sexually uncontainable, culture as disseminated through sex, and women (both African and white) as the safety valve of imperial sexual tensions.

The Silberrad scandal thus offers a prehistory of many of the key debates that characterized the construction of race and sexuality during the later colonial period. The scandal occurred at a moment when Kenyan settler culture was just developing: in 1908, there were likely fewer than three thousand whites living in Kenya—a figure that included missionaries, colonial administrators, and settlers.[10] As such, Kenyan racial formations were still in their nascent stages. However, several key components of colonial discursive formations surrounding sex are already apparent at this early date. Already, African cultures were depicted as both troublingly primitive and in need of preservation and protection from contamination. Likewise, the scandal mobilized the idea that a key part of the responsibility toward colonized peoples was protecting them from the sexual threat of colonial whites. Finally, the scandal reveals surprising commonalities between the vision of white and colonized women; both were defined through their sexuality yet evacuated of sexual desire, and both were cast as the bearers of culture and tradition, an association that, as we will see, positioned them as the embodiment of interracial conflict.

In the next section, I outline the historiography of the Silberrad case, focusing particularly on the "memsahib myth." This idea held that racial relations in the colonies were largely unproblematic until white women arrived in large numbers in the colony. The memsahib myth suggests that the establishment of greater racial barriers and the crack-down on interracial sex was an unfortunate consequence of the introduction of white women, deemed to be more racist and sexually conservative than their male peers. In reality, though, the evidence indicates that colonial administrations intentionally imported white women *precisely in order to* shore up racial boundaries. This framework thus ignores some important commonalities in women's imagined positions in colonial projects.

Historiography

The existing historiography on the Silberrad scandal is preoccupied with the question of women's function as facilitators of (in the case of African women) or obstacles to (in the case of white women) interracial harmony. It is most commonly discussed as the catalyst for the "Crewe Circular" in January of 1909, a major touchstone in the history of sexuality in the British empire.[11] The circular, named for Colonial Secretary Lord Crewe, discouraged colonial officials from engaging in sexual relationships with local women, glossed as "concubinage." As Lynn Thomas notes, "The official prohibition on concubinage, like the black peril scares, worked to construct and maintain racial boundaries by defining appropriate sexual and social relations."[12] Two versions of the circular were produced by the Colonial Office and distributed to the outposts of empire; the first version, sent to new recruits, warned civil servants that such dalliances would cost them their jobs, while the version of the circular distributed to experienced officers merely expressed the government's disapprobation of concubinage.[13]

The first scholar to discuss the Silberrad case—and the last to study it at any length—was Ronald Hyam, one of the first historians of sexuality in the British empire.[14] Hyam discussed Silberrad in several of his works, most notably in a pair of articles published in two consecutive issues of the *Journal of Imperial and Commonwealth History* in 1986. Hyam's first article on the subject, "Empire and Sexual Opportunity,"[15] laid out his thesis (later revised and elaborated in his monograph[16]) that the success of the British empire lay in part in its ability to satisfy the sexual urges/needs of British men, needs that could not be met in the increasingly Puritanical environment of the Victorian metropole. "[A]lthough sexual opportunity was generally reduced in Britain," he claimed, "the empire continued to provide for traditional expectations, at least where white wives had not penetrated."[17] The opportunity to penetrate the empire benefited not only the British men who travelled overseas, but also the empire itself since "Running the empire would probably have been intolerable without resort to sexual relaxation."[18] Additionally, sex between British men and colonized men and women "soldered together the invisible bonds of empire" and promoted understanding between the races.[19] Hyam's second article, "Concubinage and the Colonial Service," offered up the Silberrad scandal as a case study, arguing that the misguided sexual prudery of the metropole forced colonial leaders to crack down on interracial sex, with concomitant damage to race relations in the colonies.[20] His contention was that the introduction of white women to the colonies destroyed this period of sexual bliss, ending the practice of concubinage and thus introducing racial boundaries between colonized and colonizer.

Hyam's rather blatant sexism and racism were roundly criticized by a number of contemporaries. Scholars like Margaret Strobel and Mark Berger pointed out that Hyam left unspoken the significant power imbalance between colonizers and colonized, ignoring entirely issues of rape and/or coercion, the effects of venereal disease and pregnancy, and the vulnerable position of the men and women who "serviced" colonial men as concubines, mistresses, prostitutes, or even wives.[21] Another critic, Richard Voeltz, pointed out that "Hyam paid no attention to any of the accounts of the sexual experience of the colonised, even those which may have been in the reports of official commissions."[22] In fact, such testimony does exist in the Colonial Office archive and will be discussed here.[23]

Hyam was not, however, the only person to advance the so-called "memsahib hypothesis," the notion that the introduction of white women in large numbers to settler colonies resulted in the enforcement or even introduction of firm racial boundaries. As Beverley Gartrell has pointed out, in novels, memoirs, and historical accounts of colonial spaces, "Officials' wives are portrayed as narrowly intolerant, more prejudiced and vindictive towards the colonized than their men, abusive to servants, usually bored, viciously gossipy, prone to extra-marital affairs destructive to peaceful social relations, and cruelly insensitive to women of the colonized races."[24] Such descriptions suggest that the establishment of racial boundaries was a regrettable side effect of the introduction of white women to the colonies. Yet, as Ann Laura Stoler points out, colonial spaces imported white women with the explicit intention of (re)enforcing racial boundaries. "By controlling the availability of European women and the sorts of sexual access condoned," Stoler notes, "state and corporate authorities controlled the very social geography of the colonies, fixing the conditions under which European populations and privileges could be reproduced."[25]

In an operation very similar to the "angel of the house" of industrial England, the colonial wife cultivated a domestic space that served as a cultural and moral touchstone for her husband. For this reason, white women were viewed as key to the health and well-being of colonial officials and settlers: as Janice Brownfoot writes with reference to colonial Malaya, "If a man had begun a degenerative decline, however, popular opinion endorsed that his best means of salvation was to go 'Home' and find a suitable European wife."[26] Furthermore, the presence of white women created a perceived need to protect white women from the attentions of brown and Black men; this proved to be a convenient rhetoric used to police the behavior of both white women and nonwhite men.[27] Finally, by providing both a sexual outlet and by facilitating racial distance, the presence of white women discouraged the growth of a multiracial population, a population whose "cultural sensibilities, physical being, and political sentiments called into question the distinctions of difference which maintained the neat boundaries of colonial rule."[28] While the introduction of substantial numbers of white women to colonial spaces certainly changed interracial dynamics, this was not an unfortunate accident, but rather an intentional strategy deployed by colonial governments.

There is no denying that European women enacted racial violence against colonized peoples, particularly in their roles as housewives and arbiters of settler culture. (This is a topic explored more in chapter 4.) Yet while white women clearly played an essential role in the establishment and maintenance of racial boundaries, Indira Ghose has argued that the "memsahib myth" was actually cultivated to displace male anxieties about white women's power in the colonies. As in Kenya, the presence of cheap domestic labor in India allowed European women to inhabit a higher class status than they would have at home. As supervisors of a large team of servants, memsahibs exercised power and authority in their own homes. Furthermore, Ghose (following Mary Procida and Antoinette Burton) points out that white women in India were able to claim a place in the public sphere by presenting themselves as the advocates of oppressed Indian women. Because white women framed their political interventions as essential to the imperial project, it was more difficult to silence them. She concludes that "The myth of the memsahib served as a convenient means to defuse male anxieties about women's access to authority in empire."[29]

The Silberrad scandal occurred prior to the growth of a significant white settler population, and particularly of a population of white women. Yet the discussions concerning the potential role of white women in Kenya during the Silberrad Affair are particularly valuable precisely because they occur before the emergence of "a distinct colonial morality" in Kenya.[30] While Hyam argues that racial segregation was an unfortunate consequence of the entrance of white women into the colonies, at the time domestic Britons explicitly argued that white women must be brought to the colonies to preserve the morality of colonial administrators—and thereby prevent interracial sex from creating resentments among African men that would threaten the imperial project.

The Silberrad scandal was not simply a clash between the puritanical values of domestic Britain and the permissive environment of the colonial spaces. Rather, it was a nuanced debate about the ways in which sex complicated and facilitated colonial rule, and about the degree to which the principles of colonial rule could be applied to the sexual and moral realms. The remainder of the chapter explores these questions in two main sections. The first examines the scandal as it played out in Kenya. Here, authorities largely accepted Silberrad's argument that he had committed no major offense since he had "purchased" the girls through established channels. Authorities thus drew on and reinforced the larger belief that, as "chattel property," African women possessed no meaningful ability to consent to or refuse sex. The next section follows the scandal to the metropole, where a pair of muckraking ethnographers ensured that Silberrad's behavior would not be swept under the rug. While a significant portion of the metropolitan audience objected to Silberrad's actions, they did so through mobilizing the nascent discourse of primitive normativity, arguing that African women were essentially childlike and in need of protection from lascivious white men. Importantly, these critics thus *also* mobilized the idea that African women were fundamentally unable to either consent or refuse consent to any sexual activity. The final section also outlines the proposed solution to the problem posed by Silberrad's actions; both his defenders and his detractors agreed that white women must be imported to serve as the guardians of sexual morality. While settler women and African women were frequently at odds in colonial Kenya, ironically they were imagined to play a very similar role in the overarching colonial project; when it was deemed undesirable for African women to serve as "concubines," white women were imported to take over the task of containing the sexual urges of white men.

Sleeping Dictionaries: The Scandal at the Periphery

The events at Nyeri first came to the local government's attention in February of 1908, when W. Scoresby Routledge wrote to the governor of the East African Protectorate, Sir James Hayes Sadler. Routledge and his wife Katherine Pease Routledge had arrived in Mombasa, Kenya in 1906.[31] The Routledges settled in Nyeri and began research for an ethnography of the Gikuyu people.[32] While living in Nyeri, the Routledges learned of the misconduct of their District Commissioner, Hubert

Silberrad. Mr. Routledge explained the circumstances of his discovery in his letter to Hayes Sadler. He reported that he had been told by locals "whose confidence I have" that "their women were being brought to the Government 'boma' [enclosure or compound] here for immoral purposes."[33] Routledge reported that both Silberrad and his predecessor, District Commissioner C. W. Haywood, had procured African girls and lived with them.[34] The two Gikuyu girls, Nyambura and Wameisa, had also lived with Haywood; at the time the scandal broke out, Wameisa was about thirteen to fourteen years old, while Nyambura was described as being of "more mature years."[35] Nyakayena, a Maasai girl of about twelve to thirteen years, was only involved with Silberrad.[36] The complaints from local men appear to have been catalyzed by Silberrad's decision to jail Nyakayena's husband after a dispute over her. On learning of the situation, Routledge's wife Katherine went to the government house and retrieved the two girls living there, bringing them back to the Routledges' home.[37]

In response to Routledge's allegations, Gov. Hayes Sadler sent Judge J. W. Barth to Nyeri with the task of conducting an inquiry into the issue. The inquiry was accomplished in March, and in April of 1908, Barth (who was at that time stuck in the European Hospital in Nairobi, recovering from a bout of dysentery) submitted a rather lukewarm report to the governor. This report includes a record of the testimony of witnesses given during the inquiry: unfortunately, unlike other portions of the file, which are generally typewritten, Barth's report is handwritten, and quite badly at that. Elsewhere in the archive, we discover why: noting that the report on Silberrad's case is nearly illegible, one of the undersecretaries in the Colonial Office explains that "the authorities did not like to hand over a report of this kind to the Goanese Clerks for typewriting, and that no one else was available to undertake the job."[38] Presumably, colonial officials didn't want the details of a British officer's sexual misconduct to reach the eyes and ears of nonwhites, and since the lower levels of the colonial administration were dominated by Kenyan Asians, the report lands in the archive in a condition that often censors the material from the eyes of the modern researcher as well.

Several other factors complicate these records. The African witnesses would have testified in their native languages (Gikuyu or Maa) or less likely in Swahili; their answers would have been translated and then recorded by a European administrator. The testimony is thus twice filtered. Their evidence is also constrained by the questions that were asked, questions clearly indicating that those who led the inquiry felt that the girls' own interpretation of events was only marginally relevant.

Despite their limitations, these records reveal several common themes. First, in evaluating Silberrad's conduct, his adjudicators felt it was more significant to establish whether or not Silberrad had acted in accordance with Indigenous norms surrounding sex and courtship than to determine if the girls themselves had consented to live and sleep with him.[39] While authorities did express concerns about how interracial sex might lessen the prestige of British officials, the notion that Silberrad had acted in accordance with customary law was indeed viewed as a mitigating factor.

Second, to determine whether Silberrad had followed customary law, his superiors mobilized an ethnographic discourse that characterized both African women themselves and the labor they performed as property owned by male guardians. In particular, the money and/or livestock given to a bride's family by her new husband was glossed as the "purchase" of a woman. Importantly, the question of the girl's age did not become a particular focus of the discourse at the periphery: as Brett Shadle has written, "Colonial officials seemed blind to any African categories that might approximate British ideas of girlhood. They generally understood females as moving rapidly from children to women, daughters to wives, with no stage in between."[40] (This is in contrast to young African men—as Paul Ocobock has shown, the state was intensely interested in "discover[ing], defin[ing], and demarcate[ing] a precise moment when a young man was no longer beholden to his elders" and could join the colonial labor force.)[41] Despite their very young age, Silberrad and his predecessor Haywood interpreted these girls as mature enough to have sex with.

The actual position of women in precolonial Kenyan societies is a matter of considerable debate.[42] What is significant, however, is that, at this moment in Kenyan history, the social order of Gikuyu society—including the meanings of marriage and bridewealth—were being dramatically rewritten. As Luise White has shown, during the late 1890s, central Kenya underwent "a succession of ecological disasters" that "ruptured the established economics of African marriage systems by shifting wealth away from cattle owners and toward agriculturalists."[43] These included several outbreaks of rinderpest, a contagious fever that kills livestock, followed by an outbreak of bovine pleuropneumonia; together, these diseases killed as much as 90 percent of cattle—the primary social and economic currency of central Kenyans. Humans, in turn, suffered famine and disease, causing a devastating blow to populations in central Kenya.[44] As Charles Ambler notes, "The frantic struggle for existence interrupted the established relationships of authority and obligation, stretching the bonds of social order to breaking."[45]

Meanwhile, a new economy was arising associated with the establishment of the Uganda Railway and the development of colonial governance. Now, young men could make money as merchants, as agents or allies of the British colonial state, or by working on white-owned farms—meaning that power was gradually shifting from older men to a new youthful elite. These developments also caused considerable disturbance in marriage arrangements. Economically devastated communities took to "pawning" women (and sometimes children), a practice by which women could be sent to live with neighboring groups in exchange for food. As Tabitha Kanogo writes, "marriages constructed out of pawnship arrangements were in reality political alliances that enabled a community facing economic crisis to exchange some of its human social capital to acquire sustenance for the rest of the population pending the recovery of its economy."[46] Some "pawned" women attempted to run away, others were reclaimed by their kin after the period of crisis had passed, and some remained married and bore children in their new communities. Significantly, when called to adjudicate cases of disputes over pawned women, colonial officials do not seem to have felt it necessary to consult the women themselves about their preferences.[47]

Meanwhile, heavy death tolls among men meant that there was an increased supply of widowed and unmarried women, and young men who were engaging in the new economies opened up by colonialism were able to obtain brides without the consent or participation of their families. As the economy began to rebound at the turn of the century, young men engaged in these new economies had increased access to cash, meaning that more men were marrying, and causing rapid inflation in bridewealth—cash or livestock given to a bride's family as compensation for the loss of her labor.[48] Women, too, took advantage of new economies—Luise White suggests that the social and economic changes of this period led some women to engage in prostitution.[49] The irony, then, is that Silberrad and allies were developing discourses about the "traditional" status of women in Kenyan societies at precisely the moment that these traditions were being overhauled.

In particular, these narratives consistently described African women as either "chattel property" or "beasts of burden." Tabitha Kanogo's work is particularly helpful for both laying out the contours of this discourse and explaining its utility. As Kanogo writes, Kenyan African women were frequently represented "as perpetual legal minors, chattels, exploited beasts of burden, not too intelligent, gossiping, giggling, idle, shy, vulnerable, and dependent social victims."[50] For instance, Chief Native Commissioner (CNC)

John Ainsworth (an official who was actually among the most sympathetic toward Indigenous peoples) maintained that "According to Native law and custom a woman is practically a chattel, she never comes of age and although transferred from the custody of her father or guardian to some other man on payment of the so-called marriage price she still remains a chattel, her purchaser's (husband's) chattel."[51] Furthermore, while African women were viewed as uniquely oppressed, they were simultaneously depicted as the most strident advocates of the very traditions that oppressed them. Ainsworth, for instance, argued that the typical African woman was "extremely conservative in her ideas and is very often responsible for some of the backwardness found in the native areas. She is invariably a great stickler for custom and tradition and the older and more conservative it is the better she seems to like it."[52]

At first glance, constructions of African female sexuality appear curiously contradictory. On the one hand, there was a prevailing belief that African girls engaged in a number of premarital sexual activities. This sexual activity was not, however, viewed by most settlers and officials as evidence of female hypersexuality or deviance. Instead, in accordance with the discourse of primitive normativity, premarital sex play was viewed as a characteristic (and hence unproblematic) aspect of the sexuality of "premodern" peoples. The novelist Nora Strange captured the prevailing thesis when she claimed that although the lives of adolescent African girls were "crowded with amatory episodes," this did not necessarily damage their morals: "A sense of patriarchal dignity prevailed, and certain tribes exercised hygienic principles lacking in European civilization."[53] Not all white Kenyans were as sanguine about premarital sexuality—missionaries in particular viewed African premarital sexual activity as pathological. Yet even missionaries did not view African women's sexual desires as a factor: quoting Kanogo again, "missionary and government officials bemoaned what they characterized as pervasive promiscuity, on the one hand, and lack of choice and consent for girls with regard to their marriage partners, on the other."[54] African girls may have been promiscuous, the argument held, but they did so not of their own volition, but rather because they were essentially viewed as property available for use by men.

The position of African girls and women as the moral center of African life and the suitable outlet for male sexual desires was threatened, though, by their movement away from the reserves. In particular, settlers and officials consistently argued that urbanization destroyed African women's morals, leading them inevitably into prostitution—deemed nonexistent in "uncontaminated" African cultures. This supposedly occurred both because they were introduced to the evils of civilization in the "modern" space of colonial cities, but also because urbanization allowed women to escape the authority of men. Recall Jomo Kenyatta's contention that "The custom [of polygamy] also provides that all women must be under the protection of men; and that in order to avoid prostitution (no word exists for 'prostitution' in the Gikuyu language) all women must be married in their 'teens, i.e. fifteen to twenty. Thus there is no term in the Gikuyu language for 'unmarried' or 'old maids.'"[55]

While Kenyatta invoked the notion of African patriarchy in service of Gikuyu nationalism, the notion that African women were the chattel property of their male relatives served the colonial mission as well. In short, the idea that women were the moral center of African life, joined with the idea that urbanization would inevitably lead women into prostitution, allowed both African men and the colonial administration to restrict women's movement.[56] Both groups asserted that African women should remain on the reserves, or on white-owned farms to avoid the moral dangers of the city.

The idea that African women were treated as "chattel" by "their" men also enabled the colonial government to establish policies that entrenched women's position as legal minors and served the interests of the white minority. In other words, whether or not African women were truly regarded as "chattel" within Indigenous worldviews, colonial policies made them legally so on the basis that they were following "customary law." For instance, the "Hut Tax" (first levied in 1901) required African men over the age of sixteen to pay a set tax for each hut they occupied;[57] the tax had the intended effect of forcing men to leave the reserves and enter into waged labor in order to pay the tax. Because men generally built a separate hut for each of their wives, the hut tax essentially operated as a wife tax as well; in fact, even if more than one wife lived in a single hut, the man was taxed for each wife.[58] Mr. Parkinson of the Colonial Office explained that the rationale for this tax was based on the widely-held idea that Africans considered women property; although attitudes might be changing with colonization, Parkinson held that "It is however doubtful whether, in general, the natives have ceased to think of wives as chattels which are purchased; and if that is the case it might be argued that when a native can afford to acquire this property, he can reasonably be taxed upon it."[59] Ironically, while the Colonial Office critiqued Africans for their "backwards" views toward women, they simultaneously imposed a tax that defined wives as a commodity. Some went even further: a Mr. H. H. Harris argued that the colonial government ought to be allowed to purchase African girls and women from their fathers and bring them to work as laborers on white farms. Harris argued (with no apparent sense of irony) that allowing whites to buy African girls would enable them to escape a life as slaves to African men.[60]

The practice of paying bridewealth was also a much-discussed example of African patriarchy—and one that played a key role in the Silberrad case. Various witnesses reported (or were recorded as reporting) that Silberrad had "paid" the local "chief" Wambugu for the girls with livestock as a form of bridewealth. At the time, many communities in East Africa, including the Gikuyu and Maasai, exchanged livestock as part of the process of courtship and marriage. As Lynn Thomas explains, "Bridewealth established respectful relations between two families and clans. It also declared the value of women's fertility and labor."[61] After obtaining consent from both the prospective bride and her family, a Gikuyu bridegroom would present the bride's family with a negotiated number of livestock known as the bridewealth. These livestock were understood to reimburse the family for the loss of the bride's labor, but they also served as a form of insurance: if the bride proved unsuitable or wished to leave her husband, the bridewealth could be returned and the marriage dissolved.

However, the nuances of this practice disappeared when the British translated bridewealth into the "sale" of a woman by her family and the "purchase" of a wife by husband. British interpreters discussed the payment of bridewealth using language deeply imbricated in a capitalist framework. One rather striking example of this confusion occurs in an intra-office memo that circulated among Lord Crewe's undersecretaries in the Colonial Office files. At one point, Mr. Harris, rejecting the askari Mgulla's contention that Nyakayena was his wife, states that Mgulla "had previously cohabited with the girl, and considered he had a lien upon her."[62] Similar language is used in the Executive Committee's review of the other administrator involved, C. W. Haywood. After acquiring Nyambura, Haywood supposedly wished to contract another woman as a companion to her, particularly because at the time Haywood spoke no Gikuyu and hence could not speak with her at all. Lizo wa Ndegwa, a local headman working under the authority of "Chief" Wambugu, apparently then offered Wameisa, saying "that he knew of a girl whom he had a sort of option over" since he had already paid for her in goats (this may be a reference to the practice of "pawning," discussed earlier).[63] Haywood then paid Lizo back with a heifer calf and then "took the girl to live with me in the usual way."[64] (Someone—presumably a colonial official—underlined the final portion in the original text.)

The point is not that African women were equally doomed by patriarchy within their own cultures and the imperial one; while debates continue about the status of women in precolonial East Africa, colonial officials clearly did not possess an accurate or nuanced understanding of women's status. Rather, I wish to emphasize how the use of this language of trade and ownership here enabled colonial policies that entrenched the status of African women and girls as legal minors and nonagential figures. Such beliefs informed the official responses to Silberrad's misbehavior, which largely accepted his argument that he had followed "local protocol" and hence had not actually abused the girls. This indicates that, at least to some extent, they accepted his argument that the principles of indirect rule should be applied to the moral and sexual sphere.

The girls' own testimony, on the other hand, clearly indicates that they experienced their involvement with Silberrad as coercive, and that Silberrad had not, in fact, obtained the girls via sanctioned cultural channels. Instead, their testimony offers important evidence about how colonialism was already profoundly altering norms surrounding courtship and sexuality. Wameisa, for instance, stated that Lizo wa Ndegwa, the headman working for "Chief" Wambugu, had propositioned her for sex. Already, this indicates the degree to which central Kenyan political formations were changing, since there was no such position as "chief" in precolonial East Africa, where communities were led by councils of elders. Rather, because the philosophy of indirect rule required that the colonized be organized into "tribes" headed by "chiefs," the British modified local power structures to produce these identities.[65] As John Lonsdale and Bruce Berman have pointed out, "chiefs" and "headmen" tended to be selected from those who had already proved most adept at exploiting the new economies produced by colonialism, that is, those who were most willing and able to collaborate with the colonial government.[66] Wameisa testified that when she refused to sleep with the headman, he retaliated, saying "You have refused me I will go and tell a mzungu [white person] to take you."[67] The political structures imposed by colonialism, which created new positions of authority among younger men, therefore enabled new forms of exploitation of African women.

Wameisa stated that she only agreed to go live with the mzungu and act "as his wife" because she had been threatened that her family would be imprisoned if she did not go.[68] In a rare piece of testimony where the affective dimension of her experience comes through, Wameisa was questioned about whether she cried when taken away to live with Silberrad. She stated that she did cry in front of Lizo and her brother "on the occasion of the shauri [business] with the other mzungu. I did not cry about Mr. S's shauri."[69] Clearly, Wameisa did not freely consent to the relationship with the two District Commissioners. Yet, Wameisa also is recorded as saying that she "was bought by the [illegible] mzungu according to Kikuyu custom."[70] Again, the last portion of the quote has been underlined by another hand, presumably someone in the colonial office or the governor's office. Of course, Wameisa's "purchase" by Silberrad most definitely did not transpire "according to Kikuyu custom" since the fee (of forty goats and cattle) was paid to Wambugu, the "chief," rather than to Wameisa's own family. More significantly, in Gikuyu tradition, a potential suitor would generally have had to obtain the bride's consent before entering negotiations with her family over bridewealth.[71] However, the idea that Silberrad had followed local protocol was clearly important to the arbiters of the scandal, as indicated by the anonymous underlining of this portion of her testimony.

Silberrad's conduct with Nyakayena was considered to be the most egregious, since in this case he had interfered with a girl who already belonged to another man, and not just any man, but an askari under Silberrad's command. Silberrad defended himself in this regard by again asserting the importance of Indigenous tradition: he claimed that the marriage between Nyakayena and Mgulla had not been conducted according to local protocol and was hence illegitimate. Silberrad claimed that Nyakayena told him that "she was free and no man owned her beyond her brothers."[72] Upon discovering that Mgulla claimed her as his wife, Silberrad states that he encouraged Mgulla to ratify the marriage by paying "mali" [wealth] to her brothers; here he presented himself as a guardian of African tradition, insisting that Mgulla follow the rules of courtship. Nyakayena's own testimony differs vastly from this account. She stated that she had been collected by an askari and taken to the government boma. "I cried when I was taken to the bwana [Silberrad]," she recalled.[73] "He said if I cried I could not go to my husband," so she agreed to sleep in his bed where he "had connection" with her.[74] Her husband's testimony adds an important detail to her story: he stated that Nyakayena was a Maasai who had been captured by the Gikuyu as a little girl. After Nyakayena told Mgulla (also Maasai) that she was unhappy living in the Gikuyu community and would prefer to live on the police lines with him, he recalls that he "paid 4 goats and R [Rupee] 3 for her."[75] Given that Nyakayena was isolated from her family and living in a community with vastly different traditions than her own, it is likely true that she did not have a wedding that accorded with Maasai protocols. However, neither she nor Mgulla seem to have considered their union to be less official as a consequence. We can more accurately state that Nyakayena was uniquely vulnerable, having no access to her natal family or ethnolinguistic community and being compelled to arrange a marriage for herself.

But Silberrad had an answer for this too. In a letter written to Governor Hayes Sadler, he claims that Mgulla was an uncircumcised Maasai, and therefore Nyakayena's brothers[76] considered him to be an inappropriate spouse for her. (In his discussion of the Silberrad Affair, Ronald Hyam accepts Silberrad's testimony on this topic at face value and presents it as a key motivating factor: he writes that it was "unfortunate for Silberrad that the askari, Mugalla, was an uncircumcised Maasai, and, as a result, peculiarly touchy about his sex life."[77]) Silberrad never contested that he had brought the girls to live with him. Instead, he presented himself as an advocate for their interests. He stated that he had originally sent away Wameisa because she had appeared to be unwilling to live with him, and only called her back to be a companion to Nyambura. He also implied that he paid Wameisa more money than she actually earned: "She was at Nyeri exactly 28 days," he writes, "half of which time I was on safari and for the first five days I was in the boma she had her courses. I gave her R. 5 a week's pay while she was 'indisposed' and [two?] sets of clothes; she gave R2 or 3 to her brother and I told her not to let him sponge on her."[78] Silberrad argued for his generosity in paying her even when she was not able to perform sexual labor, either because she was menstruating or because he was away from headquarters. Additionally, he painted himself as her financial protector, trying to convince her not to give away her money to her "sponging" brother. Although he admitted to sleeping with all three women, he also explained that this was not his primary motive in obtaining Wameisa, writing that "I got her as I wanted her to talk Kikuyu to me, and when she would not talk I told her to return."[79] This of course conflicts with his earlier statement, as Wameisa would have doubtless been able to converse with him in Gikuyu whether or not she was menstruating at the time.

Not surprisingly, Nyambura told the story differently. In her testimony she asserted that while she had lived with the previous District Commissioner Mr. Haywood, she originally refused Silberrad's request to live with him. However, she recalled that "I was present when Wameisa was told that she should live with Mr. S by Mr. Haywood," and that she did not want Wameisa to have to live there alone. She therefore decided to return to Silberrad's compound, where she stayed until the Routledges came to take the two women away.[80] This testimony indicates that colonial administrators understood access to African women as a sort of perquisite and felt free to exchange them. However, even more importantly, it points to the kinds of solidarities that African women showed toward each other during this time of tremendous social change; Nyambura was willing to expose herself to continued sexual exploitation in order to comfort another woman in her community.

Despite these obvious indications that Silberrad *had not*, in fact, followed traditional protocols, the local government was ultimately sympathetic to Silberrad's argument that he had acted in accordance with Indigenous norms. In mid-May, Governor Hayes Sadler and a committee of the Executive Council met to discuss the inquiry's findings.[81] Judge Barth's report had been lukewarm: though he was not convinced that the girls had been unwilling to sleep with Silberrad, in the case of Nyakayena, he nevertheless believed that Silberrad could not be justified in "exercising his authority in sending the girl away from the man with whom she was living—an Askari under his command—in order that he might enjoy her himself"—a statement that once again depicted African women as sexual property to be "enjoyed" by men.[82] The Executive Council did explicitly object to the practice of concubinage as something that "must be emphatically condemned" since, in addition to its being immoral, "they consider that an English Officer who acts thus descends from the position that every whiteman should occupy in this country."[83] However, they also believed that "Mr. Haywood's transactions were those ordinarily in use in the Kikuyu country when a man wishes to live with a woman" and that Silberrad "also acted according to the native custom."[84] As such, they recommended relatively lenient punishments: Haywood should be told he could not have any more mistresses, while Silberrad's name should go to the bottom of the promotion list, and he should not be put in charge of a district for two to three years. Hayes Sadler felt that even this punishment was too severe, noting that the inquiry had found that Silberrad "did not buy these girls as slaves and that they came and lived with him perfectly freely."[85] Thus, the governor advised Lord Crewe that "a warning should suffice" to discipline Silberrad.[86]

The Colonial Office clearly hoped to prevent the Silberrad scandal from reaching the general public: shortly after receiving Governor Hayes

Sadler's recommendations, an undersecretary commented in an intra-office memo that "It is much to be hoped that Mr. Routledge will not have any of these matters brought up in Parliament."[87] Unfortunately for the Colonial Office, the Routledges were both persistent and well connected. Katherine Pease Routledge, in particular, exploited her considerable family connections in her pursuit of justice. The Pease family, who had made their fortune in railroads and woolen goods, had been politically prominent since 1832, when Katherine Routledge's grandfather Joseph Pease had become the first Quaker elected to Parliament. At the time of the scandal, two of her cousins served as Members of Parliament.[88] The Routledges were successful in bringing the issue to the attention of metropolitan politicians; shortly after their letters, Undersecretary of State for the Colonies Colonel Seely was forced to field questions from eight MPs in the House of Commons regarding the case.[89] Even the distribution of the Crewe Circular in June of 1909 did not quash the scandal: it was discussed again in the House of Commons the next month.

As I show in the next section, the metropolitan discourses that appeared in the press and in the two parliamentary debates on the scandal presented the British public as the guardians of African women's sexual welfare. However, they did so in ways that evacuated the possibility of African women/girls' sexual agency; instead, they argued that African women were so vulnerable that they were not capable of consenting to sex with a colonial official. Such discourses showed how the discourse of primitive normativity could present African women as both sexually promiscuous and fundamentally asexual. Furthermore, these discourses seemed to concur that white men could not be expected to control their sexual desires unless an appropriate sexual outlet was provided for them. The proposed solution to the problem of concubinage—the importation of white women—situated white women as that outlet.

Mobile Metropoles: The Scandal in Britain

Silberrad's defenders had suggested that the girls' consent was irrelevant because they were essentially property to be traded between men. His critics, meanwhile, tended to argue that it would have been impossible for the girls to give consent, due to the power disparities between themselves and colonial officials. While the latter argument certainly seems more in line with twenty-first-century understandings of the nature of power and consent, it took place within the larger framework of primitive normativity. This framework positioned all Africans as "childlike," but also emphasized the notion that African *women* could never be understood as agential adults within the (often imagined) regimes of "customary law." Thus, while Silberrad's critics opposed his abuse of the three girls, they did so in ways that reinforced the notion that African women were essentially powerless and unable to make meaningful choices about their own sexuality.

A significant number of Silberrad's detractors argued that Silberrad had abused his position as a colonial officer. Their comments indicate that they understood consent in much more nuanced terms than we might expect from an early twentieth-century audience. For instance, during one of the parliamentary debates, the MP Mr. Lyttelton pointed out that although the girls did seem to eventually yield to the advances of Mr. Silberrad, "I should imagine that such yielding would be natural to the most powerful man in the district, seconded by one of the most powerful chiefs."[90] Mr. Stuart Wortley put the question more directly, stating that since it was illegal for an official to use his position to obtain sex, "There is no question of consent. Consent is a matter that is immaterial."[91] Another MP, H. J. Wilson, went further, suggesting that the African men who facilitated the relationship had also been coerced. While accusing the officers of using "native pimps" to "procure and bring an assortment of girls for his selection," he argued that even they could not be held totally responsible for Silberrad's actions since "it is very possible that the chief could hardly refuse the demand of a man in such a position."[92]

For these MPs, a disparity in power between a man and his sexual partner negated the possibility of a consensual encounter. Katherine Routledge agreed, entering the ongoing debate in the "letters to the editor" pages in *The Spectator*: "At best," she wrote, "all native women, thus confronted with power, education and wealth, are in the condition of girls at home under sixteen years" and declared that "*Noblesse oblige* is a lesson which still requires to be learnt in British East Africa."[93] Positioning herself as an advocate for African women, Routledge ascribed all African women with a status as adolescents in questions of sex and consent; her comparison of African adult women to European girls evoked the evolutionary narratives that situated all "primitive" peoples as children. Her reference to *noblesse oblige* translates this racial language into terms of class; like the old lord of a landed estate, the benefits of wealth and status came with an obligation to care for those lower on the social scale. Silberrad's detractors rightly acknowledged the operation of power in interracial relationships. However, in presenting themselves as trustees of voiceless and perpetually immature African women/girls, they too viewed the girls' own experience as irrelevant.

The construction of African women as permanent minors, for whom sexual contact with white men would be disastrous, existed alongside a second belief: that white men in the colonies required a sexual outlet if they were to successfully do the work of empire. Thus, as members of the British parliament and the press considered whether African women could freely say yes to sex, a parallel question emerged: Could white men say no? Could white officials, isolated from women of their own race and living in stressful conditions, be expected to abstain from sex? The debate in *The Spectator* increasingly honed in on this question, beginning with the rather colorfully named article "A Canker in Imperial Administration."[94] "We fully recognise," it stated, "that in an Empire as great as ours there must often be cases in which men living under the very trying conditions that result from isolation, from the absence of a healthy public opinion, and from the special temptations which surround the possessors of unlimited power over a naturally slavish population, yield to those temptations."[95] (The reference to an "absence of a healthy public opinion" anticipates the key role that white women were seen to play in importing British sexual morals to the periphery.) However, it continued, if "we were once to allow the notion to get abroad that men charged with the duties of administration can be permitted to exercise the tremendous powers placed in their hands to gratify their animal passions," it would "mean nothing short of ruin to the Empire" and represent "a prostitution of the trusteeship" with which Britain had been entrusted.[96] The focus on "animal passions" is revealing, as it is applied not to the African wards but to the European (male) guardians. The notion that such abuses of power amounted to a "prostitution of the trusteeship" obligations incurred by the British explicitly tied the realm of sexuality to administrative policy.

A few days later, *The Spectator* printed a letter to the editor signed "One Who Knows" that elaborated on the "canker" metaphor. The author warned that "Britons at home must not allow themselves to rest content with the thought that the 'open sore' so much lamented by Livingstone has been permanently healed when it has, in fact, broken out in a more virulent and malignant manner in the form of a different, but far more insidious, slavery."[97] The open sore that Livingstone had referred to (supposedly as he lay dying in Central Africa) was that of the slave trade; in fact, one central legitimization of the British colonial presence in late colonial

Africa was that they supposedly played a key role in ending this trade. One Who Knows borrows Livingstone's phrase to portray concubinage as a kind of syphilis spreading its malignant cankers across British imperial Africa. The implicit threat was that sexual intercourse with African women would impair and weaken the body of the empire itself.

One Who Knows continued by condemning "such a state of affairs as that which permits a British official to exercise his prerogative of passing judgment upon natives accused of adultery and theft, when he has himself a harem within a stone's-throw of his judgment seat," a statement that evoked the much hated figure of the "Oriental despot" whose sexual excess was seen to symbolize a more general tyranny.[98] The danger of such a practice was clear: "When one considers that the native is a keen observer of human nature, that he is possessed of a natural proclivity for imitation, and that, in the absence of any literature, his sole evening occupation is to sit round the fire and gossip (chiefly about the European who may happen to live near him), it is only too apparent what a far-reaching effect the example and conduct of his administrators will have upon the natives in that and neighbouring districts."[99] Here, One Who Knows suggested that African observers would not only lose respect for white officers who engaged in illicit relationships with African women but might even be inclined to imitate them. Since many East African communities practiced polygamy, One Who Knows was worried not about the likelihood that an African "imitator" would establish his own harem of African wives, but rather that he might be inspired to seek out sexual relationships with white women.

How could this canker be healed, thus preserving the prestige and security of the imperial project? Many commentators agreed that the best solution was to increase the salaries of colonial officials. In part, this salary rise was intended to ensure that men from a higher social class would enter the service. In its original "Canker" column, The Spectator had advised that colonial administrators must be paid more, so as to attract a better "stamp of men": they argued that "it is impossible for a white man, and an Englishman living in Africa, to be what we want him to be—a mixture of benevolent despot, upright Judge, and high-minded official—at a salary of from £200 to £300 a year."[100] In a statement foreshadowing later concerns about the growth of a "poor white" population in Kenya, the paper suggested that living in less-than-English conditions would lower the moral standards of colonial civil servants. In fact, at this time, the colonial service was beginning to actively recruit officers with more training and from a higher class background.[101]

But most importantly, increased salaries would allow colonial officials to bring their wives out to live with them; these women would provide both a sexual outlet and serve as the embodiment of domestic British morality. A letter to the editor of *The Spectator* on December 26, written by a man identifying himself as a former official in Nyasaland (now Malawi), stated that "A married man gives up much in accepting an official appointment in these outposts of the Empire, even if he takes his wife out with him, has infinitely more at stake, and is much more likely, from a health point of view, to prove an efficient public servant than a single man, who, often young, in full vigour, and without any control, finds full vent for the play of his animal passions in the tropics, with very often attendant disastrous results to his health, and consequent efficiency."[102] He noted that his own wife had happily accompanied him to his rural outpost, proof that "even women of refinement and culture are not to be deterred from accompanying their husbands where duty calls them to the uttermost parts of the earth, as you say, to 'face hardships, solitude, and the risk of life from dangerous climates' little known to those who remain in the homeland."[103] Yet "Without help, either in the way of increased salaries or what amounts to the same, assisted passages for wives both ways, it is a very heavy call on the poor pay meted out to junior officials in our Protectorates to take out a wife. Many cannot afford to; hence in great measure the 'canker.'"[104] Again, the "canker" metaphor works on multiple levels; just as monogamous marriage to a chaste woman would protect white men from venereal disease, it would also prevent the outbreak of moral ailments in the colonies.

Although self-control was seen as a distinguishing feature of "civilized men," these discourses suggested that such discipline was perhaps not possible without the presence of white women. T. F. Victor Buxton, who was himself a settler in the EAP, wrote a letter to *The Times* on January 9, 1909, in which he stated: "All honour is due to those members of the service who by self-control are proving their fitness to exercise authority over uncivilized peoples; but the conduct of others, to which recent correspondence has drawn attention, merits the strongest reprobation."[105] Buxton suggested that the presence of white women facilitated this "self-control" by providing an approved outlet for the sexual appetites of white officials and bringing the moral environment of the metropole to the colonies. Buxton praised the example given by Governor Hayes Sadler who, along with his wife, "is doing his best, by the wholesome influences of English family life, to promote a high tone among his subordinates, and to help those who, away from home and friends, have to face the temptations of life in the tropics." He noted that "The refining influence of ladies' society has already done much for our East African Protectorates, but it might with advantage be greatly extended."[106] His references to "high tone" and "wholesome influences" points to the ability of white women to reproduce British families and moral ideologies in the outposts of empire. White women served the empire not only by redirecting the amorous advances of officials away from local women; they were far more important in their capacity as a metonym of British cultural norms as a whole.

Another letter to the editor, published in *The Spectator* on December 19, elaborated on this point: the author, "D.S.S." inquired "Will you believe one who has spent long years in such places, there would be less drink and immorality among men in the outlying parts of the Empire, deprived of the refining influence of their country women, if only some of the latter would go there too?" Introducing British women would "refine" the morals, manners, and habits of British men, and even promised an extra benefit: D. S. S. believed "there would be less ultra-feminist unrest among our women at home if the surplus went abroad."[107]

In fact, Silberrad did manage to acquire a white wife, a fact that his advocates viewed as a sign of his successful reformation. One of Silberrad's strongest defenders in Parliament, the Scottish MP Mr. Cathcart Wason, noted that Silberrad "has come home after this reprimand, and not only has he laid his sins at the foot of the Throne, but he has gone to an English lady and told her the whole story, and she has consented to be his wife and to go out to Africa with him, there to help him lead a higher and purer life."[108] Colonel Seely had also emphasized Silberrad's marital status when he responded to questions in Parliament, suggesting that Silberrad had acted honorably since "he told all to his future wife."[109] The new Mrs. Silberrad promised to guard over the morals of her husband once he was returned to an imperial outpost, and her forgiveness of Silberrad's misbehavior was viewed by certain of his supporters as a sufficient form of absolution. In fact, some of the MPs seemed rather sorry for the young couple: J. D. Rees stated "I personally deplore the fact that this gentleman, who committed a fault and was punished and went back to his duties a married man, absolved from all his past transgressions, should be haled [sic] before the House to-day as a malefactor, and that all these circumstances should be raked up to the pain and ignominy of himself and his wife."[110] Even Lord Balfour, who strongly believed that Silberrad had abused his position and used his authority to procure mistresses, felt the need to assure the House that "I am really not trying to impose upon officials everywhere a code of morality and purity, whatever it may be called, which, no doubt, is violated in our own country and in our own society . . . On the contrary, I admit the fact of their isolated life and all the rest of it. We know there are special difficulties."[111]

If African women, then, were constructed as always already available for sex, these discourses suggested that male officials were fundamentally unable to control their sexual urges without the restraining influence of white women. These officials required an outlet to express their biological imperatives—a discourse that challenged the primacy of self-control in the "civilized" sexual personality. In part, white women in their role as wives would provide such a sexual outlet, but even more significantly, the company of other whites, both male and female, would encourage officials to maintain certain cultural standards, including those that insisted on a strict segregation between Africans and whites. When I refer to white settler women as "mobile metropoles," I mean to point to their perceived value as bearers of tradition and norms within their own bodies. These discourses established an interesting relationship between the duties performed by colonial men and women: the colonial "man on the spot" served to convey information about a foreign territory back to the metropole. The "woman on the spot," meanwhile, reversed this directionality, bringing metropolitan values to the periphery. The languages of gender and geography come together in this discourse; colonial men and women played a complementary role in knitting the colonies together with domestic Britain.

The Aftermath

Despite the extensive publicity surrounding his actions, Silberrad suffered few long-term consequences. Officials in the Colonial Office actually *reduced* the punishment proposed by the government of the EAP: Silberrad lost only one year of seniority and was not to be put in charge of a district for two years.[112] Some felt that even this reduced punishment was too severe. The MP Sir Clement Hill noted that the publicity surrounding the scandal amounted to a very strong punishment: "whatever the nominal weight of the punishment, the publicity given to it must seriously affect, if it does not ruin, the career of the official implicated." He would be surprised if such punishment did not act as a deterrent to future crimes.[113] In a letter printed a few weeks later, Mr. Routledge pointed out that had he

not written to *The Times* and provided Silberrad's name, the publicity surrounding the scandal would not have had any effect on Silberrad's career
prospects; in effect, the punishment had been meted out by himself and
not the Colonial Office.[114]

In fact, Silberrad's career seems to have survived intact; in December of
1908, he was given a position as the Assistant District Commissioner of
Kiambu, just fifty miles away from the site of his indiscretions at Nyeri. He
was later moved to Nyasaland (now Malawi) where he served as a District
Commissioner.[115] A notice in the *Nyasaland Times* reported the birth of a
child to Silberrad and his wife in February of 1912.[116] Wameisa, Nyambura,
and Nyakayena drop out of the archival record after the scandal; we can
only speculate about the long-term effects that the Silberrad Affair had
on their lives. The scandal did live on in the work of Norman Leys, an
anticolonial author and former colonial official in Kenya: in 1924, Leys
referenced the Silberrad case in his book *Kenya* as an example of the corrupt nature of British imperialism in East Africa.[117]

The Silberrad scandal is important to this book in several ways. First,
these discourses suggest that sexual morality was site and space specific.
Although sexual self-control was a defining feature of European cultural/
sexual superiority, Britons worried that these traits would dissolve in the
distant corners of the empire. As bearers of tradition, white women were
viewed as a panacea to this dangerous disorder; by importing domestic
morality to colonial spaces, they prevented sexual disorder. In fact, as we
will see, when a significant settler population did develop in Kenya, they
crafted their own site-specific discourses surrounding sex and race. Anglo-
Kenyan settlers did not simply import a moral sphere; rather, they constructed one in relation to events at the periphery.

Second, the Silberrad scandal mobilized the language of indirect rule
and trusteeship in ways that indicate the inherent tension between them.
Silberrad's rather ingenious defense was premised on the logic of indirect
rule: If customary law held sway in colonized spaces, how could Silberrad be punished for following it? This argument was countered by those
who invoked the trustee duties of the colonizer. The language of ward and
guardian conjured a relationship of dependency, parentage, and even kinship. Interracial sex blurred the lines between ward and guardian, creating
an incestuous relationship that discredited the guardian's claims to act in
the interest of the dependent.

Finally, we see the first suggestions of East Africa as a space of white
sexual deviance, and African sexual vulnerability. While one strand of

discourse characterized African women as property to be exchanged at will between men of any race, an equally prominent thread presented Silberrad as the corruptor of innocent African women and girls. The total absence of any language about female sexual desire contrasts strongly with the representation of African women as lascivious and sexually excessive in other parts of Africa and the African Diaspora. Rather, the Silberrad Affair foreshadows the association of whiteness with sexual excess and disorder, which would come to predominate in colonial Kenya. The next chapter offers another example of this discourse of white sexual disorder, this time arising from members of Kenya's substantial Indian population. During the so-called Indian Crisis, prominent Kenyan Indians argued that, because of their superior sexual morals, they were the population best suited to govern Africans. As the debate raged between white and Indian settlers over who was the most sexually normative, and hence best suited to rule, Africans were racialized as innocent and vulnerable to contamination.

THREE

"Stoop Low to Conquer"

Primitive Normativity and Trusteeship
in the Kenyan "Indian Crisis" of 1923

IN 1923, the Kenyan Indian newspaper editor Sitaram Achariar caused a near-riot when he published a column impugning the chastity of European women. Achariar's paper, *The Democrat*, was responding to anti-Indian statements made in a white-owned paper, *The East African Standard*.[1] Specifically, Achariar wished to dispute the claim that Indians should not be granted equal political status in Kenya since they kept their wives in purdah, married child brides, and refused to allow widows to remarry. "We are not going to support either the custom of child marriage or of purdah which obtains amongst certain sections of our countrymen," Achariar wrote. Yet: "If the earth of India is soaked with the tears of her child-widows, the very atmosphere of England is poisoned by the sobs of the unmarried. It is no exaggeration to say that the great majority of Englishwomen have usually one or two 'abortions' before some one comes along to conduct them to the holy alter."[2] If child-marriage was not an ideal system, Achariar implied, neither was the European trend of late marriage since it led to extramarital sex and the aborting of unwanted offspring. Countering accusations of Indian sexual and moral deviance, Achariar implied that European civilization produced equal or greater evils, especially for women and children.

The *Democrat* article appeared at the height of the so-called "Indian Crisis," a period in the early 1920s when Kenyan Indians demanded a more equal position with the colony's white settler population. The debate quickly became a referendum on which of the two "immigrant races" were more suitable guardians of African wards. Each side presented its opponent as the enemy of the African. Whites accused Indian traders of cheating and overcharging rural Africans, Indian clerks and artisans of stealing jobs that would otherwise go to Africans, and Indian households of posing a sanitary threat to the health of cities. Indians, meanwhile, pointed out the hypocrisy of whites who claimed to serve the best interests of Africans while demanding that the government supply them with cheap African labor to work their farms—farms that had previously been occupied by Africans who had subsequently been relocated to "Native Reserves."

But more importantly for this study, the two "immigrant races" also debated which population would prove to be a more effective guardian of African *sexuality*. In doing so, they mobilized the rhetoric of primitive normativity to present themselves as trustees of African sexual welfare. The imperial philosophy of trusteeship characterized the British state and its agents as benevolent guardians who held land and resources "in trust" for a colonized population that was not yet sufficiently modern for self-government. As Brett Shadle has noted, the language of trusteeship reached an apex during the Indian Crisis, with both Indians and whites positioning themselves as the most suitable guardians of Indigenous peoples.[3] Both groups annexed trusteeship to sexuality, arguing that they were uniquely qualified for the task of protecting the sexual practices and health of African people. During the Indian Crisis, this sexualized vision of trusteeship bore an additional weight, as Kenyan Indians tied their community's ability to enjoy the full rights of British subjects to their (suit)ability to protect the morality of less "civilized" colonial wards. The discourse of primitive normativity privileged sexuality as a key gauge of modernity, and thus political maturity; the Indian Crisis offers a case study of how the narrative of African sexual "innocence" was used to advance the interests of settler groups.

Historians who have looked at the Indian Crisis have generally overlooked the sexualized rhetoric used by Achariar and others. Scholars like Christopher Youé, Robert Gregory, Dane Kennedy, Bruce Berman and John Lonsdale, and Sana Aiyar have written insightfully about the political and racial implications of the Indian Crisis, but without attending to its gendered and sexual dimensions.[4] Aiyar, in an otherwise excellent discussion of Indians in Kenya, goes so far as to claim that "Indian political discourse was largely unconcerned with sexuality, religious practices, and other cultural preoccupations."[5]

However, by paying attention to the sexualized dimensions of trusteeship, we begin to see how issues of sexuality and gender were continuously evoked both by Indian and European settlers. White settlers recirculated discourses of Indian sexual deviance that had originated in the Raj, claiming that Africans would be contaminated by contact with Indian sexual cultures. As Achariar's column indicates, Kenyan Indians responded to this rhetoric by attacking the morals of white settlers, asserting that Indians were more suitable trustees of African sexual welfare. The discourse circulated around two central nodes—the rhetorical figure of the (variously racialized) woman and the (feminized) African—both of whom were constructed as childlike wards in need of protection. As each side depicted its opponent as immoral, African sexuality was being constructed by proxy: primitive normativity envisioned Africans as innocent of sexual depravity and therefore vulnerable to sexual contamination by more civilized, and hence more deviant, colonizers.

It is also significant that, in making their argument for equal status with whites, Indians picked up on the language of evolutionary racism and attempted to deploy it to their own ends. Colonial discourses consistently placed Indians ahead of Africans on the evolutionary timescale—they were supposedly more advanced than Africans, although less civilized than Europeans. In fact, evolutionary narratives about the "westward march of civilization" stressed that Indians had at one time held the position at the apex of civilization, before degenerating to their current state—this is why they were viewed to be particularly prone to forms of sexual deviance such as "the Oriental vice" (sodomy).[6] However, during the Indian Crisis, Kenyan Indians reworked this narrative in several ways. First, they argued that if they were more evolutionarily advanced than Africans, they ought to be allowed to participate in their colonization. Second, they played on fears of white degeneration, suggesting that the Europeans who settled in Kenya were of debased stock, and that Europe as a whole was falling prey to the dangers of racial deterioration. Sexuality was key to this rhetoric because sexual practices were so closely linked to evolutionary racism—with particular sexual practices and prohibitions being associated with the various evolutionary stages. Significantly, Kenyan Indians did not contest the value or legitimacy of colonialism, at home or in Kenya. Rather, they attempted to deploy evolutionary narratives to claim a role in the colonization of a "more primitive" people.

This chapter also therefore offers an opportunity to see what happens when different timescapes of colonialism come together in a single geography. According to the evolutionary discourses of the day, white settlers were civilized people living in a primitive landscape; Indian settlers were the degenerated legacy of a civilized past, yet still more advanced than Africans; and Africans occupied a primitive past left behind by both immigrant groups. In asserting their civic rights, the Indian settlers demanded that the temporal promise of trusteeship be upheld—the promise that when a colonized people were capable of "self-rule," they would no longer be subject to colonization. It is significant that the Kenyan Indians attempted to make good on that promise not in their own space of India, but in the timescape of a "more primitive" people. Sexuality works as a central metaphor that mediates and marks these timescapes because of the belief that the kinds of sex a group supposedly engaged in signified where they stood on the spectrum from primitivism to civilization. It is not so much that Kenya contained competing timescapes, but more that all of these timescapes coexisted in one physical location—this is, in fact, what makes Kenya such an interesting space to explore.

In what follows, I first offer an historical overview of the Indian Crisis, explaining the major points of contestation, as well as the solution proffered by the Colonial Office. Next, I describe the narrative deployed by white settlers to discredit Indian claims to inclusion. Specifically, white settlers recirculated existing colonial discourses about the sexual immorality and gendered disorder of Indian cultures. The twist, though, was that they deployed this narrative not only to counter Kenyan Indian claims for civic inclusion but also to present Kenyan Indians as unsuitable guardians of Africans. In the final section I turn to the Indian response, focusing especially on Achariar's article. Achariar skillfully deployed fears about white degeneracy to argue that white settlers posed the true threat to African sexual morality. Throughout, I emphasize how the debate between the two "immigrant races" relied on a vision of African primitive normativity. Ironically, the one point that both sides of the debate agreed on was that African cultures were too primitive to be deviant; this primitive normativity also indicated that they were not yet sufficiently developed to govern themselves.

The Indian Crisis

Indians first began to settle in inland Kenya in the 1890s, when the British government imported laborers to work on the Uganda Railway: by the time the railway was completed in 1901, just under thirty-two thousand Indians had been imported as laborers, primarily from the Punjab but also from Sind and the Bombay Presidency.[7] About seven thousand Indians remained in the protectorate, most becoming traders, artisans, owners of small shops (dukas), and clerks.[8] Migration continued throughout the colonial period.[9] These migrants came from a wide range of regional, religious, and social backgrounds. Punjabis and Gujaratis were prominent, but migrants also came from Goa and Bombay. The Indian community included Hindus, Muslims (including a sizable community of Ismaili Muslims), and Christians. The Indians imported to work on the railroad included both unskilled laborers and artisans, but the most prominent figures in the Kenyan Indian community tended to be wealthy merchants. Because Kenyan Indians were not allowed to own land in the most fertile parts of the colony, there were relatively few farmers. Indians were, however, very prominent in the lower levels of the colonial administration (they were not allowed to serve in the upper levels).[10]

The Indian population continued to grow throughout the colonial period, always outnumbering whites. In 1921, for example, there were 9,651 Europeans compared with 25,253 Asians, 10,102 Arabs, and roughly 2.5 million Africans.[11] As discussed in the introduction, Europeans dominated the Legislative Council, while the Indian community could elect only two members.[12] Elections were conducted according to a "communal roll," with each enfranchised racial community (Europeans and Asians) voting exclusively for representatives from their own race.

Racial divisions were reflected not only in the electorate but in the colony's land policies. The Crown Lands Ordinance of 1903 set the stage for an appropriation of African lands by white settlers, allowing Crown Lands to be leased to European settlers for a period of ninety-nine years.[13] The fertile area known as the "White Highlands" became the exclusive preserve of Europeans as Africans were removed to Native Reserves, or employed as "squatted labor" on white-owned farms.[14] Another Crown Lands Ordinance in 1915 gave the governor the power to veto the sale or lease of land in the highlands to nonwhites—notably, Kenyan Indians.[15] Thus, both Africans and Indians were excluded from owning the most desirable land in the colony—the significant difference being that these lands had all originally belonged to Africans.

Kenyan Indians responded to these racial inequalities by establishing several organizations to advocate for their position in the colony. One of the most prominent of these organizations, the East African Indian National Congress (EAINC), was formed in 1914 by several wealthy and influential Indian traders.[16] From the beginning, the EAINC represented only those Indians who had proved—by virtue of their wealth and education— that they had attained a comparable "civilizational status" to the British; as Aiyar notes, elite Kenyan Indians "highlighted their civilizational progress to demand rights for themselves, not for the poorer and uneducated working-class Indians whom the Congress did not represent."[17]

In their pursuit of "equal rights for all civilized men," Kenyan Indians made a specific set of demands.[18] First, they sought the right to own land in the White Highlands, not only because this was the most desirable land for farming but also because they viewed segregation as an insult to educated middle- and upper-class Indians. Indians opposed restrictions on immigration but stressed that they supported only the immigration of a certain class of their countrymen and women; in a meeting with Governor Coryndon, M. A. Desai reassured him that "there is no influx of Indians likely; we do not want the coolie class in this country."[19] Finally, they objected to the "communal" voting roll, advocating instead for a "common roll" with Indians, Arabs, and Europeans forming a single multiracial electorate. They did not, however, advocate that *all* Kenyan Indians be allowed to vote, only those who were educated property owners.[20]

Wider shifts in imperial politics abroad also shaped the Indian Crisis. Mrinalini Sinha has argued that the First World War brought significant changes in British imperial policy toward the Raj. In 1917, India was rewarded for its contribution to the war effort with a declaration in the House of Commons favoring "the progressive realization of responsible government in India as an integral part of the British Empire."[21] The meaning of "responsible government" was left deliberately vague; few British politicians actually supported granting India dominion status akin to that enjoyed by white settler–ruled spaces like Australia or South Africa.[22]

The postwar period also saw new waves of activism, including Gandhi's noncooperation movement. As the noncooperation movement began to gain steam, lobbying by metropolitan organizations like the Indian Overseas Association and the Imperial Indian Citizenship Association connected the plight of Indians in the diaspora to the fate of domestic Indians.[23] Kenya was considered to be a particularly important site in this debate because it was a Crown colony, and hence under the direct control of the Colonial Office. It was bad enough for Indians to be discriminated against in territories with responsible self-government like South Africa,[24] but for Britain to allow racial discrimination against Indian subjects in a Crown colony gave the lie to British claims to preparing Indians for "progressive realization of responsible government."[25] A document published by the Kenya Indian Delegates in 1923 explained that allowing Indians to be placed in inferior status in a Crown colony like Kenya "would deal the death-blow to the hopes of Indians and their trust in the good faith of the Imperial Government and the British people."[26]

Despite these broader trends, white settlers in Kenya were not prepared to cede or share power. In fact, frenzied white settlers were threatening to take "direct action" in the colony should the Indian demands be met; they even devised a plan to kidnap Sir Robert Thorne Coryndon, the governor of Kenya, and deport all the Indians in the colony to Mombasa, from whence they could be shipped back to India.[27] Christopher Youé has argued that the prospect of a white settler rebellion loomed large in the Colonial Office, which was eager to avoid a situation in which African soldiers in the Kings African Rifles would be called upon to shoot at white Kenyans; such an order, Youé argues, would be "political suicide for the Conservative government."[28] The Colonial Office was put in a difficult position; if they conceded to the Kenyan Indians' demands, the settlers might revolt, yet they also needed to avoid stoking anticolonial discontent in India.

The solution the Colonial Office found for this problem was "the doctrine of native paramountcy." In 1923, the Duke of Devonshire, then Secretary of State for the Colonies, released a White Paper introducing a new philosophy of administration in colonial Kenya. The so-called Devonshire Declaration rejected the demands of Kenyan Indians for civic inclusion on the basis that in colonial Kenya "the interests of the African natives must be paramount, and that if, and when, those interests and the interests of the immigrant races should conflict, the former should prevail."[29] The Declaration neatly sidestepped the issue of Indian equality by asserting the primacy of African interests, that is, "native paramountcy."

Scholars who have written about the Devonshire Declaration have been rightly cynical about the motivations of the Colonial Office in declaring native paramountcy. What appears on the surface to be a commitment to prioritizing the welfare of colonized people was in fact the outcome of careful maneuvering by a Colonial Office determined to appease white settlers without offending mainland India. "The press in India had assumed a threatening tone, Africans in Kenya were restive, and Europeans there were laying plans to kidnap the Acting Governor," concludes Robert Gregory. "In this tense situation native paramountcy appeared to be the only plan acceptable to all parties."[30]

Interestingly, as Gregory has pointed out, the concept of native paramountcy was first elaborated in the colony itself.[31] In Kenya, pamphlets, government reports, minutes of colonial organizations, and especially colonial newspapers consistently framed the Indian Crisis as a question of which group, the Indians or the white settlers, would better serve the interests of Indigenous Africans. Full civic inclusion in Kenya, then, was premised on inclusion in the "civilizing mission."

By placing the Indian presence in Kenya in the context of broader transnational politics, Wambui Mwangi shows why Indian demands provoked so much anxiety in the white settler community.[32] Because Kenyan Indians were so crucial to the colony's economy, it became "possible for colonized Indians to presume an equality that extended to a desire for the particularity of the positions reserved for the British."[33] That is, Kenyan Indians began to equate equality with the right to colonize more "primitive" peoples. However, as Mwangi explains, the notion of Indians serving as "sub-imperialists" represented both the logical conclusion of the colonial "civilizing mission," and an outcome that would undermine the distinctions that structured the colonial enterprise:

> For Indian colonialism to have quite literally represented British colonialism would have meant that British colonialism in India had succeeded in producing the essential colonized subject—a pure subject constituted only by the fact of having been colonized and existing only within the terms of reference of this colonization. Paradoxically, the requisite degree of faith in such re-creation, and the attendant sanguine acceptance of the notion of the Indian colonizer, would inescapably have led to the surrender of the crucial distinctions between colonizer and colonized. It would have suggested that Indians could be mimetically representative of, equal to and indistinguishable from the British in East Africa.[34]

The idea that Indians were fit to rule others would also imply their fitness to rule themselves—thus undermining the legitimacy of British rule in the Raj. Conversely, if Indians were proved unsuitable to hold authority over Africans, then they could not be accepted into the ranks of colonizers.

In determining fitness to rule—either the self or others—sexuality and gender were touchstones returned to again and again. During the Indian Crisis, both Kenyan Indians and white settlers focused on sexuality as a metonym of colonial trusteeship. The next section examines how white settlers used tropes of Indian sexual depravity to oppose Kenyan Indian demands, arguing that they were acting in the interest of vulnerable African wards. In particular, they emphasized Indians' supposed cruelty to women, the prevalence of deviant sexual practices in Indian cultures, and the effeminacy of Indian men as markers of their immorality. More significantly for this project, they did so in ways that consistently contrasted Indian deviance with the primitive normativity of colonized African subjects. The discourse of sexual trusteeship thus allowed whites to oppose Indian political demands while positioning themselves as guardians of African sexual welfare.

Kenyan Indian Deviance

White settler discourse about Kenyan Indians revolved around a seeming contradiction: while Kenyan Indians were consistently constructed as more sexually deviant than Africans, they were also presented as more evolutionarily evolved. In fact, the concepts were deeply related. Because sexual deviance was associated with degeneration, only those societies that had attained a certain level of civilization were considered to be capable of developing deviant sexual practices. Thus, by constructing Kenyan Indians as sexually deviant, white settlers essentially conceded that they were more evolutionarily "advanced" than Africans. This concession might have logically led to the expansion of certain civic rights to Indians, but instead it took a different route—by presenting Indians as a threat to the sexual morality of the colony's more "primitive" African wards, the white settler population mobilized sexual trusteeship as a duty that only whites were capable of fulfilling.

The construction of Indians as sexually deviant and immoral has a long history. In India, imperialists pointed to the supposed sexual immorality of Indians as evidence that they required the benevolent intervention of British guardians. As scholars Mrinalini Sinha, Antoinette Burton, Tanika Sarkar, and Padma Anagol-McGinn have shown, nineteenth-century imperialists frequently justified colonialism as a means of protecting vulnerable Indian subjects—particularly women—from practices like purdah, sati, and child marriage.[35] Such traditions were viewed as symptomatic of a larger culture of sexual degeneration in India: as Mrinalini Sinha explains, proponents of imperialism tied "the alleged sexual obsession of the Hindus that was manifest in practices such as child marriage and premature maternity, as well as in rampant masturbation and homosexuality" to the unsuitability of Indians for self-rule.[36]

The notion of Indian sexual depravity was also closely tied to evolutionary racism and particularly to the discourse of degeneration. The so-called Aryan race theory (popular amongst philologists and Orientalists in the nineteenth century) in fact posited that Europeans and Hindu Indians shared a common ancestral past, with the key difference that Asian civilizations had declined (due to climate, intermarriage with more "primitive" groups, or the influence of Muslim conquerors) while Europeans had progressed.[37] As Sinha notes, while "this scholarship had very little impact on actual race relations in colonial India . . . it formed the basis for popular colonial explanations of contemporary Indian society in terms of a fall or decline from the glories of an ancient Aryan past."[38]

The characterization of Indians as culturally backward and sexually deviant traveled relatively intact across the Indian Ocean with two key differences. First, the policy of divide and rule meant that in India the British recognized and even produced a number of divisions, based on caste, religion, ethnicity, and so on, within the colonized population marked as "Indian." However, in Kenya, South Asian immigrants tended to be treated as a single group. Likewise, Kenyan Indians themselves tended to eschew internal differences in the interests of presenting a united front—as in the East African Indian National Congress, which represented all members of the Kenyan Indian population.[39]

The second major difference in the use of the discourse of "deviant Indians" was that, in East Africa, it was used not only to discredit Indian self-rule but also to demonstrate their incapacity to rule Africans. The report of the 1919 *Economic Commission of Enquiry into Post-War Development*, for instance, characterized Kenyan Indians as unsanitary and criminal. However, the Economic Commission went beyond simply opposing the "decadent civilisation of India" by comparing it to the more primitive, and hence more innocent, sexuality of Africans: the Commission noted that "The moral depravity of the Indian is equally damaging to the African, who in his natural state is at least innocent of the worst vices of the East."[40] By contrasting Indian "depravity" with African "innocence," the report invoked the narrative of primitive normativity to discredit Kenyan Indian claims.

By presenting Indians as a threat to the morality of Indigenous Africans, white settlers sought to establish trusteeship as a sacred duty exclusive to whites. *The Mombasa Times* opined that "To allow participation in the administration of a race distrusted by the aboriginal inhabitants would lower the status of the whites, and not raise that of the exotic black, the sum total result would probably be the loss of the colony and its reversion to heathenism of a worse type than ob[t]ained before the advent of civilisation."[41] The idea of a "reversion to heathenism" implicitly evoked the association of Indians with degeneration—to allow them to participate in the governing of the colony would be to reverse the temporal course of the civilizing mission. Similarly, in a 1923 interview with the *Manchester Guardian*, the prominent Anglo-Kenyan missionary Dr. John W. Arthur (who also served as the representative for African interests on the colony's Legislative Council) asserted that "Our responsibilities and our trustee-ship for the natives could not [be] carried out if there was unrestricted immigration from India and if the influences of Eastern civilisation and morality were to become paramount."[42] White settlers argued that, to fulfill their duties as the trustees of vulnerable Africans, they must protect them from contamination by "Eastern" cultures.

In particular, white settlers recycled the trope, already used to great effect in the Raj, that Indians mistreated women and girls. This was viewed as an indication of their low evolutionary status and their unreadiness to take on the burden of either self-rule or the rule of others. Critics pointed, for example, to the practice of polygamy among some Kenyan Indian communities as evidence of their unsuitability for civic inclusion. In a letter to the editor of the *East African Standard*, Elizabeth Coxoni offered some "Knotty Points to Consider" in relation to Indian franchise. For example, she asked, "how many wives of Indians of Mahomedan faith would be entitled to vote? If only one then who settles the knotty question of the owner of the vote; if the head of the harem, quite obviously he will chose [sic] the wife of the least mutinous and rebellious disposition!" But Coxoni also objected to the idea of granting the vote to all the wives, saying "the experience of the average Indian woman does not, as yet, entitle her to take part in public life. That a few Indian women have become more or less emancipated is true but they are so very few in number that they do not affect the bulk of the population, nor is it easy to see how they can do so even in the distant future unless the main tenants of their religions are forsaken and the status of Asiatic women is entirely altered."[43] Coxoni's concern about the dangers of granting suffrage to Indian women is particularly interesting when we consider that European women had only gained the vote in Kenya four years earlier, in 1919.

The notion that Indians mistreated women was also extended in ways peculiar to the Kenyan colonial situation—Indians were not simply too immoral for self-rule, but more importantly, they were depicted as likely to corrupt and contaminate Africans. The East African Women's League (an organization formed by the wives of settlers and officials)[44] explained the unsuitability of Kenyan Indians for enfranchisement by contrasting them with the more "primitive" Indigenous population: "The customs of the average African are far more wholesome and sanitary than those of the low caste Indian, who is so conservative that he will not learn decent habits even when he comes in contact with uplifting influences."[45] The EAWL juxtaposed the more "wholesome" African customs with those of their Indian peers, driving home the point that Indians could not gain access to equal rights unless they proved themselves capable of serving as trustees of African sexual welfare.[46] The EAWL also added a particularly Kenyan spin to the rhetoric of Indian misogyny by claiming that Indian women were too sheltered to provide benevolent care to vulnerable Africans. "The native has on the whole taken very kindly to the rule of the white woman," they claimed. "The Native has learned to look on the British Woman as his friend and to turn naturally to her in times of trouble, and sickness. The Indian woman by the limitations of her Eastern education has not been trained to cope with the everyday emergencies that arise on farms in outlying districts."[47] The League questioned Indian women's ability to provide medical care to ill Africans, a task they associated closely with their role as colonial women.[48] Of course, the construction of Indian women as powerless bolstered white women's self-perception as essential agents in the colonial mission.

The consistent references to Indians' supposed misogyny are particularly interesting given that African societies, too, were constructed as deeply abusive to women. The reference to the demoralizing influence of polygamy is a case in point, given that most East African communities were, at the time, also polygamous. Furthermore, as the previous chapter showed, Africans were consistently derided for exploiting women's labor, treating them as "beasts of burden," and "selling" them into marriages. The fact that Kenyan Indians could be portrayed as a poor moral example to a community that was consistently derided using the very same terms is not so much a contradiction as an object lesson in how discourses of race and sexuality function: these discourses can be endlessly malleable, frequently incoherent, and often internally inconsistent without sacrificing any of their rhetorical power. As Gloria Steinem rather succinctly put it, "Logic has nothing to do with oppression."[49]

As white settler discourses sought to establish that Indian misogyny rendered them unsuitable mentors for African wards, they also suggested that Indian sexuality was inherently degenerate and likely to contaminate African communities. For instance, the "Memorandum on the Case against Indians in Kenya" (written by prominent settlers Lord Delamere and C. K. Archer) highlighted the sexual threat posed by Kenyan Indians to African colonial wards. The memorandum quoted Dr. Burkitt, a private MD and former medical officer in India, who claimed that "Venereal disease, in peoples following such debasing religious customs [as Indians do], I need hardly say, is rampant, more rampant probably than anywhere else. . . . The same may be said of bestial sexual offences, also generated by these religions and which *are almost unknown among primitive peoples.*"[50] Dr. Burkitt excluded Indians from the category of the "primitive" by virtue of their deviance, and consigned Africans to primitivism based on their inability to veer from the sexual norm.

A settler named Spencer Tryon also made a distinction between the sexual habits of Indians and Africans in his 1921 letter to the Anti-Slavery and Aboriginal Protection Society, a London-based humanitarian group that had taken an interest in the Indian Crisis. Tryon suggested that Indians spread both plague and venereal disease to Africans, and that relationships between Indians and African women were responsible for not only the spread of disease but also the corruption of previously morally upstanding Africans.[51]

To this presentation of Indians as misogynistic and sexually deviant, white settlers added a third offence: Indian men were insufficiently masculine to govern Africans. Thus, even as whites attacked the morals of Indians, they also rehearsed the paternalistic position of whites as the protectors of effeminate and weak "Orientals." In a letter to the *Standard*, Lionel Lawford, a commander in the Royal Navy, recalled a visit to an estate where 140 African men were working. After asking one worker for his opinion about Indians, Lawford claimed to have been told "Master, if the white men forsake the native and leave the Indian here to rule us there will be very few Indians left in a weeks time."[52] Lawford concluded that the British were not only the protectors of Africans, but "we are also the protectors of the Indian community who at the moment we oppose, for remove the Government of this country, the white man as the holders of justice and peace and leave the Indian as the ruler of this country and I stake my reputation of ten years experience of the native and Indian relationship of this Colony that a rising will be seen which will shake this country to the core."[53] Indians were merely "the pretenders of the moment," he continued, "who unable and untried in the art of Government, seek to take from a nation of tried colonists the reins of emancipation of a race which they are entirely incapable of handling."[54]

The notion of the effeminate "Oriental" was also exploited in a lecture entitled "The Thermopylae of Africa. Kenya Colony's Responsibility in the Conflict of the Primary Races" given by E. Powys Cobb, a prominent settler and member of the Legislative Council and the Convention of Associations.[55] Cobb wrote that "it is difficult to picture so grotesque a thing as the timid Indian ruling the manly war-loving African native. Certain it is that his rule would be corrupt and oppressive, for his veneer of Western democracy would soon wear off leaving exposed the Eastern despot."[56] Furthermore, it was likely that the Indian would intermarry with Africans "as he did with the negroid tribes of Southern India, so adding a bastard breed to the horrors of his misrule."[57] Not only did their supposed effeminacy render Indians unfit to govern Africans, but they also posed a sexual threat poised to disrupt African primitive normativity. The threat of "intermarriage" in particular raised the powerful specter of racial degeneration. The Indian threatened the African; the African threatened the Indian; only the benevolent white colonist stood in the way of their mutually assured destruction.

By contrasting the Oriental decadence of Indian culture with the primitive normativity of Africans, white settlers sought to prove that Kenyan Indians were unfit to serve as trustees of African sexual welfare. By doing so, they hoped to preserve their privileged position in the colony, where they wielded political influence far beyond their numbers. What is perhaps more surprising is the degree to which Kenyan Indians also adopted the language of sexual trusteeship. As Aiyar notes, Indians in the imperial diaspora "straddled the discursive division between colonizer and colonized."[58] They were therefore less likely to oppose the British colonial project than Indians on the subcontinent. Instead, they viewed their full recognition as British subjects as contingent on their inclusion as fellow colonizers of Africans. And to make this case, they activated very similar discourses to those produced by white settlers: whites were unfit to rule (feminized) Africans because of their mistreatment of women and because of their debased sexual practices.

"The Scum of England and Europe": The Kenyan Indian Reply

In her book *Politics of Time*, Prathama Banerjee makes the following observation about the shifting timescapes at play in colonial spaces: "[T]he
colonizer, being more 'advanced', claimed to possess a greater cumulation
of history and experience and claimed to harness a greater length of time
for themselves. In response, the colonized claimed, for their own history,
the length of time which was greater still. If they were not as 'advanced' as
the rulers, they possessed a more antique past—granting them a right to
a temporal depth far greater than that of the self-consciously modern nation."[59] While Banerjee is discussing Indian civilizational claims at home
on the subcontinent, her observations are equally salient for understanding the Kenyan Indian response to the discourses highlighted previously.
Kenyan Indians made claims to a higher evolutionary standard then either
their fellow immigrant populations, or the Indigenous African population. Given the primacy of sexual and gendered language in the white settler
discourses, it's perhaps not surprising that Kenyan Indians also centered
gender and sexuality in their arguments for why they were, in fact, more
suitable trustees of African sexual welfare than Europeans.

Perhaps the most outspoken critic of white claims to sexual trusteeship
was Sitaram Achariar. His article "Stoop Low to Conquer," with which
this chapter opened, was penned as a response to letters published in the
East African Standard, in particular a letter in which Reverend W. H.
Shaw asserted that Indians were unsuited for citizenship as they were "alien
in mind, colour, religion, morality."[60] Achariar pointed to the deviousness
of white settler tactics as a way of impugning their claim to higher civilizational status. The statement "alls fair in love and war," he claimed, must
have been coined during "the dark days in England when the people wore
hides like the highlanders of Africa and had their bodies tottooed [*sic*]."
Although most of the British had since "outgrown these medieval ethics,"
he noted that "there are still some 'black sheep' who would not be civilized,
and who to-day exhibit the same frame of mind and follow the same school
of ethics which characterized their ancestors in the dark ages. True, they no
longer wear skins and hides but their mentality is awfully behind the times
they live in. Unfortunately, there are quite a few white people in Kenya
who come under this category—the scum of England and Europe."[61]

Achariar's characterization of Kenyan whites as atavistic and
primitive—analogous, in fact, to "the highlanders of Africa"—fits into a
larger civilizational discourse characterizing the "primitive" as politically

immature. It also tapped into fears of white degeneration, suggesting that those whites who migrated to Kenya represented "the scum of England and Europe," people whom the European march towards civilized modernity had left behind. Accusing the Europeans of using malicious tactics to resist Kenyan Indian demands, Achariar noted that "The Indians could do the same if they want to stoop so low, but as it happens they have much longer and more civilized traditions behind them and it is therefore difficult for them to make up their minds to resort to such medieval and barbarous tactics."[62] Realigning the hierarchy of civilizations, Achariar placed Indian civilizations on top, and the "medieval and barbarous" culture of white Kenyans well below.

In denigrating European claims to civilizational perfection, Achariar turned specifically to the question of sexuality. "Sexual morality has reached such a lowered ebb in Europe, particularly in England," he writes, "that thinking people are striving their best to devise ways and means to minimise it. . . . Syphilis and other venereal diseases are fairly common and although there a number of hospitals maintained by the State and by the Public to cleanse the nation of this poison, the demand always exceeds the supply."[63] As discussed at the beginning of this chapter, Achariar responded to criticisms of child marriage and purdah in India by suggesting that delayed marriage among white women resulted in premarital sex and abortions. "We say this in no vindictive spirit," he assured the reader, "but only to show that marriage several years after puberty is just as bad as the Indian child marriage" both for the women themselves and for the unfortunate babies that the wealthy aborted or abandoned, while "the poorer classes consign their product of shame and infamy to the tender care of the Thames."[64] He concluded his attack with the assertion that "Incest is fairly common in England-a crime which is unheard-of in Oriental countries."[65] In these few sensational paragraphs, Achariar assembled a compendium of European vices, from indiscriminate sex to infanticide. Perhaps most strikingly, Achariar countered the characterization of sodomy as an "Oriental vice" by insisting that the crime of incest was an Occidental vice unknown in the East.

As Brett Shadle has noted, the settlers' response to Achariar's column was largely framed as a defense of the prestige of white women.[66] In the days following the column's publication, local settler-owned newspapers filled up with letters from outraged whites, advocating Achariar's arrest and deportation on the grounds that he "has overstepped the bounds of decency" and "attempt[ed] to sully the fair name of the white women of Kenya.[67] In characterizing Achariar's column as an attack on women, white Kenyans implicitly drew on the narrative that Indians mistreated women—and that this was a sign of their lack of civilization. While authorities did end up arresting Achariar, they claimed that they did so to protect him from white mobs that were out to lynch him.

Indians in Mombasa responded to Achariar's arrest with a hartal, closing all shops and parking all taxis, effectively shutting down all business in the city in protest. A Nairobi Barrister named K. S. Chowdhury wrote a letter to the *East African Standard* pointing to the injustice of Achariar's imprisonment: White Papers had published accusations about the treatment of Indian widows that "was all provoking and painful lies, but no step was taken because the writer happened to be an European, and above all because it was against Indians. But if an Indian spoke some truth based purely on Historical facts and figures, I can not understand why the European people should be . . . so much upset as, to apply for Deportation."[68] He concluded his letter: "I pray to the Almighty God to give us 20 new Editors like the one of the 'Democrat' who is now in the clutch of those persons who wrongly do not like him."[69] The *East African Standard* responded to Chowdhury's letter by suggesting that Achariar's letter had been pornographic and that Indians supported him out of a desire to read illicit material; the *Standard* claimed Indians "may even enjoy reading what can only be termed indecent literature of this description. To judge indeed from the letter of an Indian barrister which we print in this issue, it would appear that they would like more of it." The paper concludes with the outraged observation that "these are the people who wish to assist in governing Kenya. These are they who would guide the Native mind and character."[70] The idea that Indians might teach Africans to view white women as sexually loose and to take erotic pleasure in stories of their licentiousness represented the ultimate threat, the specter of "Black Peril."

Achariar was freed in early March, largely due to the activism of the Indian community, and the government made the unpopular decision not to deport him. It seems that the Colonial Office instructed Governor Coryndon how to proceed; a letter from Major E. A. T. Dutton, the governor's private secretary, referred to Achariar's "deliberate, malicious and false attack on the honour of our women and, by the release of Achariar without any suggestion that he should withdraw, the attack has been justified; and this in a native country, Good Lord!"[71] The colonial officials thus reworked Achariar's statement in more rhetorically volatile terms; what was in fact an attack on white (male) supremacy in the colony was rewritten as a *sexual* threat to white women. The settlers agreed with this contention that Achariar's release represented an invitation to the sexual harassment and violation of white women by men of other races. In response to his release from jail, white settlers held a public meeting at Mombasa Club, on March 10, 1923, to decide whether or not to resort to direct action against Achariar. Ultimately, they decided against it but advised the government to more strictly police the press. The *Mombasa Times* reported this decision against direct action with outrage: the meeting had resolved "to take the advice of His Excellency to let the matter drop. In other words, European women may be libelled; but because politics are supreme, their honour must be subservient to political exigencies. It is on such an occasion that one hails the Suffragette movement. After all, women appear to be chattels, where men rule."[72] An unavenged attack on the morals of white women rendered them "chattels," the very word used so often to criticize the position of Indian and African women. A column in the *East African Standard* suggested that Achariar's libel of European women was in fact designed to provoke whites into violence, thereby gaining the sympathy of the Colonial Office: "Our Indian friends are ready to make any sacrifice whether of truth, or even decency, to enable them to goad some European into taking 'direct action', so that they may find an excuse for fresh inflammatory cables [to India and the Colonial Office], or confirmation for those already sent."[73]

Ultimately, neither Kenyan Indians nor white settlers resorted to violence. Nor was Achariar scared away from politics; he continued to publish *The Democrat*, and when Jomo Kenyatta established his Gikuyu-language paper *Muigwithania* in 1928, Achariar served as his printer.[74] Although the furor over Achariar's column ultimately died down, an examination of the column and its context gives us important insight into how racial discourses worked as social hierarchies of power in 1920s Kenya. As the controversy evolved, spokespersons on each side made their arguments within an increasingly restrictive framework. It became impossible to discuss Indian civic inclusion without making a claim about the effect, positive or negative, that such inclusion would have on the moral and sexual lives of Africans—that is, whether it would protect or threaten the "primitive normativity" that supposedly characterized African sexuality. Achariar titled his article "Stoop Low to Conquer" as a way of indicting whites for the lengths they would go to discredit their Indian peers; however, he framed his own response in accordance with the discursive framework established by settler papers, that is, a framework that translated the question of colonial belonging into a language of sexual morality.

Furthermore, it's significant to note how women became the central node around which this discourse turned; at various stages, women of all races were singled out as the potential victims of political disorder. At the same time, Africans of *all genders* were implicitly feminized by this discourse, presented as vulnerable to the sexual predations of the more "civilized" immigrant classes and in need of protection. While the previous chapter laid out the unsexing of African women, this chapter suggests a similar ungendering of African men, who appear in the discourse primarily as victims whose vulnerability to corruption signals their status as wards and minors. Women of all races and feminized Africans appear as the silent but central nodes around which the entire debate turned.

By restricting the terms of the debate to which population would make better colonists, the discourse of sexual trusteeship implicitly foreclosed the idea that Africans might be capable of representing themselves: the possibility of Africans participating in the democratic process was only held up as a disastrous possible consequence of the battle between Indians and whites. Ironically, while the language of sexual trusteeship tied sexual morality to civic inclusion, it also characterized those who practiced the most "natural" sexuality as the least fit to rule. Importantly, then, the language of sexual trusteeship was a way of defining not only colonial guardians but also wards in relation to their sexual evolution. Ironically, by correlating sexual innocence to political immaturity, sexual trusteeship suggested that because Africans were sexually uncontaminated, they were also destined to be ruled by more corrupted cultures.

It would not be accurate, however, to say that African voices were completely silenced. Over the course of the crisis, there were several letters and telegrams published in the press and widely discussed that purported to be authored by Africans.[75] Like the Indian- and white-authored sources analyzed previously, African-authored sources followed a highly restricted discursive framework that largely limited them to a discussion of which population would make a preferable colonial authority.

A case in point is the special supplement to *Sekanyolya*, a Luganda-language paper edited by Z. K. Sentongo, a Ugandan expatriate living in Nairobi. As Michael Twaddle explains in his article on Sentongo, a sizable community of educated Ugandans lived in Nairobi at the time, where they took advantage of the higher wages available to them.[76] The supplement in question had been translated from Luganda to English "for the benefit of the many European subscribers to this paper," indicating that the message was tailored to appeal to a settler audience.[77] Sentongo claimed that

Indians had done nothing for the education of Africans and asserted that the influence of two civilizations (British and Asian) on Africans would lead "to a confusion of ideas on conduct, morals, etc."[78] It continues:

> If the current rumour of equal rights for Indians with Whites in Kenya Colony materialises, then the educated Africans in Kenya and Uganda will have to press for similar rights. It is true that we educated Africans recognise the great superiority of Whites over Africans and are willing to learn and obey their laws, but the idea of being subjected to a race whom we do not admit to be our superiors, who would then come to our shores in their thousands and prevent us from learning trades and useful work, and therefore robbing us of our livelihood, and ever keeping us in the dark, would be an unjust, intolerable law and opposed to our sense of justice, because it is our wish to learn from the White man and to form a big African Nation.[79]

Interestingly, Sentongo asserts that Africans would be compelled to demand equal political rights *only* if Indians were granted them first; he therefore holds up African enfranchisement as a threat rather than a demand, playing on white settlers' fears that enfranchising Indians would lead to the extension of rights to Africans. Sentongo also reproduces paternalistic arguments about the role of whites in the colonial "civilizing mission." Sana Aiyar dismisses the supplement as the product of a Muganda expatriate who was hostile to Indian business interests.[80] While Aiyar is correct to contextualize the *Sekanyolya* source, it is nonetheless important to recognize that no source is more "authentically African" than another. Rather, all represent viewpoints that emerged out of the complicated and varied engagements of Africans with colonialism. For the author of *Sekanyolya*, the decision to reiterate the rhetoric of white paternalism may have been a strategic one.

The source that most explicitly echoed white settler rhetoric appeared as a letter to the editor of the *East African Standard*. The author, Obner Owyo son of Obiero, objected to the enfranchisement of Indians on the basis that they were untrustworthy and sent all their money back home to India. More interestingly for the purposes of this chapter, however, Obiero also echoed the EAWL's contention that the status of Indian *women* presented an obstacle to their colonizing ambitions. He noted that Indian "women cannot look after hospitals nor touch a sick person, while the English ladies are doing all this sort of things without saying that she being a European lady cannot attend to a black man, as the European lady sees the sick person feels very pity on him just the same as he was one of her own child."[81] The white editors of the *Standard* likely viewed this letter with approval since it recirculated settler discourses privileging white women as the source of charity and maternal care, the very image that organizations like the EAWL hoped to convey.

A few African-authored sources, however, explicitly rejected the notion that Africans were incapable of representing themselves; ironically, these sources were quickly dismissed as "unrepresentative." The clearest example is a telegram sent to the Colonial Office by the East African Association, an early African nationalist organization led by Harry Thuku, at the end of May 1923, that reads as follows (for the sake of clarity, I have filled in the words that were left out in the original telegram):

> [The] East African Association consisting [of] Young Kikuyu Kavirondo Nandi [and] other natives wish [to] represent grievances [by] sending [our] own delegation. [We have] No faith [in] Dr. Arthur [and] believe he [will] harm our cause [and] favour white settlers our troubles emanate [from] white settlers only. We [are] afraid [to] declare our mind here [and] fear imprisonment transportation or hanging. [We] Request [to be] afford[ed the] opportunity [to send] representative natives [and] wait upon you before taking [a] decision regarding [the] fate [of] our country [We] want [to] remain [a] Protectorate not [a] white colony. [We] Understand chiefs [were] influenced [or] coerced [to] sign certain documents [and we] disassociate ourselves [from the] contents thereof."[82]

Here, the members of the East African Association identify themselves as the appropriate representatives of African opinion; they stress their multiethnic composition and express their lack of faith in both Dr. Arthur, the missionary appointed to represent Africans during the discussions in London, and the chiefs who attested (apparently under duress) to their antipathy to Indian enfranchisement. The Colonial Office dismissed the telegram as being "unofficial" and therefore regretted that it could not possibly consider its proposal to send African delegates. A cable from Nairobi to the Colonial Office asserted that the telegram had been sent to the Colonial Office "WITHOUT KNOWLEDGE OR APPROVAL [of] CHIEFS"; rather, the "EXECUTIVE INDIAN CONGRESS HAVE DISTORTED THESE FACTS TO SUGGEST NATIVE REPUDIATION OF DEPUTATION AND THIS DOUBTLESS ORIGIN CABLE."[83] The cable reported that Indians were now organizing a meeting with six hundred Gikuyu in an attempt to gain belated support for their claims.[84] The Colonial Office rejected African demands for meaningful representation by claiming that the telegram had not been authored by Africans at all. Rather, Indians had manipulated the East African Association into representing their case and were continuing to rile up otherwise docile colonial subjects.

The local press was similarly dismissive of these claims. In an article somewhat ironically titled "The Voice of Africa," the *East African Standard* insisted that, while most Africans were illiterate, they would surely side with Europeans if they could. "Natives to-day are for the most part inarticulate," the *Standard* claimed, "but they will not always be so. There will come a time when they will judge us for our actions to-day, and thank us for doing the right thing, or blame us bitterly for betraying their interests."[85] Here, the white settler paper proclaimed the impossibility of Africans speaking for themselves, even as its own claim to represent Africans effectively silenced them.

Thus, even when African voices did make it into the discourse of the Indian Crisis, they were always mediated through the rubric of "authenticity." Unsurprisingly, those statements that aligned most closely with a colonial vision of white paternalism were those most likely to be deemed authentic. Indeed, settlers believed that part of their obligation as "trustees" of African welfare was to determine which African voices could be considered authentic. For the historian, this is also a reminder that locating and highlighting "African voices" will not allow us to access any authentic truth about colonized perspectives; African voices, like all others, are mediated by and produced in relation to discursive regimes, and Africans occupied complicated and contradictory positions within colonial hierarchies. Rather than attempt to recover the "authentic" voice of the colonized, we might do better to consider how such voices were structured by regimes of power.

Conclusion

During the Indian Crisis, Kenya's two "immigrant races" argued over which group was more suited to serve as trustees of African welfare. Significantly, sexuality became a central metaphor of fitness to rule, and the discourse of primitive normativity was invoked by both sides to bolster their claims. Both Kenyan Indians and white settlers accused their opponents of sexual depravity; both suggested that this depravity could be spread to vulnerable African wards. The duties of sexual trusteeship were mobilized in this debate in ways that presented Africans as childlike, vulnerable, and incapable of self-representation. African voices were included in the debate only to the extent that they supported the colonial civilization mission; any more trenchant critiques of colonialism were dismissed as fraudulent or inauthentic.

While this chapter has examined a discourse where two competing populations accused each other of sexual deviance, the next chapter explores a rhetoric of white sexual dysfunction that emanated from *within* the white community. An outbreak of alleged assaults on European and Asian children by African men produced a surprising rhetorical response; both administrators and settlers blamed white women for generating deviant sexual desires within their African employees through their own lewd behavior. Through an analysis of the intersecting languages of age, race, and consent, I show how the discourse of primitive normativity structured interracial relations within the intimate space of the settler home.

FOUR

White Peril

Rape, Race, and Contamination

IN 1920, what appeared to be a spree of assaults on white children by African domestic servants prompted outcry from within the Kenyan settler community. The colonial government responded by appointing a "Special Committee on Sexual Assaults of Natives upon Europeans" to investigate the problem.[1] As part of their study, the committee compiled all the available data on sexual assaults of white and Indian girls and women by African men and boys. Despite widespread concern about the alleged assaults within the settler community, the committee's report, completed on July 22, 1920, determined that "sexual offences by natives upon European women and children, so far from being prevalent, are quite exceptional in this protectorate and that there is no reason to think they are on the increase."[2]

In his testimony to the Special Committee on Sexual Assaults, Kenya's Chief Native Commissioner (CNC) John Ainsworth accounted for the relative rarity of rapes in the colony by maintaining that it was a practice not often found in Indigenous African societies. In Kenya, he asserted, "sexual assaults by natives on native children are unheard of, and that while such offences upon adult native girls are not unknown, they are extremely rare owing to the prevalence of free love among various tribes."[3] In other words, because the practice of "free love" allowed African men to access sex whenever they liked, there was supposedly no motivation for crimes like rape.[4] The committee determined that no further legislation was needed to deter such crimes.[5]

This chapter examines how the narrative of primitive normativity shaped discourses surrounding interracial intimacy and sexual violence. Settler homes were key spaces of quotidian interracial intimacies between white settler women and African domestic servants. The ability to keep a large staff of African domestic servants was viewed as an essential perquisite of Kenyan settler lifestyles, yet the daily cross-racial and cross-gendered interactions in settler homes troubled the boundaries of the settler state. White settlers thus needed to devise a discourse that policed these daily cross-racial intimacies while preserving the ability of housewives to manage large staffs of African domestic servants. The solution to this problem was the development of a narrative depicting *white women* as a potent threat to the sexual morality of the African men and boys who worked in settler homes, a concept that I refer to as "White Peril."[6]

"White Peril" rhetoric held that white women who promoted excessive "familiarity" with their African servants created a desire for the white female body that was absent in the "uncontaminated" African mind. This included behaviors that, although not inherently or clearly sexual in nature, were perceived as promoting undo "familiarity" in African servants and thereby creating desires for sexual contact with white women or girls. Importantly, the groups deemed most likely to behave with excessive familiarity were poor whites and ethnically marginal whites, especially those of South African origin. White Peril discourses thus intertwined ideas about class difference with sexual, gendered, and racial rhetoric.

Unlike the term Black Peril (which refers to allegations of the sexual assault of white girls or women by Black men), White Peril was not a term generally used by colonial Kenyans. However, in naming this phenomenon—and especially in naming it using terms that play on and extend the scholarship on Black Peril—I want to bring attention to how this unnamed but highly visible discourse suffused colonial rhetoric about interracial intimacies, especially in the space of the settler home.

The discourse of White Peril served the needs of the settler state in four ways. Maintaining a large domestic staff was an iconic and cherished feature of settler life in the Kenyan highlands. White Peril rhetoric ensured that this practice could be continued by producing a narrative suggesting that the threat of sexual violence could be contained if only white housewives would behave appropriately. Second, White Peril discourses acted as a mechanism to discipline the behavior of white women, who were depicted as the vanguard of white prestige. The discourse of White Peril suggested that white women could indirectly cause the rape of their own children through poor management of their household staff—a powerful motivation for maintaining strong racial boundaries within settler homes. Third, because poor/marginal whites were viewed as most likely to contaminate their servants, the discourse of White Peril supported the larger colonial opposition to the development of a population of "poor whites" in Kenya. Finally, the discourse of White Peril served what is arguably the central goal of colonial states in African history—the control of African mobility. Settlers deployed White Peril discourse to force through legislation that increased juridical control over Africans, as well as limiting their ability to leave unsatisfactory jobs.

I want to be careful to acknowledge that this was not the *only* discourse surrounding rape: the more familiar narrative of African sexual disorder and excess also appeared with some frequency. Yet while White Peril was not the only available narrative surrounding interracial sex, it was nevertheless a prominent one. Perhaps *precisely because* it seems to fly in the face of what we think we know about colonialism and narratives of sexual danger, an examination of White Peril discourses can help us make sense of how discourses of race and sexuality were site specific and flexible enough to evolve to meet the needs of each place and time. In particular, the narrative that Africans only became capable of certain forms of sexual violence when corrupted by contact with white settlers and/or settler culture follows the logic of primitive normativity by suggesting that rape was yet another form of (heterosexual) deviance that was linked to degeneration and, thus, to civilization.

In what follows, I start by providing some background on domestic service in Kenya as well as highlighting scholarship on the role of the domestic sphere in imperial projects. I also review the historiography surrounding interracial sex and imperialism. Both of these bodies of work suggest the ways that narratives surrounding interracial intimacy attempted to discipline *both* white women *and* Black men. I then unpack the key elements of White Peril discourse. These include the contention that rape was conspicuously rare among "raw natives," and the corollary claim that white women could "contaminate" their servants through particular kinds of intimacy. Such intimacies—which included both excessive familiarity and excessive discipline—supposedly *created* the capacity for sexual violence in African men and boys. This discourse drew on a conception of Africans as "childlike" and therefore prone to corruption by more "adult" cultures (a conception that the very practice of referring to domestic servants of all ages as "boys" underscored). In the final section of this chapter, I spell out more explicitly how the rhetoric of White Peril served the goals of the colonial state. Ironically, the contention that sexual assaults were rare did not impede settler efforts to push through legislation designed (ostensibly) to prevent it. In reality, these legislative efforts extended control over African laborers in ways that served the settler state.

A final note: I make no claims here about whether allegations of sexual assault were true or not. It would be fair to say that domestic servants were extremely vulnerable to such allegations, and that cases of abuse or incest by white men could be easily dismissed by blaming the "houseboy." As in the rest of this book, I am much less invested in tracing actual sexual practices than in establishing the discursive frames that tied sexuality to race and evolutionary status and showing how these frames served the purposes of the settler state. In writing a history of sexuality, but not one of sex, I am self-consciously hijacking our attention away from the materiality of bodies and swinging the wheel in the direction of discourses, racial and gendered imaginaries, and fields of power.

Troublesome Intimacies: White Women and African "Houseboys"

When European settlers began to arrive in Kenya in large numbers, circa 1910, they primarily settled in the central highlands, where the land was most fertile for farming, and where the high elevations granted cooler temperatures. There they set up homes resembling a microcosm of genteel British country living, with one significant difference: large numbers of African men and women lived alongside whites on Kenyan farms. The spatial arrangements of the farms produced some separation—African workers lived in huts on the "native lines" some distance from the main house. Yet the settler home itself remained a site of constant contact. The availability of cheap domestic labor was one of the major attractions of living in Kenya, particularly after World War I when it became increasingly difficult to obtain or afford domestic servants in Britain.[7] However, the specter of white women and Black men working daily side by side with no supervision posed a clear opportunity for anxiety about interracial contact. Settlers needed to develop a discourse that would manage these anxieties but still enable them to employ African domestic servants.

An obvious solution to the anxieties caused by the pairing of African men and white women in Kenyan settler homes might have been to hire

African women rather than men as domestic servants, but this was rarely the case in colonial Kenya. In part, this was because women's agricultural and domestic labor was simply too valuable to African households to be sacrificed. But, as Dane Kennedy notes, African men also worried that their wives, sisters, and daughters would be harassed or assaulted in settler homes.[8] This evidence suggests that the anxiety about cross-racial and cross-gendered contact was shared by both colonized and colonizer.

Since the early 2000s, scholars have increasingly emphasized the significance of domestic spaces to the larger imperial project. In particular, Ann Laura Stoler has argued persuasively that "it was in the disarray of unwanted, sought after, and troubled intimacies of domestic space that colonial relations were refurbished and their distinctions made."[9] Likewise, in a recent collection devoted to the project of "decolonizing domestic service,"[10] Claire Lowrie and Victoria Haskins argue for the conceptualization of colonial homes as "a kind of microcosmic contact zone . . . where colonization is rendered close-up and personal."[11] Of particular note is Lowrie's chapter on Chinese "houseboys" in Darwin and Singapore in the 1910s–1930s. As in colonial Kenya, Lowrie finds that white women were frequently blamed for inculcating bad behavior in their servants through ignorance and mismanagement.[12] In the African context, Karen Tranberg Hansen has examined how colonists in Northern Rhodesia viewed domestic service not only as necessary to the running of white households but also as a means of "domesticating" African men.[13] As such, domestic service was incorporated into the larger "civilizing mission" of British imperialism.[14]

In addition to scholarship on colonial domestic service, the literature on "Black Peril" scares supports the argument that the presence of white women was used as an excuse to shore up threatened racial boundaries, particularly in domestic spaces. The scholarship on Black Peril has been particularly influential on histories of the postbellum United States, where scholars have shown how accusations of rape were used to keep a newly emancipated Black population from achieving economic or political independence. According to Crystal Feimster, "the portrayal of black men as beastly and unable to control their sexual desire served to justify the practice of lynching, segregation laws, and disfranchisement of black men."[15] This discourse also proved useful to controlling the behaviors of white women, as it circulated the narrative that "the New South was a dangerous place for women who transgressed the narrow boundaries of race and gender."[16] Furthermore, the focus on the (usually fictional) assaults of white women by Black men helped deflect attention from the sexual abuse committed by white men against Black women.[17]

Yet in her examination of cases of interracial sexual assault in Virginia, Lisa Lindquist Dorr has shown that accusations of sexual assault were not universally or unquestioningly accepted: while "being accused of an assault by a white woman placed a black man in considerable jeopardy," the cases she examined indicated that a number of factors influenced whether or how severely the accused was punished.[18] These factors included the social class and sexual reputation of the white woman in question: "Not only did some women bring their assaults on themselves, some whites seemed to believe, but some white women's characters were already so compromised that their having been violated did not represent a threat to the social order."[19] Black men who had connections to prominent white men or who were perceived to "know their place" within the racial order were also less likely to suffer harsh punishment. Thus, "Black Perils" were as important to controlling the behavior of white women as that of Black men.

The work on "Black Peril" cases in colonial Africa supports this contention. In a study of the 1938 election in South Africa, Jonathan Hyslop has noted that Afrikaner nationalists exploited the specter of interracial marriage to discredit their opponents. This rhetoric was particularly appealing because the 1920s and 1930s saw trends (like urbanization and industrialization) that increased the independence of white women. "The Nationalists' apparent hysteria about 'mixed marriages,'" he notes, "in fact performed an important role in re-establishing gender hierarchy. By portraying white women as sexually threatened by black men, Afrikaner males claimed the role of protectors of women, thereby reasserting their patriarchal control."[20] Likewise, Jock McCulloch has argued that "In Southern Rhodesia discourses about sexual pathology helped to decide the most fundamental of bourgeois rights: the legitimate claims of men to property, which included control of the bodies of women, headship of a family, and citizenship."[21]

A number of scholars have focused particularly on the relationship between white settler women and their African domestic servants, showing that contemporaries blamed the excessive "familiarity" of white women for cases of assault. In an analysis of a "rape scare" in Natal in 1886, Jeremy Martens notes that "the panic firmly laid the blame for 'outrages' on female settlers who failed to conform to the domestic ideal expected of white women in a racist and patriarchal society, and on African men who subverted accepted gender norms."[22] As in Kenya, the scare was also used to extend control over the movement of African men; the colonial government responded to settler demands by establishing a system of "native registration" and by establishing the death penalty for the crime of rape.[23] In keeping with the broader rhetoric of the threat of "detribalization," African men who "were independent of 'tribal' restraints and had put on 'a spurious veneer' of civilization" were believed to be the most likely to assault white women.[24]

Consensual interracial sex between white women and African men was also seen as a contaminating force. Diana Jeater has shown that settlers in Southern Rhodesia believed that "sex across the colour bar brought out the inherent perversity of African male sexuality and led to assaults on other European women."[25] Again, poor whites were viewed as particularly prone to engaging in interracial sex.

Historians of colonial Kenya have also looked closely at cases of interracial rape. Three studies deserve special mention because they rely on many of the same sources I examine here. The first is David Anderson's 2010 article "Sexual Threat and Settler Society: 'Black Perils' in Kenya, c. 1907–30," which examines three separate episodes of "Black Peril" in the colony: in 1907, 1920–1922, and 1924–1926.[26] Despite relying on some of the same archival documents, Anderson arrives at several conclusions that I will dispute here. First, Anderson argues that in southern and eastern Africa, "whites were urged to guard against the polluting influence of black sexuality—African men were widely presented as a diseased and degenerate menace, African women as wanton, lustful symbols of uncontrolled sexual behaviour."[27] Although this vision of African sexuality did sometimes appear in "Black Peril" discourses, it was not the only—or even the most prominent—one. Furthermore, the idea that African *women* were hypersexual was not especially prominent in Kenya; rather, as Brett Shadle points out, Kenyan African women were more often portrayed as asexual and non-agential victims of sexual and economic exploitation.[28] Likewise, Megan Vaughan asserts that in East Africa "the sexuality of African women only became a subject of distinct interest when it could no longer be contained by African men—when, for instance, women moved to towns and cities as migrants in their own right."[29]

A second important source is Dane Kennedy's comparative study of settler societies in Rhodesia and Kenya, *Islands of White*.[30] While Kennedy usefully points out parallels between the two African colonies, his comparative approach sometimes minimizes differences between the two spaces. For instance, Kennedy suggests that "Most settlers were convinced that, as one Rhodesian legislator proclaimed, 'the male native more or less has a tendency to commit rape'"—while a few pages later he discusses the prevalence of the belief in Kenya that "the blame for black assaults lay with the ignorant impropriety of some white women."[31] While a full discussion of the differences between the two spaces is beyond the scope of this chapter, it is important to note that "Black Peril" scares were more frequent in Rhodesia than in Kenya and occurred at an earlier date, reflecting differences in patterns of settlement.[32] Kennedy conceptualizes "Black Peril" scares as a response to new waves of immigration or periods of economic downturn: "when pressures set white setters at odds among themselves, when circumstances frayed the racial threads that bound them into a cohesive community, the specter of black peril arose to instruct and remind white settlers of their common needs and their common fears."[33] Yet the fact that cases of "Black Peril" in Kenya were blamed on particular subsets of the white settler community—women and poor whites—suggests that such discourses were actually *divisive*, in that they separated the responsible, knowledgeable settlers from those who, by virtue of their ignorance or carelessness, created an environment of sexual danger for everyone.[34] Interestingly, while both Kennedy and Anderson acknowledge the narrative that blamed white women for the introduction of deviant desires in African men, they subsume it within the more familiar framework of "Black Peril"—a testament to the dominance of the Black Peril narrative in studies of colonial sexuality.

The latest work on settler culture in Kenya is Brett Shadle's 2015 *The Souls of White Folk*. Shadle includes a discussion of "Black Peril" in Kenya that supports many of the conclusions of this chapter.[35] In particular, he notes that white women and whites who were marginal because of ethnicity or economic status were blamed for creating the threat of "Black Peril." Shadle centers his discussion around the notion of white prestige, the idea (prominent among settlers) that the superior civilizational status of whites ensured the wary respect of Indigenous people. Such respect could, however, be impaired by the misbehavior of individual whites; "In Kenya," Shadle notes, "prestige was connected to race such that any white person's *individual* failure to maintain prestige threatened the prestige of *all* white people."[36]

Shadle's focus on prestige is useful to understanding why settlers were so concerned with policing the behaviors of errant whites. Yet my research reveals that Kenyan settlers focused not just on loss of prestige but also on the idea that Africans had to be taught to desire white women, and that they had to be deeply contaminated by white "civilization" in order to commit sexual assault. The competing timescapes of the settler state—the "primitive" Indigenous and "civilized" settler worlds—raised fears about the dangers of "detribalization" and particularly its effects on sexuality. By placing the discourse around sexual assault within the broader context of primitive normativity, this chapter helps us understand how a narrative that asserted the absence of deviance in African cultures could be deployed to control African communities. By shifting the focus from the threat of Black Peril to the danger of White Peril, we begin to see how anxieties about the sexual contamination of African domestic servants fit into the larger rhetoric about the duty of whites to preserve the morality of Africans. We also see how this rhetoric, in turn, facilitated a number of measures that extended the power of settlers over African laborers, white women, and poor white settlers.

"Unmoral Creatures": Rape and Detribalization

In 1921, Hildegarde Hinde, the wife of a doctor working for the Kenyan colonial government,[37] published an article for the *Empire Review* titled "The 'Black Peril' in British East Africa. A Frank Talk to Women Settlers."[38] She began by discussing the Grogan case, which, she noted, had been falsely classified as a case of "Black Peril." In 1907, Colonel Ewart Grogan (known as Cape-to-Cairo Grogan in recognition of his journey by foot across the length of Africa in 1898–1900)[39] was sentenced to one month's imprisonment and a fine of five hundred rupees after publicly flogging rickshaw drivers in front of the Government House.[40] Grogan claimed that the drivers had insulted their two white female passengers by jostling them excessively, and, when they complained, forcibly removing them from the vehicle.[41] The case was treated as an incident of Black Peril because of the belief that such an insult, if tolerated, could lead to actual sexual assaults.[42] Yet, Hinde stated that such a classification was ridiculous since, at that time, "the danger [of Black Peril] was non-existent. None of the primitive natives were capable of visualizing such a possibility. It was entirely beyond their physical desires as it was beyond their mental imaginings—neither their minds nor their bodies could have evolved such ideas."[43] Since those early days of colonialism, however, Hinde conceded that Black Peril cases had become possible. In accounting for this change, Hinde placed the blame firmly on white women for encouraging familiarity with their servants through thoughtless behavior. "It is quite usual," she claimed, "for a white woman, in the absence of her husband, to call the boy [servant] into her bedroom to fasten her dress, and, in a hot climate, the scantiness of the garments is a further point to be taken into consideration."[44] Because "native servants of both sexes are absolutely un-educated, and . . . have no knowledge of European morals and standards other than those their employers have shown them," these thoughtless housewives were responsible for the inculcation of sexual desires in their servants.[45] Hinde noted that "It is reported constantly in the anti-native local newspapers that there have been cases of rape—the rape of young female children by natives."[46] Yet "These acts must be regarded as the out-come of the conduct and the attitude of the Europeans themselves, for had more decorum been observed on the part of white women, they would have been in no danger of physical assault from the natives."[47]

Hinde's article neatly encapsulates some of the key elements of the discourse of White Peril. While the danger of interracial sexual assaults was a topic frequently discussed in settler publications, it was consistently framed as the result of contamination by thoughtless settlers. Drawing on the broader discourse of primitive normativity, White Peril rhetoric maintained that rapes rarely occurred in "traditional" Indigenous spaces. White settlers—and especially white women—were blamed for inculcat-ing sexual desires in their servants through excessively "familiar" behavior. In particular, poor white women were viewed as a threat to the sexual mo-rality of their male servants. In this section, I attend to each of these tropes in turn to sketch out the rhetoric of White Peril.

The notion that rape was rare or absent in Indigenous African societies tapped into a changing consensus about the nature of "primitive sexual-ity" in anthropological and sexological circles. There were two primary explanations for the supposed normativity of "primitive" sexual practices: that it was healthy because of strong social controls or because of the ready access to "normative" sexual outlets. Both explanations informed colonial Kenyan responses to cases of interracial violence. The latter interpretation was typified by Ainsworth's comments from the report that opened this chapter—recall his opinion that rapes were "extremely rare owing to the prevalence of free love among various tribes."[48] Yet, elsewhere, Ainsworth seemed to favor the former explanation, which held that Africans did not commit deviant sexual acts because of the strong degree of social control supposedly exercised within traditional African communities. While maintaining that Africans did not have any "moral aversion" to sex (as evidenced by the supposed practice of "free love" in Indigenous societies), British administrators and settlers believed there were strict rules governing sexual behaviors, especially behaviors that might cause damage to a woman or girl-child's marriage prospects and thus render her less valuable to her father. It was not that the African man possessed a strong sense of sexual morality, but rather that certain kinds of deviance would never occur to him: another colonial observer summarized the popular attitude well with his statement that "the average native is simply an unmoral creature, and as a general rule he becomes immoral only after contact with certain forms of civilization, either Eastern [i.e., Indian or Arab] or Western."[49]

Thus, in his own writings, Ainsworth both argued that the control of "tribal elders" preserved the well-being of Africans and warned that this control was weakening as a result of colonialism. For instance, he warned that Christian missions were alienating Africans—especially among the Gikuyu and Luo—from their traditions. Such detribalized Africans, he suggested, had "in consequence of their association with Christian Missions, arrived at a stage of confused thinking consequent on their being subjected to teachings which their unformed minds have not yet been able to assimilate. The danger in this is that they are liable to break away from tribal control before they are ready for an individualistic form of existence, and so may become ill-informed wanderers and possible agitators."[50]

The reference to agitation is significant, since it so directly characterizes the "threat" posed by detribalization as a threat to the stability of the settler state. Similarly, an article published in a settler paper in July of 1920 also blamed whites for the outbreak of sexual violence, stating "We don't think the growing practice [of assault on white children] is tribal or racial; it is simply the effect of a closer intercourse with Europeans and their children; in other words, increased opportunity bereft of the drastic tribal punishment imposed more from the material damage done to the female than to any moral aversion."[51]

Ultimately, however, it was less important for officials to pin down the reason that rapes were supposedly so rare in "traditional" African societies than to declare that detribalization threatened to introduce the practice. The author of a memo submitted to the Kenyan government circa 1920 offered competing explanations of why white women were not sexually desirable to the rural, "traditional" African. He pointed to the "well established fact that the white woman appeals very little to the normal native, while the extraordinary immunity from assault and violation of the wives and families of Europeans, during native, and especially slave, raisings, is a striking testimony to either *the self-restraint or the lack of desire* on the part of the natives of Africa where European women are concerned."[52] The reference here to self-restraint is significant since this was a concept annexed to civilization. In fact, the supposed *inability* of Africans to delay gratification was a central feature of anthropological discourses. The author's indecision over whether the rarity of rape was due to self-restraint or lack of desire reflects the broader anthropological debate over whether the sexuality of "primitive peoples" was characterized by strong social controls or consistent access to socially sanctioned sex. However, the author was clear that in responding to the recent attacks, the government was "dealing then not with the ordinary and average native, and still less with the unsophisticated savage, but with the abnormal type."[53]

Likewise, a 1926 article in the *Daily Standard* expressed outrage at recent cases in which African domestic servants had allegedly assaulted white children, but nevertheless blamed detribalization. In particular, the author maintained that "Tribal institutions are breaking down gradually and the creation of others more in keeping with the ideas of western civilisation is taking place more slowly than the disappearance of the older sanctions. The African, particularly the detribalised native, is left without the moral support which is so essential to him in this stage of transition."[54] This statement is typical of the discursive tightrope that the discourse of detribalization carefully walked: the problem was not necessarily that Africans were being "modernized"—after all, this was one of the stated goals of twentieth-century colonialism—but rather that this modernization was occurring too rapidly. Detribalization thus handily allowed settlers to oppose "modernizing" practices while still adhering to the colonial civilizing mission.

The discourse of White Peril thus reflected a larger systemic problem characteristic of settler colonialism, which both asserted the need to respect (and maintain) essential differences between colonized and colonizers *and* required daily contact between African laborers and settlers. This tension was particularly marked in settler homes—viewed as bastions of British values, they were simultaneously sites of daily intimacies that crossed racial and gendered lines. It is not surprising, then, that the settler home became a central focus of White Peril discourse. While the preceding discussion has highlighted how the discourse of White Peril characterized African men, the next section examines its portrayals of white women. Because White Peril discourse tended to blame white women—and especially poor women—for inculcating deviant desires in servants, it served as a potent form of social control for white women as well as African men.

"To the Everlasting Reproach of the Mother": White Peril's Construction of White Motherhood

Kenyan whites disagreed about why rape was supposedly so rare within African communities. There was consensus, however, on how such deviant desires were introduced into African minds. White women—particularly mothers and poor whites—were consistently singled out as the cause of the contamination of their African servants. The discourse of contamination was central to the larger discourse of primitive normativity—the idea that "civilization" was a corrupting force supported larger efforts to limit the mobility, education, and activism of African men and women in the name of preventing detribalization. This section, however, looks at how White Peril discourses functioned as a mechanism of social control over white women.

Elsewhere, I have discussed the problem of the daily intimacies of the settler home, which required collaboration and cooperation between two supposedly distinct groups, white women and African men.[55] Here, however, I want to focus on the idea of colonial motherhood as a way of explaining why mothers were consistently blamed *not only* for not protecting their children from sexual assaults, but for inculcating previously unimaginable sexual desires into the minds of their African "houseboys." As mothers of the nation, white women had the responsibility both to ensure the well-being of the next generation of Kenyan settlers and to properly interact with "childlike" Africans. This dual motherhood also had a significant sexual dimension, as white women were tasked with protecting both their own children and their "childlike" servants from sexual contamination. White Peril (and primitive normativity itself) were highly relational discourses—always holding in tension the dual timescapes of "civilized" and "primitive" sexuality.

In her now canonical essay on imperial motherhood, Anna Davin outlined a preoccupation with the problem of motherhood that emerged at the turn of the twentieth century. Declining birth rates and high mortality rates raised concerns that the future of the British "imperial race" might be in question. The solution proposed was to compel British mothers (especially those of the working classes) to take better care of their children—a solution that ignored the role of structural issues related to poverty in both maternal and infant illness. As Davin explains, "Middle-class convention of the time took for granted that the proper context of childhood was the family, and the person most responsible the mother. So if the survival of infants and the health of children was in question, it must be the fault of the mothers, and if the nation needed healthy future citizens (and soldiers and workers) then mothers must improve."[56]

In colonial Kenya, a similar discourse centered around the need to "educate" mothers in order to prevent injury to their children. Likewise, Kenyan discourses tended to focus particularly on poor mothers as the target of their ire. However, in Kenya, white women were held responsible not only for raising future settlers but also for "raising" African employees, who were consistently depicted as childlike and evolutionarily immature in colonial discourses. In the periphery, then, imperial motherhood was not only about producing a healthy "imperial race" but also about preserving the moral well-being of the colonized.

This was especially true in cases where white children were allegedly assaulted by African domestic servants. For instance, the report of the Special Committee placed the responsibility on white parents—and particularly mothers—to properly care for their children, stating that they "fe[lt] it incumbent upon them to warn parents of the grave danger of entrusting little girls to the care of native boys of an age at which sexual instincts are beginning to develop."[57] The committee noted that in two of the cases of assault on white children, the presiding judge "expressed the opinion that there had been grave negligence on the part of the parents concerned in leaving their female children in the sole charge of totos [children] little older than themselves."[58] While the committee focused especially on assaults committed by adolescent African boys, the same discourse held when the accused was an adult. For instance, a letter to the editor of *The Leader*, titled "A Woman's View," worried about the effects of leaving children in the care of Africans. Despite her morbid recommendation that rapists be punished with "operation [i.e., castration] and branding," to be inflicted without anesthesia, she conceded that "There are always two sides to a question, and I often wonder if in some cases the mothers are not to blame, in many instances children are left to the care of natives. . . . Any mother doing this is asking for trouble, as no native is to be trusted, and through her ignorance it eventually leads to the child suffering and very often being ruined for life, to the everlasting reproach of the mother."[59]

The letter from a settler from Kisumu specifically attributed the blame for the corruption of Africans to the influence of careless Europeans, stating "I am also of the opinion that these crimes against women are very largely caused by the action of the Europeans themselves" who "make themselves cheap in the eyes of the natives."[60] He then offered a numbered list of incidents in which whites had negatively influenced their African servants, citing "a prominent settler [who] had one of the rooms in his house hung round with pictures from Bocaccio, depicting white people of both sexes together, in every sort of lewd position," women who allowed native servants to dress or bathe their young female children, a woman who allowed her African servant to enter her bedroom "while she was lying in bed, with nothing on but a nightdress which practically exposed her as far as her waist," women who allowed African servants to remove jiggers[61] from their feet, and those who allowed Africans to read publications like *The News of the World*, which were filled with lewd photos of white women.[62] He concluded by asking, "Would anyone in their sense at Home allow the butler or chauffeur to bathe their female children, or to escort them to the lavatory, or to attend their views in their bedrooms when they (the wives) were in a state of dishabille? Why do they do it here? They seem to think a native has no feelings."[63]

Interestingly, the author's comparison to butlers and chauffeurs "at Home" indicates that he was equally concerned with the maintenance of social distance between employers and (male) subordinates and with the maintenance of racial boundaries. However, his concern about the public display of "lewd" images also reinforces the notion that Africans had to be taught to desire white women—and his anxiety that white women were incapable of properly managing their servants.

In accounting for the emergence of deviant sexual desires in African men, White Peril rhetoric particularly targeted poor whites. The same memo mentioned earlier made this point explicitly, claiming that "such crimes are seldom or never committed in out districts [districts far from the city] by raw and unsophisticated savages" and that the recent events were "but a sign of the times and an inevitable concomitant of the opening up of the country and the spread of that aspect of so called civilization, represented by the influx of Europeans of low social standing, without conceptions of justice where the native races are concerned and lacking the most rudimentary instincts of the correct methods for dealing with such."[64] While the author of this memo acknowledged that the contamination of Africans was "in part due to the growth of Nairobi and the education they have derived from the War," he maintained that "it is also largely the effect of their having been brought far more frequently than before, especially during the War period, into direct contact with a lower and different class of European to that to which they had previously been accustomed."[65] Poor whites who employed African laborers and domestics alternated between treating their employees with "gross familiarity and coarse severity."[66] Neither approach inspired the proper respect for white prestige.

The idea that lower-class whites would be destructive to race relations was quite common in Kenya, reflecting larger concerns about the dangerous consequences of allowing a population of poor whites to develop in the colony. As mentioned earlier, after World War I, domestic servants were increasingly difficult to find or afford.[67] Thus, some of the settlers who came out to Kenya were in the position of maintaining a large staff of servants for the first time. Elite Kenyan settlers consistently worried that such settlers were unsuited to manage a large household of domestic servants. Settlers often pointed to South Africa as an example of the disastrous consequences of allowing a poor white population to develop.[68] (And in fact, South Africans living in Kenya were often viewed as the worst offenders in this category.)[69]

Poor whites and newcomers to the colony were viewed as being more likely to mistreat or abuse their servants—and hence lower the prestige of Europeans as a whole. As Brett Shadle explains, self-control was understood to be a distinctive feature of middle-class identity; thus poor settlers (and especially those who had emigrated from South Africa) were perceived to be the most likely to discipline their workers with "excessive" violence.[70] Importantly, though, marginal Europeans were criticized for *both* excessive violence *and* excessive intimacy: as one source put it, "Nothing can be more deleterious to the character of the native than the treatment so often meted out to him by Europeans of this type, alternating as it does between gross familiarity and coarse severity, the one following the other with bewildering rapidity."[71] Importantly, excessive intimacy was viewed as the other side of the coin of excessive violence—both betrayed a lack of social distance between ruler and ruled and a dangerous lack of civilized self-control.

Poor white women were also viewed as the most likely to fraternize with Africans. For instance, in October 1934, the settler Nellie Grant wrote to her daughter, the author Elspeth Huxley, complaining that the East African Women's League was making too much fuss about the "problem" of Black Peril. "If the E.A.W.L. would work more at the eugenics of the white population," she wrote, "it wd [*sic*] be much more constructive than at-tempting to contravene justice, & demanding public hangings etc. There seem to be some 300 white children getting no education at all, & all the wrong people breeding like rabbits, & of course these sort of people will always get raped etc."[72] The idea that uneducated, poor white women were the "sort of people [who] will always get raped" reflected the widely held belief that poor whites were incapable of maintaining proper racial bound-aries with African men. As Will Jackson has shown, in Kenya poor whites were frequently decried as having excessively familiar relationships with nonwhite men. Until World War II, poor whites could be deported from the colony as "Distressed British Subjects." Poor or marginally white women could also be declared insane and sent to the colony's mental asylum due to their relationships with African men.[73] As Will Jackson puts it, poor whites were viewed as problematic in part "because their debased position entailed the kinds of contact with non-Europeans that jeopardized in turn the underlying human distinction between colonisers and colonized."[74]

In reality, the "poor white problem" was more of a strawman in colonial rhetoric than an actual threat. Until 1945, the Kenyan government was largely successful in its efforts to prevent the growth of a "poor white" population; large capital requirements prevented those without money from immigrating to the colony, while poor whites already living in Kenya could be "repatriated" to Britain or other colonies.[75] Yet while the actual numbers of poor whites in the colony may have been small, they held an outsized place in colonial rhetoric. As Jackson puts it, "The 'degenerate' and the 'poor white' . . . were staple terms of colonial discourse—the anti-thetical alter egos of the archetypal European."[76] Identifying the misman-agement of servants as a *classed* issue, therefore, added to its rhetorical power. That is, white women who behaved with excessive intimacy toward their servants not only violated racial and gendered boundaries but also displayed déclassé behavior in a culture that was deeply preoccupied by issues of social status.

Perhaps the best evidence of the contention that rape (or at least inter-racial rape) was rare among "uncontaminated natives" was the consistent concern about publicizing cases of sexual assault. For instance, after pass-ing the 1926 Criminal Law Amendment Ordinance, which made rape a capital offense, the colonial administration circulated a manifesto, written in both English and Kiswahili, to the Native Reserves explaining that "any man (whatever his race or creed) who commits rape on any woman may be condemned to death by a Judge of the Supreme Court and may be hanged."[77] A settler from Kisumu wrote a letter to the Provincial Commissioner's office expressing the opinion that it would be a bad idea to circulate the manifesto, since "I do not think the bulk of the natives in the Reserves know anything about these crimes, & publishing the Manifesto will only make them think about them."[78] The phrasing suggests that rape would never occur to Africans living in rural communities. "So far as I know," he continued, "the persons who commit these crimes are more or less detribalised natives, who are under the control of no headmen or elders, and have learnt to do such things from their association with our so-called civilisation."[79] Likewise, a memo submitted to the colonial government suggested that, if not executed, African rapists should be exiled to "prevent the possible contamination by him of his fellow countrymen, and any display by the latter, on his release from prison, of an unhealthy interest in his exploit."[80]

Settlers also worried that hearing testimony about the rape of white women would contaminate "native assessors," the "tribal elders" who provided nonbinding opinions on customary law in Kenyan courts.[81] The 1920 Report of the Special Committee, while declining to recommend harsher punishments for rape, suggested "that the law should be amended so as to allow cases of sexual assaults by natives on Europeans to be tried by a Judge alone as it considers that the presence of native assessors in such cases is both unnecessary and undesirable."[82] An article from July 1920 responding to the rape of a seven-year-old girl expressed the opinion that "native assessors" should not be used in cases involving a European victim, both because of doubts about the usefulness of their opinions and because they worried about the impression such cases would make in the minds of the assessors.[83]

Importantly, there is evidence that Africans also adopted this rhetoric. In their response to the 1926 rape of an elderly woman in Kijabe, the Nyeri District Council echoed the prevailing rhetoric about the dangers of detribalization, framing the assault as foreign to Indigenous African custom and as the result of their own loss of control over increasingly "civilized" men. The council wrote a letter to the governor expressing their shock that "a member of our tribe could have so far forgotten our tribal laws and custom, as well as the honour and good name of the tribe. We would like to express to Your Excellency our opinion that those who commit such crimes are those who have forsaken their tribal authority and over whom we, as representative of the tribe, ceased to be able to exercise any control."[84] This statement follows the rhetoric of White Peril in asserting the absence of rape in Indigenous African societies. It is possible that the memo was influenced by the District Commissioner who would likely have attended District Council meetings. It also, however, served the interests of Indigenous elites by stressing the importance of maintaining their control over members of their ethnolinguistic community. The assertion of "tribal authority" is thus framed within the broader discourse of White Peril, but in ways that serve the interests of African elites.

Ultimately, the trope of the thoughtless housewife was convenient because it allowed colonial commentators to dangle the threat of interracial sexuality while simultaneously neutralizing the notion that white women might desire their African servants. The problem was not that white women were seducing their servants; rather, interracial sex was so far from their minds that they failed to recognize their "houseboys" as adult men. Simultaneously, such texts continually reasserted that the uncontaminated "native" was incapable of desiring white femininity; he had to be taught to view her as a sexual subject. This discourse cleverly circumvented the possibility that white women and Black men might desire sex with each other, at the same time as it deployed the specter of interracial intimacy to control the behavior of white women.

But the discourse of White Peril was *not only* about exerting control over white women—it also enabled policies that facilitated control over the mobility of African workers. In the final section, I outline the instrumental uses of White Peril rhetoric, mapping a direct line from the narrative of contamination to policies and legislation that prevented Africans from leaving unsatisfactory or exploitative employment and increased the juridical power of the state.

Instrumental Uses of White Peril Discourse

At first glance, there seems to be a significant divide between settler and official responses to interracial sexual violence. Both groups tended to characterize sexual violence as the purview of "abnormal" Africans, but while officials maintained that no further legislation was required to deter would-be rapists, the settlers consistently demanded harsher punishments and more social controls. In this section, I first describe some of the rather draconian policies white settlers proposed to tamp down on the burgeoning threat of interracial rape. In particular, I show how some of the same commentators who maintained that cases of interracial rape were rare nevertheless asserted the necessity of harsh measures to prevent them. I then turn to a discussion of the policies that were actually implemented. The Kenyan government's management of this manufactured crisis is typical of settler colonialism in that it subordinated the interests of the Indigenous population and facilitated settler goals. Yet, there is one difference: while the white settlers tended to propose measures that extended their individual control over their African laborers, the legislation adopted by the settler state facilitated the larger goal of limiting African mobility and increasing state surveillance.

The most common demand in the settler press was for the establishment of the death penalty in cases of sexual assault. For instance, an article entitled "Children's Peril" published in the *Daily Leader* in April 1920 responded to a recent case in which a white girl was allegedly assaulted by two African men. The article asserted that "In British East Africa the natives are still in that semi-sophisticated stage and too near their tribal conditions to present overmuch social danger, and, as a matter of fact, as far as has been made public these awful incidents of outrage on European women and children have been extremely rare."[85] However, the article warned that such cases would inevitably increase "as familiarity brings less awe into the native's mind."[86] The *Daily Leader* offered two key rationales to support its contention that the death penalty ought to be established for the crime of rape. First, it hinted that, in absence of legislative deterrents, settlers would be compelled to turn to extrajudicial means to secure the safety of women and children; while asserting that lynch law did not appeal "to the law-abiding Englishman," the article nevertheless dangled the threat of lynching should authorities not concede to settler demands.[87] More interestingly, the article suggested that the death penalty was needed to bring the penal code into line with existing customary law: "Among many, if not most, native tribes the crime of seduction and outrage spells death. And if it were a wife or daughter of a Chief such death would not be a very easy one. As the native understands these things, are we to appraise our own womenkind at less than the native does himself?"[88]

This statement drew on the notion that "tribal constraints" prevented rape within "traditional" African communities. At the same time, it asserted that any penalty short of death would communicate to Africans that white women were not valued. This might be interpreted as a reversal of the standard narrative of African misogyny—one that suggests that Africans actually valued women *more* than settlers did. However, it is more likely that the author was invoking women's status as property in both

African and white societies, as his reference to "appraising" the value of women suggests. This passage thus offers insights into how comparisons between "primitive" African cultures and "civilized" white ones promoted conservative gender ideologies: the continual assertion by settlers that African women were understood as "chattel" facilitated measures that treated white women as property as well.

The *Daily Leader's* assertion that rape was treated as a very serious crime within African communities was not, however, universally accepted. In fact, the settler community as a whole tended to argue that African women were not as profoundly affected by sexual assault as white women and, hence, proposed that the death penalty was only warranted in cases where a white woman or girl was assaulted. Extracts from a debate held in the Kenyan Legislative Council in June of 1926 reveal some of the views on the necessity of racially specific legislation. Lord Francis Scott, one of the most prominent white settlers, argued that "you cannot get away from the fact that the result of some of these offences to a European woman is worse than death, while in some of the tribes it is a matter of comparatively small account."[89] Another member of the Legislative Council, Captain E. M. V. Kenealy agreed that rape was more harmful to a white woman than her African peer. Kenealy painted a rather macabre picture of the consequences of the rape of a white woman by an African man: "Let us consider a woman in child who is assaulted by a native unsuccessfully. He does not accomplish his purpose. He fails in that, and he is tried for attempted rape. That unborn child may die, or be insane, after the man is tried. The woman may be driven mad and the child may be deformed. I think the average man is incapable of realising the enormous possibilities of such a crime on the woman. I can appeal only to the medical community to give us details of such things."[90] Here Kenealy invoked the concept of maternal impression, or the idea that a pregnant woman could transfer negative influences to her fetus, causing deformity. Importantly, Kenealy centered his horror story around the "unsuccessful" rape of a white woman; an attempt alone was sufficient to drive both mother and child to insanity.

For an African woman, however, Kenealy felt the situation was very different; "A European woman," he argued, "would rather lose her life than her chastity, it is the dominating factor in her life; in a native woman, owing to their tribal thoughts and customs, chastity is measured in terms of other property."[91] While the *Daily Leader* suggested that African women's supposed status as "chattel" informed harsh penalties for their violation, Kenealy exploited the same discourse to dismiss the effects of a rape on their psyche.

This latter interpretation was also echoed in a memo submitted to the 1920 Special Committee, which hinted at the troubling frequency of the assault or seduction of African women by *white men*. "That members of the European community are not usually guilty of such [sexual] offences against the native population in East Central Africa may be true de jure," it stated, "but the somewhat lighthearted manner in which the moral aspect of such affairs are regarded by the natives, the age of the native girls concerned, their ready obedience to the wishes of their relations and the overwhelming pressure exerted automatically by the disparity in status of the man and the girl, render these crimes de facto of almost common occurrence."[92] While gesturing toward the factors that might complicate consent for Indigenous women—their age and the disparity in power between Indigenous women and white men—the memo dismissed the effects of such coercive relationships on Indigenous women; the "lighthearted" attitudes toward sex that supposedly prevailed in Indigenous societies would protect Indigenous women from the worst effects of assaults.

The death penalty was not, however, the only proposed palliative for the threat of interracial rape. An article from February 1920 entitled "A Black Peril. Wanted a Curfew Hooter; and Decency in our Streets" suggested the establishment of a 9 p.m. curfew for all Africans living in Nairobi. The author blamed "the lax treatment of the hordes of natives who are now overrunning our streets" for introducing the threat of violence into the cities.[93] Even as he pathologized Africans as unruly "hordes," however, the author asserted the essential innocence of rural Africans. While objecting to "the indecent method of blanket and cloth attire which can be seen daily and hourly in the streets of this supposedly civilized Christian City," the author conceded that "It is only fair to point out that these blanket-attired natives [are] like Adam and Eve of old who, being so attired, do not realise that they are naked."[94] In a very direct invocation of primitive normativity, the author argued that Africans presented a threat to public decency precisely because they occupied a prelapsarian timescape where sexuality was as yet unknown. The author concluded by suggesting that the government needed to teach Africans to be ashamed of their nakedness, which would serve the dual purpose of covering their bodies and forcing them to work to earn money to buy clothes.[95] (Following the logic of the Adam and Eve example, it also rather ironically positions Europeans as the Satanic snake whose machinations cause Adam and Eve to realize their nakedness.) This is a stark example of how narratives of African innocence could be instrumentalized to serve the economic goals of the settler state.

To some extent, settler agitation was successful. In 1926, the colonial government passed a Criminal Law Amendment, which increased the penalty for rape to include the death penalty. There is considerable evidence that the government agreed to such legislation, despite their belief that it was unnecessary, to cater to settler demands. Governor Edward Grigg (one of the colony's most pro-settler governors) wrote a letter to Leo Amery, the Secretary of State for the Colonies, describing the sequence of events that convinced his government to make rape a capital offense. He begins by quoting the Report of the Special Committee of the Legislative Council's conclusion that cases of interracial assaults on white children were rare.[96] Accounting for several cases of assault that had inspired outrage in the settler community, Governor Grigg echoed the contention that white mothers were primarily to blame: "The difficulty of safeguarding children against immorality on the part of native house boys and ayahs," he remarked, *"even if it be immorality only by suggestion and gesture*, is one of the most powerful elements in the demand for strong deterrent legislation."[97] Grigg also seemed to concede that the legislation was necessary to prevent the outbreak of mob violence on the part of the settlers. In June of 1926, he sent a telegram to the Colonial Office stating "I am convinced that drastic change in the law is necessary not only as a deterrent to possible offenders but in order to maintain respect for the law if another offence is committed."[98]

While acceding to settler demands for harsher penalties, the colonial government opted to produce a racially neutral bill that made rape of any woman punishable by death.[99] This decision proved controversial. For instance, the members of the Convention of Association expressed their gratitude to the government for raising the penalty for rape to death but disapproved of the penalty being applied to all communities. One member, Captain Anderson, maintained that no deterrent was needed to discourage rape among white or Asian men, nor to discourage rape within "native" communities: only interracial sex or sexual assault, he maintained, was of concern.[100] Some members of the Convention of Associations, however, acknowledged the negative press that a racially discriminatory law could earn the colony.[101] Captain Schwartze responded to Captain Anderson's speech, worrying that it would be reported back home in Britain.[102] Besides, he argued, there was no need for racially specific legislation since no Kenyan court would hang a white man for raping an African woman. He concluded with an appeal to the press to avoid publishing the contents of the meeting.[103]

The non-settler members of the Legislative Council also expressed discontent with the legislation, but for different reasons. Mr. Shams-Ud-Deen, one of five members elected to represent the Kenyan Indian community,[104] questioned the need for the legislation. "My own personal opinion," he stated, "as a result of my residence in this country for the last 26 years is that the natives of this country are really not, from the settler's point of view, such a dangerous criminal body as the world at large might think from the passing of this Bill."[105] He lamented the introduction of the bill "because it is not a good advertisement for the country for intending settlers, either from Europe or British India."[106] Reverend Dr. J. W. Arthur, the member appointed to represent African interests on the council, also questioned the necessity of the increased penalty, claiming that most of the chiefs, elders, and

> the young manhood of Kenya, who are law-abiding members of Society, do resent such crimes of violence and punish them severely according to their own tribal customs. While it is true that today there is a lack of discipline in some instances amongst the young manhood of some Tribes, yet I believe it is equally true that in some ways there is a growing self-discipline amongst many of these Tribes in the matter of sexual offenses. There are thousands of young men and young women in the tribes of Kenya who in this very matter of sex relationship have learned and are learning what self-discipline means. When one thinks of the lustful life of such young people in their own tribal life as it was and as it still is amongst so many, because it is tribal custom, I stand amazed at the self-discipline amongst young men and women which is manifested today.[107]

At first glance, Arthur's statement seems contradictory; it both asserts that rape is punished severely according to the "tribal customs" of traditional African life, yet also posits that young Africans were only just learning "what self-discipline" means. In interpreting this statement, it's important to remember that the discourse of primitive normativity presented Africans as unlikely to commit rape not because they possessed self-control, but rather because they enjoyed unlimited access to sex with willing partners. Arthur seemed to be suggesting that the negative influences of "civilization"—which destabilized tribal controls—would also introduce the kinds of "self-control" necessary to prevent deviant behaviors in detribalized Africans. Arthur also hinted at the misbehavior of white men, noting that "If we desire the Africans to respect our women folk, we must also respect the African women."[108]

The other major piece of legislation introduced in response to settler demands was the establishment of the Registration of Domestic Servants Ordinance, also passed in 1926. As David Anderson explains, this legislation "regulated the movement of servants between employers, ensuring that those lacking satisfactory references of employment would be denied labour permits and forced to return to their home areas."[109] The legislation was amended in 1931 to apply to government departments that employed servants as well as to private citizens.[110] Thus, despite the fact that the narrative of White Peril blamed *white women* for the outbreak of sexual violence in settler homes, it nevertheless extended control over the mobility of *African men*, limiting their ability to leave an unsatisfactory or exploitative job and asserting the looming threat of "repatriation" to rural reserves at the whim of white employers.

Thus, while there was a stark difference in opinion between the colonial administration and white settlers about the degree to which interracial rape was a problem in the colony, the discourse of White Peril nevertheless enabled settlers to demand legislation that extended their control over African men. At the same time, as I discussed earlier, it proved useful to policing the behavior of white women and to asserting the need to prevent the growth of a "poor white" population in Kenya. White Peril was thus a discourse that enabled multiple forms of social control at once. The next chapter continues to explore the space of the settler home, as well as anxieties about interracial intimacies, but from a different point of view. Rather than focusing on discourses surrounding African sexualities vulnerable to outside contamination, I use a series of romance novels to explore concerns with European sexual degeneration—and to sketch out Kenya's place in British sexual imaginaries.

FIVE

Queering Settler Romance

The Reparative Eugenic Landscape in
Nora Strange's Kenyan Novels

IN NORA STRANGE'S 1933 novel *Kenya Noon*, a raucous party of Anglo-Kenyan settlers, gin and tonics in hand, exchange limericks satirizing the bad reputation of their community. One "bright young thing" entertains the crowd with the following offering:

> *Adam and Eve after the Fall*
> *Settled in Kenya. Now lis'en all!*
> *Draped in a skin up to the shin,*
> *While he fashioned a boma,*
> *She danced in n'goma*
> *And let in original sin.*[1]

The scene, typical of Strange's oeuvre, plays with the popular curiosity surrounding the (mis)behavior of elite Anglo-Kenyan settlers. In fact, Strange was one of the primary producers of the "stories of bed-hopping settlers, men and women marrying, taking lovers, divorcing, and starting the whole process over again with new partners" that entertained a domestic British audience during the interwar period.[2] It would therefore be easy to dismiss her work as simple sensationalism, and her choice of Kenya as the setting of her novels as a way to project illicit desires onto the colonial periphery.[3] Yet a closer examination of this scene reveals an interesting preoccupation with colonial Kenya as a pure and uncontaminated space. As an Edenic paradise where "Adam and Eve" could settle, Kenya seemed to offer overcivilized Europeans the opportunity to reconnect with their primitive roots. Importantly, while the limerick depicts the Anglo "Adam and Eve" appropriating elements of East African cultures—dressing in skins, building domestic compounds or "maboma," and participating in "n'goma" or dances—it also posits that it is only with the arrival of non-Africans in the paradisiacal space that "original sin" is introduced.

This chapter explores Strange's novels as key cultural texts for understanding Kenya's place in larger discourses about European degeneration and decline. Here I move beyond the geographic limits of Kenya itself to consider how it was envisaged in metropolitan contexts. Strange's work tapped into the discourses of degeneration and decline that preoccupied Europe during the 1920s and 1930s, presenting the reader with characters who failed, in a variety of ways, to live up to their reproductive potential. The Kenya of Strange's novels provides these dysfunctional settlers with a cure: the confrontation with the "primitive" space of wildest Africa either cures her characters of their queerness or eliminates them altogether. While the rest of the book examines events at the periphery, this chapter thinks more about how the discourse of "primitive normativity" traveled, and how an imagined Kenya provided Strange with the opportunity to rehearse the same narratives about sexual deviance and normativity that had already proved so consequential in East Africa itself.

Over the course of her career, Nora Kathleen Begbie Strange authored an enormous opus of romance novels, including twenty-five texts set partly or entirely in Kenya. Published between 1924 and 1970, her novels covered almost four decades of colonial rule and a decade of Kenyan independence. Her primary publisher, the London-based company Stanley Paul, specialized in low-cost thrillers and romances, and Strange's novels appear to have obtained a fairly wide readership.[4] *A Wife in Kenya* (1925) went through three editions in its first year, while *An Outpost Wooing* (1925) was in its fifth reprint in 1927. While certainly not regarded as high-brow literature, her works were sufficiently popular to be reviewed in major papers: *An Outpost Wooing* received reviews from *The Morning Post*, *The Times Literary Supplement*, *The Daily News*, *The Methodist Recorder*, *The Illustrated London News*, and *The Sketch*. While never a leading light of the British literary scene, she was famous enough to merit inclusion in the British National Portrait Gallery.

Yet, we have only minimal biographical information about Strange, most of which comes from her nonfiction study of Kenyan politics, *Kenya Today*.[5] Born in Bombay in 1884, she was the daughter of William Lumisden Strange and Rose Fanny Cobbold. Strange was part of an established Anglo-Indian family—both of her paternal grandparents were born in Madras.[6] She first came to Kenya in 1913, where she worked as the first woman stenographer in Nairobi.[7] In 1919, she left Kenya to join her brother in Karachi. She married Edward Gower Stanley, who was born in Lucknow and served as the executive engineer in India's Public Works Department.[8] Strange returned to Kenya only once, collecting the material for *Kenya Today* during a six-month visit in 1932. Despite the fact that she lived most of her life in India, Kenya seems to have captured her literary imagination to a much greater degree.

This chapter examines the production of settler sexuality in several of Strange's novels, a set of sources that have been almost entirely ignored in histories of Kenyan colonialism.[9] Her novels fashion Kenya as a eugenic landscape where the "right sort" of settler could reclaim sexual health through contact with a "primitive" space. Her profound concern with the moral, physical, and psychic decline of contemporary Britons echoed broader discourses in twentieth-century Britain, where eugenicists worried that the sexual self-control associated with middle-class Europeans might breed problematic sexual dysfunctions. Frigid women and neurotic men could not reproduce—and as Anna Davin has shown, contemporaries believed that low rates of reproduction among the most "fit" posed a threat to the maintenance of the empire.[10] Such anxieties were heightened in the space of the settler colony, where the reproduction of the "ruling race" was key to the maintenance of white supremacy. Strange's novels reflect these anxieties by continually returning to a central theme, which I term *queer settler sexuality*—an aversion to heterosexual sex produced by an excess of "civilized" self-control. This sexuality was queer to the extent that it was seen as disordered, dysfunctional, and nonreproductive.

Settler queerness was problematic because it threatened the future of the colony: if white settlers could not reproduce, the settler state would fail. Importantly, however, Strange's novels also provide a solution for queer settler sexuality—the *reparative landscape*. Placed in contact with the fecundity of the African terrain, the "overcivilized" settlers reconnect with their sexual urges and embrace an earthy reproductive heterosexuality. Importantly, this "reconnection" is often achieved through marital rape; abandoning outmoded notions of honor or restraint, the husband demands sexual access to his wife. The wife often resists this access, until the primitive Kenyan landscape supplies a near-death experience that threatens her or her husband's life. The threat of death awakens the wife to sexual desire and romantic love; the biopolitical imperative to reproduce is thereby ensured.

Eugenically unfit settlers, however, meet a different fate in Strange's books. Settlers whose class status renders them unfit to serve as wards of colonial guardians (either because they are too poor or too aristocratic) are weeded out through disease or disaster. Importantly, these were also the classes that eugenic discourses identified as most prone to degeneracy and deviance. In colonial Kenya, they were also the classes deemed most likely to mismanage their African laborers. In a remarkable mirror of the colonial discourses surrounding interracial rape discussed in the previous chapter, Strange depicted these unfit settlers as parading their sexual foibles in front of an observant audience of colonial subjects, decreasing white prestige and contaminating colonized Africans in the process. Strange's preoccupation with the African gaze—the ability of domestic servants to observe white misbehavior—plays with the idea of panoptic disciplinarity and performs a striking reversal of the typical directionality of colonial surveillance. In her novels, Kenyan whites are constantly observed by the silently judging panopticon of African domestic servants. This domestic panopticon, however, serves the colonial project by figuring the colonized as an extension of the eye of the state. In other words, the watchful eye of the domestic is *in service* not only to the colonial household but to the colonial state writ large.

The sexually indiscreet settler who paraded his/her deviance in front of the watchful eye of the servants posed a threat to the sexual order of the settler state. Yet, as in the case of the frigid married couple, the reparative landscape provides a eugenic solution to this brand of settler queerness. While eugenically "fit" settlers are opened to reproductive sex through their encounter with the primitive space of Kenya, "unfit" settlers fall prey to a striking array of wild animal attacks, tropical diseases, rickshaw disasters, and wildebeest stampedes. The reparative landscape solves the problem of settler queerness by enforcing the "survival of the fittest"—which in this case specifically refers to the fitness to colonize. Thus, while the near-death experience opens the eugenically fit settler to reproductive futurity, thereby ensuring the continuation of the settler state, the unfit settler does not survive his/her encounter with the landscape.

Responding to the call for histories of colonial sexuality that attend to the specificities of settler colonialism, I use the novels of Nora Strange to conduct a queer reading of settler reproductive futurity in Kenya.[11] I first elaborate on the idea of settler queerness and explain its stakes. Because of the unique nature of settler colonialism in Kenya, a space where a relatively tiny white population[12] sought to establish itself as the dominant political force in the colony, the reproductive capacity of the settler population was key to ensuring the continuation of white rule. Settler queerness—which I define as sexual habits, orientations, or affects that direct the settler away from heterosexual, endogamous, reproductive sexuality—thus posed a direct challenge to settler futurity. The majority of the chapter is devoted to a close reading of settler sexuality in several of Strange's novels, focusing particularly on how the landscape is envisioned as a curative for settler queerness. By putting the "overcivilized" settler back in touch with his/her innate sexuality, and by exposing him/her to the dangers of disease and wild animals, this reparative eugenic landscape opened the settler to sex and reproduction—thus ensuring the continuation of the settler state. This contrasts with the final section of the chapter, where I explore the fate of the eugenically *unfit* settler. The degenerate settler, signaled through social class or marginal whiteness, is unable to survive in the primitive landscape of Strange's novels. Importantly, the elimination of unfit settlers *also* serves the project of reproductive futurity in that it ensures that those settlers whose queerness cannot be reformed will not survive long enough to contaminate the next generation.

Readers will note the relative absence of African characters in the analysis below. This is reflective of the fact that Africans generally do not appear as developed characters in Strange's work. Where they do appear, they tend to be treated as *part of the landscape*. This rhetorical elimination is reflective of the actual treatment of African populations in Kenya. Because the Kenyan economy was so heavily dependent on African labor, the colonial state did not want to eliminate Indigenous peoples. Yet because settlers occupied African land, it was important for the state to nullify African claims to land ownership. By assimilating Africans into the landscape, Strange is able to depict them as both omnipresent and lacking any real claims to authority—a depiction that reflected quite closely colonial approaches to the management of African populations. The narrative structure of the novels (re)produces the imperial project writ small. Thus, in key ways, Strange's novels not only *reflected* but also *performed* colonial biopolitics.

The High Stakes of Settler Sex(uality)

If Strange spent most of her life in India, why did she choose Kenya as the arena in which to explore themes of colonial sexual dysfunction?[13] One potential answer lies in the distinctive nature of the settler colony—questions of sexual health are key to settler colonialism because of the biopolitical imperative to (re)produce further generations of settlers.

Scholars have stressed the distinctive approaches to the management of Indigenous populations in settler colonies. Lorenzo Veracini, for instance, has emphasized the differing relationship to Indigenous labor in settler colonies, ruled by a small minority of white farmers and entrepreneurs, versus franchise colonies, those ruled from the metropole by an imperial government. Because franchise colonies relied on Indigenous labor, they tended to adopt biopolitical strategies that encouraged population growth. What Veracini terms "settler colonial phenomena," on the other hand, are defined as "circumstances where colonisers 'come to stay' and to establish new political orders for themselves, rather than exploit native labour."[14] Settler colonies, he argues, therefore generally eliminated Indigenous populations—whether through genocide, necropolitics, or assimilation.

Colonial Kenya was distinctive in that it occupied an intermediate zone between the pure franchise and pure settler colony. The small white settler population that developed there had disproportionate power, yet they never achieved their goal of obtaining "responsible self-rule," that is, white minority rule. Furthermore, while settlers lived on land expropriated from Africans, they also relied on Indigenous labor to work their farms.[15] As Ronald Horvath noted in his essay "A Definition of Colonialism," Kenya thus represented a unique form of colonialism "in which settlers neither exterminate nor assimilate the indigenes."[16] Kenyan colonialism necessitated the removal of Indigenous peoples from their land, and then their return as dispossessed squatters. In Kenya, the process of settler colonialism first evacuated and then repopulated the landscape with Africans—destroying African claims to land ownership in the process.

Simultaneously, this process of removal and return bolstered white claims to belonging. In settler colonies, European migrants underwent a process of indigenization "driven by the crucial need to transform an historical tie ('we came here') into a natural one ('the land made us')."[17] Strange's preoccupation with the landscape as an agential character is thus reflective of a broader discursive trope of settler colonialism. The process of indigenization had clear gendered and sexual valances, as claims to land

and belonging were facilitated through the production of "a gendered order, a focus on mononuclear familial relations and reproduction, and the *production* of assets transferable across generations."[18] The biological imperative was particularly pronounced in Kenya, since (with the exception of the Soldier Settlement Scheme of 1919) the British government did not actively promote white settlement in Kenya.[19] In the absence of large-scale immigration, reproduction became *the* essential method of ensuring the future of the settler state.

Far from being a unique preoccupation, Strange's eugenic angst was reflective of larger contemporary discourses of European "degeneration." As discussed in chapter 1, from the early nineteenth century, many eugenicists argued that non-Western peoples had "degenerated" from the Caucasian racial ideal; racial difference was thus explained as a result of evolutionary backsliding. As Europe industrialized, anthropologists and eugenicists drew explicit connections between the urban poor, women, and nonwhite peoples. As Daniel Pick notes, "degeneration in the second half of the nineteenth century served not only to characterize other races (for instance in the view that other races had degenerated from the ideal physique of the white races), but also to pose a vision of internal dangers and crises within Europe. Crime, suicide, alcoholism and prostitution were understood as 'social pathologies' endangering the European races, constituting a degenerative process within them."[20] The discourse of degeneration was thus not only a method of producing a racial Other (and thereby providing ideological support to profitable ventures like slavery and imperialism) but also a method of policing the sexual and moral behavior of marginal Europeans.

Simultaneously, eugenicists began to worry that the sexual self-control that allowed middle-class couples to limit the size of their families would also cause them to be outnumbered by the more fecund, but less racially fit, urban poor and racialized Other. Anticolonial rebellions in India, Ireland, and New Zealand, the Boer War, and the horrors of the first World War raised questions about the ability of Europeans to rule potentially more virile peoples, and prompted many to question the value of technology and modernity.[21] As Ann Laura Stoler has pointed out, fears about European sexual degeneration were explicitly linked to the colonial project; if the European "race" was dysfunctional, how could it hope to maintain control over a fertile and functional colonial populous?

The contrast between the unrepressed fecundity that supposedly characterized "primitive" sexuality and the neurotic dysfunctionality of the middle-class European also set the stage for the development of a queer settler sexuality. In his work on the US settler colonial state, Morgensen argues that settler colonialism necessitated the production of particular narratives of normative sexuality. Morgensen develops the idea of distinctive "'settler sexuality': a white national heteronormativity that regulates Indigenous sexuality and gender by supplanting them with the sexual modernity of settler subjects."[22] However, as shown earlier, the concept of degeneration implied that the "sexual modernity of settler subjects" was precisely what rendered them problematically queer, unable to fulfill their biopolitical obligations.

The Kenyan example thus offers an interesting counterexample to Morgensen's vision of queer settler sexuality. While Kenyan settlers certainly viewed their sexuality as more modern than that of Africans, they did not rate their own sexuality as more (hetero)normative. On the contrary, as I have been arguing throughout this book, they consistently described African sexuality as more primitive and, hence, *more normative* than that of more "advanced" civilizations. In her books, Nora Strange invoked this discourse of African primitive normativity and echoed the contention that misguided whites had the potential to contaminate Africans. In her nonfiction study *Kenya Today*, she claimed, for instance, that colonization had introduced prostitution to Kenya, and maintained that rape was "exceedingly uncommon" among Indigenous communities.[23] Although she allowed that "Free love certainly was, and is, practised in village communal life," she maintained that "a sense of patriarchal dignity prevailed, and certain tribes exercised hygienic principles lacking in European civilization."[24] Here, she echoed the prevailing discourse that it was "free love" that protected "primitive" peoples from the sexual neuroses that plagued their more "civilized" colonizers: because Africans always had access to sex, they were supposedly immune to the damaging effects of repression.

Strange also embraced the belief that exposure to more "civilized" cultures threatened the sexual purity of Africans; forces like urbanization, mission education, and Christianity caused Africans to become alienated from Indigenous social norms. It was these "detribalized natives" who were seen as most likely to adopt Western vices and, significantly, to protest colonial rule.[25] As Strange put it, "Those who best understand native psychology realise that the detribalised native is a source of danger both to himself and the community" since he inevitably "degenerates into a loafer or a criminal" or "a political malcontent."[26]

Yet Strange was far more preoccupied with exploring the nature of European sexuality. It's not surprising that Nora Strange embraced the format of the romance novel—a genre that is inherently invested in the dynamics of love, marriage, sex, and reproduction—to explore these themes. Romance novels are distinctive in that they find solutions to problems through the matrix of heterosexual coupling and reproduction.[27] Because the genre situates romantic love and sex as central objects of study, the romance novel was a particularly useful venue through which to explore anxieties about the effects of "civilization" on sexual health. Strange's novels can therefore help us produce an analysis of settler sexuality that accounts for the complexities of race, sexuality, and statehood in colonial Kenya. It can also help us sketch out what meanings Kenya held for that great majority of Britons who never set foot in the colony yet accessed it (through texts like Strange's) as a referent for a more pure and natural sexuality.

Curing Settler Queerness

In her study of race and psychoanalysis, Celia Brickman summarizes the role of the "primitive" in the European imaginary: "The term *primitive*," she writes, "anchored in the meaning of temporal or structural beginnings, placed its subject at the historical origins of human development. Close to—or part of—nature and untrammeled by the burdens of society and history, the primitive was seen and idealized as the embodiment of an undeveloped, innocent, and uncorrupted nature, still living in a terrestrial paradise before the fall."[28] In the late-imperial mindset, Kenya "functioned as a primordial space of natural purity, a sort of Edenic wild garden of open spaces teeming with wildlife"—an association that was bolstered by the belief of some anthropologists (notably Louis Leakey) that East Africa was the home of the first human beings.[29] Strange capitalized on this vision of Kenya by depicting the Kenyan landscape as an agent that forced overcivilized Europeans to reconnect with a more primitive, natural sexuality. Placed in touch with the fertile Kenyan landscape, her male characters shed some of their excessive self-control and assert sexual eminent domain over their wives—a form of staking a claim to sexual territory that closely mirrors colonial relationships to land.

Strange was not the first to use the theme of what we might call "reparative rape" in her novels.[30] In her study of romance novels and readership, Janice Radway notes that rape serves an additional ideological function in the ideal romance novel: "because the hero initiates the sexual contact that the heroine later enjoys," she writes, "it is ultimately he who is held responsible for activating her sexuality. She is free, then, to enjoy the pleasures of her sexual nature without having to accept the blame and guilt for it usually assigned to women by men."[31] In Strange's novels, marital rape served a similar function, although more explicitly tied to the sexual mandate of settler reproduction. The medium of rape opens previously frigid women up to sexual pleasure, enabling them to fulfill their obligation to reproduce future generations of settlers. Interestingly, in her novels, rape is also the medium through which settler *men* reclaim sexual pleasure; Strange depicts the assertion of dominion over sexual territory as a curative for male frigidity as well.

Strange takes up the theme of reparative rape in her very first novel, *Latticed Windows* (1924).[32] Roger Brunton, a white businessman in East Africa, marries Doreen Trevor, the daughter of impoverished aristocrats, who works as a secretary and is in love with her boss. Although Doreen agrees to marry Roger for financial reasons, she is not interested in sleeping with him, and Roger is too honorable to demand his marital rights. When he tells Doreen that he is taking her to Kenya, he remarks: "You probably won't like it, you may have to rough it and you're pretty certain to be lonely, but you've got to learn to become a woman—a wife. Your high falutin' notions have softened you. You're over civilised. If I didn't respect you, I'd have taken you long ago whether you liked it or not, but though I don't go about talking about 'em I have got—notions—ideals too, and I want you to come to me willingly."[33] In essence, Kenya will teach Doreen how to become "a wife"—that is, a heterosexual woman who craves sexual contact. Roger admits, however, that this is a risky venture, as Kenya "makes good colonists of some men and beasts of others," and for women "it makes nerve-driven creatures of some, courtesans of others, and real live good women of a few."[34] If the Kenyan landscape will sort the "real live good women" from the rest, it will also teach Roger how to become a husband by allowing him to abandon the "notions" and "ideals" that have prevented him from demanding his conjugal rights.

Once in Kenya, Doreen is struck by the "lack of restraint" in her surroundings, where "nature cried aloud to civilisation—'You may restrain me for the moment but you can't hold me for long.'"[35] Their house, too, reflects the primitive sexual space they have entered: while their flat in London "stood for civilisation—restraint!" their new bungalow represents "nature, primitive unadorned nature, when man sought woman as a mate and not as a mere companion and figurehead of his household."[36] Roger, unable to withstand his environment, is seduced by a Dutch woman named Kätie van Doorne.[37] After spotting Roger and Kätie in a passionate embrace, Doreen tells Roger that she is willing to grant him a divorce. Instead, Roger decides he will start raping her: "consumed with a burning desire to hurt her by thrusting her from the fastness of her inhuman virginity," Roger is "stirred by a primitive impulse. He wanted to drag her from it with the remorselessness of a cave man. He cursed civilisation and all it stood for."[38] Doreen's lack of sexual desire is "inhuman" to the extent that it denies the imperative to reproduce. Roger's desire to hurt his wife, meanwhile, represents at once a reversion to the "cave man" origins of the species and a cure for her overcivilized frigidity. The transformation is visible in Doreen's body: "Not happy altogether and certainly unsettled," after the rape Doreen was "yet curiously more alive. Sometimes too astonishingly vivid and lovely. No wonder Roger looked so possessive and dominant."[39] Doreen becomes more "alive" and more attractive as she is forced to engage in sexual activity; this "un-queering" of her frigid sexuality in turn makes her husband all the more domineering.

If the Kenyan landscape provides the impetus for Roger to enforce his sexual imperative, it also provides the mechanisms by which Doreen comes to accept and even embrace her fate. In another reoccurring theme, Strange exploits the notion of East Africa as a space of danger and disease as a plot device. Doreen, who has developed a keen hatred of her husband/ rapist, undergoes a rapid about-face when he saves her from a charging buffalo. Doreen then falls in love with her husband, just as he falls ill after helping to treat a family of Kenyan Indians with the plague. Doreen subsequently catches the disease while lovingly nursing him back to health. Luckily (for them), they both survive, and at the end of the novel Doreen is happily pregnant with their first child.

It is significant that Doreen's problematic queerness is resolved through two forces associated with the East African landscape. She comes to admire her husband's mastery of nature when he shoots the animal that was attacking her; her love is reinforced when they succumb to a tropical disease. These near-death experiences (a trope that Pamela Regis has suggested is central to romance novel plots)[40] emphasize the vulnerability of white settler lives, and therefore the imperative to produce more settlers through heterosexual coupling. Roger's statement that Kenya either brings out the best in men and women or utterly destroys them is in keeping with Strange's vision of Kenya as a eugenic space. By providing a sexual curative for settler queerness, the landscape ensures that those who (by virtue of race and class) are fit to colonize the space will survive and reproduce empire.

The theme of reparative rape is taken up again in *Kenya Dawn* (1928).[41] This time, however, it is the male protagonist whose outmoded moral qualms prevent him from embracing his reproductive duties. The novel centers around Sybil Dean, a young woman of the jet-set who must escape a scandal back home. Caught at a London night club with a married man, Sybil is packed off to Kenya to live with her cousin Elizabeth and Elizabeth's husband Sir the Honourable Claude Maynard. The Maynards epitomize the "younger son" type of colonists, those "smart young couples who found Kenya supplied to a certain extent what post-war England could no longer provide them with on war-depleted incomes—hunting, shooting, polo, race-meetings and, up to a point, the lighter social side of life."[42] Sybil quickly falls in love with Colin Grant, a sturdy and tanned Kenyan-born settler. However, after Sybil confesses the foibles of her past to Colin, he rejects her, constrained by an overwrought vision of sexual morality. Sybil, in contrast, maintains a more rational (and eugenically helpful) outlook on sex, viewing it "with something of the bald simplicity of the average man, by accepting it for what it was worth, and in this respect she was essentially healthy-minded, and had as much contempt for the vaporisings of the sex-possessed as she had for the crudities of the unsexed."[43] Neither "unsexed" nor "sex-possessed," Sybil is in touch with her innate sexual drives. While Sybil's sexual virility makes her an outcast at home in London, it makes her an asset to a space like Kenya where white reproduction is central to imperial success. Like the big-game trophies that were often hunted by whites in Kenya, Sybil thus represents a desirable form of prey whose pursuit will convey masculinity and prowess on the hunter.

This hunting metaphor is elaborated through the three attempted rapes that Sybil survives over the course of the novel. The first occurs at the hands of Louis Schultz, a "slick type of half-educated Boer with a thin veneer of polish."[44] This "closely-set-eyed Dutchman" earned a bad reputation for mistreating his African laborers after "one of his native herds died from the effects of a thrashing," although he was exonerated by a white jury.[45] Strange based Schultz's character on Jasper Abraham, a Kenyan settler of British, not Dutch, origin (and the son of the Bishop of Norwich) whose African servant died after being flogged for riding Abraham's horse. An all-white jury found Abraham guilty only of "grievous hurt" after his defense claimed that the victim had simply given up the will to live—a view that was famously echoed by Karen Blixen in *Out of Africa*.[46] It is significant that Strange rewrites the story with a Boer antagonist, as it fits into a larger discourse in colonial Kenya that held that Afrikaner settlers were both more racist and less suited to manage an African population than their British-born peers.[47] His "closely-set eyes" also signal a eugenic failing, a symptom of degeneration and a sign of his moral failings. Sybil resorts to booby-trapping her bedroom to prevent Schultz from forcibly entering—a strategy that again calls to mind the practice of big-game hunting.

After a night at Nairobi's Muthaiga club, Sybil faces another set of attempted rapes, this time at the hands of Colin and her cousin's husband, Sir Claude Maynard. Strange compares the two men: the aristocratic Maynard "standing sulking in the background looked artificial compared to Colin, the primitive male bent on capture."[48] Colin's connection to his "primitive" urges renders him more authentic than the more restrained Maynard. To Sybil's exclamation that "We are civilised people," Colin responds "I, for one, am not feeling particularly civilised this evening."[49] Although Sybil claims that she "would rather die than yield to Colin in his present ugly mood," the evening ends with Colin kissing Sybil passionately—and consensually—on the porch of her boarding house.[50] Sybil successfully fends off the attacks of two men who are eugenically unfit—Schultz because of his marginal claim on whiteness and Maynard because of his upper-class background—but finds herself surrendering to Colin, the hearty, unaffected settler. Colin's ability to abandon his "civilized" sexual restraint is portrayed as positive because he is the "right sort" of Kenyan settler: hard-working, physically fit, and with an unsullied claim to whiteness.

As in *Latticed Windows*, nature ultimately intervenes to bring the two together. Colin and Sybil face a final challenge when Jasper Grantham, the married man with whom Sybil had become entangled back in England, emigrates to Kenya and decides to purchase land directly next to Colin's farm. Colin intends to propose a duel to fight for his right to Sybil, but Jasper is attacked and killed by a lioness before he can put his plan in action. The duel, a highly ritualized and aristocratic practice based in outmoded notions of honor and virtue, becomes irrelevant in the Kenyan landscape, which eliminates those unfit to inhabit it. The novel ends with Sybil and Colin happily in love. With their settler queerness cured through their encounter with the Kenyan landscape, the couple are ready to produce a new generation of sturdy Kenyan settlers.

Strange's vision of healthy sexuality, however, did not amount to a wholesale rejection of white self-control. Rather, self-control was a double-sided coin; while too much self-control interfered with the reproduction of the race, too little self-control could prove damaging to interracial relations. Here, Strange was tapping into a larger colonial discourse that, in the words of Ann Stoler, "tied personal conduct to racial survival, child neglect to racial degeneracy, the ill-management of servants to disastrous consequences for the character of rule."[51] Strange was particularly concerned with those settlers whose lack of self-control might blur the racial boundaries of the colony. She echoed the discourse of primitive normativity discussed in more orthodox historical sources, depicting Africans—particularly domestic servants—as vulnerable to contamination from Westerners.

In the next section, I examine Strange's concerns about the risks posed by the inherently intimate relationships between colonial whites and their domestic servants. Readers will note that this section tracks closely to the discussion of interracial contact in the previous chapter, with a key difference: while the sources discussed in chapter 4 were directed at colonial women, Strange's novels were far more likely to reach a metropolitan British audience. As such, we can read them as engaging in broader debates about white degeneration and its potential impact on Britain's ability to hold on to its overseas colonies. Strange depicts African servants as constantly watching and learning from their white employers. In her novels, eugenically unfit colonists pose a moral threat to the Africans they interact with, introducing them to forms of deviance that were supposedly alien to Indigenous Africans. The reparative landscape responds to this threat by eliminating unfit settlers—settler queerness that cannot be cured is eradicated, thus ensuring the future of the settler state.

White Contamination, African Observation

Strange is one of several novelists who have explored the problematic relationship of colonial whites with their domestic servants. Doris Lessing's *The Grass is Singing* depicts the gradual corruption of an African servant by his neurotic mistress, while Ferdinand Oyono's *Houseboy* is abused after discovering that his mistress is having an extramarital affair.[52] But while these novels aim to critique the colonial project through the microcosm of the colonial household (the latter perhaps more explicitly than the former), Strange's novels focus instead on the importance of importing the right type of settler to the colonies, and avoiding the exposure of colonized people to marginal whites whose marginality was defined, by in large, by their class backgrounds. While *too much* self-control could threaten the reproductive viability of the middle class, a lack of self-control among upper- or working-class settlers could contaminate the watchful Africans with whom they lived side by side. The eugenic discourses of the late nineteenth and early twentieth centuries defined both working- and upper-class Europeans as degenerate. Such degeneracy was particularly problematic in a settler colony, where reproduction was essential to claims of settler belonging. However, Strange's novels depict the Kenyan landscape as having an innate eugenic capacity that solves the problem of settler queerness. Her Kenya is a space where the unfit do not survive long enough to reproduce; thus while the colony helped *fit* settlers tap into their reproductive potential, for *unfit* settlers the landscape exacerbated degeneration and provoked disaster.

Strange's concerns about the class background of potential settlers tapped into existing anxieties about the potential for developing a poor white population in Kenya. As Dane Kennedy puts it, "The 'poor white problem,' as it came to be called, was one of the central bogies of colonial society, rivaling the black peril [the alleged sexual assault of white women or children by African men] in its power to induce anxiety."[53] In fact, the two "bogies" were intrinsically connected in the minds of colonial whites: Will Jackson, following Stoler, points out that poor whites were seen as more likely to engage in interracial sex than their wealthier peers, besides which "their debased position entailed the kinds of contact with non-Europeans that jeopardized in turn the underlying human distinction between colonisers and colonized."[54] Such contact was increased in a colony like Kenya, where African laborers lived on white-owned farms and worked in settler homes.

The problem was also exacerbated by the fact that in Kenya, as in many other African colonies, domestic servants were predominately male. As discussed in chapter 4, while Kenyan settlers tended not to worry that white women would engage in sexual relationships with their male servants, they did show considerable concern about how colonial housewives might inadvertently produce sexual desires in their servants through thoughtless behavior.

Strange's 1928 novel *Kenya Calling* explores this fear that housewives, particularly those of unsuitable class backgrounds, might contaminate their domestic servants through their careless behavior.[55] The novel is revealed to us through the eyes of Sheila Marsden, a widow who goes to Kenya to live with her husband's cousin Helen. Sheila develops a friendship with her neighbor Lucille Logan, a white settler woman of lower-class background who is neglected by her playboy husband. Helen explains to Sheila how the marriage came about, assuring her that Mr. Logan is "a *sahib* [gentleman] right enough. Son of a Gunner colonel, public school-boy—Marlborough, I think—but his people bundled him off to Kenya when they discovered he had married a little waitress in a teashop"—that is, Lucille.[56] The reference to his officer parent as well as his education at Marlborough, an elite boarding school, places Mr. Logan firmly within the ranks of the upper class. His decision to marry a common teashop girl already marks him as a degenerating subject, but his unfitness is signaled further: Helen uses explicitly eugenic language when she wishes that "the type of parent who packs off unsatisfactory sons to the colonies could be exterminated. Moral even more than physical weaklings, especially when they are handicapped by foolish wives, are the last people wanted in a colony, more especially so when it is a relatively new one."[57] Importantly, both the working-class Lucille and her upper-class husband are marked as disabled subjects; he is a "physical weakling," while she represents a "handicap" to white settlement.

Helen's analysis proves to be prescient, as Mr. Logan's preference for drinking and fun over working his farm combine with his wife's "foolishness" to produce profound racial disorder in their household. Lucille's "foolishness," in fact, can be ascribed almost entirely to her class. Sheila is appalled by the state of Lucille's house, realizing that she "had not the slightest conception of how to run a house, much less of how to manage the native servants, whom she alternatively stormed at in shrill Cockney or allowed to loaf about and cheat her."[58] Lucille is unprepared to manage servants and unable to maintain British prestige with her common accent and cheap clothes. In fact, Lucille's clothing is another major point of contention between her and Sheila, who notices that "she invariably found Lucille in a once gawdy, now frayed and stained, kimono, giving a liberal display of a cheap, and not too clean, lace and crêpe-de-Chine nightdress, while her bare feet were often as not thrust into faded brocade, very high-heeled shoes."[59] Lucille's choice of cheap, dirty, and immodest clothing points to her inability to dress or consume in a middle-class fashion; likewise, her tendency to lounge in her nightclothes suggests a deplorable lassitude and a failure to embrace her duties as a colonial housewife. Yet Sheila is even more concerned about the impact that Lucille's scantily clad body might have on her African servants. Sheila asks Lucille whether she minds her servants seeing her in her nightclothes. When Lucille replies that "savages don't notice what you wear," Sheila insists "I think natives *do* notice what we—white women—wear . . . In fact, I think they are always noticing how we behave."[60] Here, we see Sheila (and by extension Strange) invoking the notion of a constantly observant African gaze as a means of disciplining Lucille's behavior.

Sheila is particularly disturbed by the observation of Lucille's servant Abdullah; she notices that every time she visits Lucille "she had been conscious of Abdullah's figure in the background—watching, listening, and, infinitely worse, understanding Lucille's invariably indiscreet conversation."[61]

Since Mr. Logan spends most of his time in Nairobi, cavorting with "bright young things" at parties, Abdullah has begun to be "the dominant factor in the Logans' slipshod *ménage*."[62] Abdullah is presented as particularly dangerous because he is part Arab; according to colonial racial logic, this rendered him both prone to "Eastern vices" and possessed of a certain exotic allure. Sheila is disgusted with Lucille when she remarks that Abdullah "is almost handsome for a native" and "look[ed] like some of those Sheik heroes in those exciting novels."[63] (This is a reference to Edith Maud Hull's bestselling novel *The Sheik*, published in 1919 and made into a film starring Rudolph Valentino in 1921.)[64] After making this remark about Abdullah, "for fully five minutes an unwilling Lucille had to listen to what a fellow white woman thought of another woman who admitted a native, a personal servant above all things, to the slightest degree of intimacy."[65] Sheila chastens Lucille that "You are not only laying up for trouble for yourself, but you are lowering the prestige of the white woman in a country populated mainly by natives who only a short time ago were savages."[66] Lucille dismisses Sheila's lecture as "unkind—narrow-minded—unjust" and classes her as one of those women with "nasty minds."[67]

The plot reaches its climax when Abdullah gets in a drunken fight with Lucille; Sheila hears a gunshot and discovers too late that it was "Abdullah, maddened by drink or jealousy, or both, murdering his mistress."[68] The dual meaning of the word mistress here conveys some of the discomfort with the degree of intimacy inherent in domestic service, particularly in the colonies; Lucille is an inadequate mistress, in the sense that she is unable to appropriately control and command her servants. Her failure as a mistress in this register opens up the possibility that she may have become Abdullah's mistress in another sense. This, however, is a possibility that Sheila vehemently denies. In the government inquiry that follows the shooting, Sheila testifies that, although she was much too familiar with Abdullah, Lucille never actually slept with him. Abdullah, overcome with guilt, eventually shoots himself. Toward the end of the novel, Strange reflects on the ability of the Kenyan environment to separate the fit from the unfit, characterizing it as a space "which brought out the strength and weakness in people, and which allowed no one to remain stationary, much less neutral. Kenya, which had made such a splendid, purposeful woman of Helen; Kenya, which had broken the poor, frivolous, good-natured Lucille Logan like a butterfly on the wheel."[69] Lucille's queerness—marked by her déclassé behavior as well as her misdirected sexual desires—is eliminated through her encounter with Africa, with Abdullah appearing as an extension of the reparative landscape.

While Lucille's gender rendered her sexual desires particularly suspect, poor white men as well as women suffered in Strange's Kenya. Her 1925 novel *A Wife in Kenya* features the character of McDougall, an alcoholic farm manager. McDougall's impropriety is signaled by his tendency to fraternize with the African laborers whom he managed. Corrupted by drink, McDougall physically degenerates over the course of the novel; one notable scene features McDougall crawling on all fours with "the shamble of a bear."[70] "Maddened by drink," McDougall takes on the characteristics of a "beast," a "pitiful wreck of a man; a shambling, unkempt figure, whose sloping shoulders and long inert, loosely-hanging arms produced the unpleasant effect of a huge baboon."[71] Returning to his primate roots, McDougall gradually declines and eventually dies, unable to survive in a primordial space still ruled by the survival of the fittest.

Lucille and McDougall prove to be eugenically unfit because of their lower-class backgrounds. Strange, however, was equally concerned with the lack of self-control displayed by aristocratic settlers. A scene in *A Wife in Kenya* also indicates concerns with the effect of strong drink on upper-class settlers. At a tony Nairobi club, a drunken woman, spurred on by the aristocrat Mr. Le Mesurier, begins to dance on the table in full sight of the African staff: "Nothing loath, she mounted the table, and with a lighted cigarette between her lips, swaying from the hips, executed a bacchanalian dance to the accompaniment of cheers and laughter from her friends. Once again, as she neared the edge, le Mesurier held out his arms to catch her, but she evaded him, and with a wild shriek, bordering on hysteria, snatched the bottle from her head and hurled it against the opposite wall, where it shivered into a thousand pieces."[72] As the words "bacchanalian" and "hysteria" suggest, the dancing woman loses all vestiges of self-control after submitting to the influence of sex and drink. Strange was far from a teetotaler; all of her characters drink—and perhaps rather more than a contemporary reader might think wise. The point is not that settlers ought not to drink but that only eugenically fit settlers possess the requisite self-control to imbibe appropriately. Watching the dance, another character Pierce Napier (whose surname marks him as an experienced colonist)[73] points to the door "at which a number of Goanese and native stewards were congregated, watching the sahib-log disport themselves."[74] He instructs le Mesurier to "Tell your friends, if any of them are sober enough to take it in, that if there is ever trouble with the natives in this country, we shall have to thank them for it."[75] White exhibitionism is construed as a form of contamination, one that may awake desires in the Asian/African man to possess white women (or to revolt against colonial rule). Importantly, it is assumed that this desire does not exist until it is introduced through the carelessness of whites and the constant observation of the colonized.

In Strange's novels, the misbehavior of white settlers has the potential to produce not only cross-racial desire but also same-sex desire. One of her most interesting characters is Hugh Barron in *The Clinton Heritage*.[76] As his surname suggests by mimicking the title of a "baron,"[77] Barron comes from the British elite. He marries Daphne Clinton, the daughter of aristocratic parents, but maintains an ongoing affair with a three-time divorcée named Araminta. He is also described as being a "blood-brother" with the Maasai, a description borrowed from colonial Kenya's most prominent settler, Lord Delamere.[78] Barron rejects his son Nigel who is born with one leg shorter than the other, a detail that not only underscores Barron's cold-heartedness but also perhaps suggests the eugenic decline of the upper class.

The most interesting element of the novel is Barron's relationship with his domestic servant, a Somali man named Saleh.[79] Saleh bosses Barron around and refuses to do any work, behavior that Barron rewards with presents. Mildred Merton, the moral compass of the novel and a devoted servant who has served the Clinton family for several generations, observes Barron's behavior. At first, Mildred finds that their relationship leaves her only "vaguely disturbed and nauseated," but her nebulous suspicions are confirmed one morning when she finds Barron sitting on the veranda in his pyjamas, sharing a chair with "the handsome lithe Somali lad" Saleh.[80] Barron demands to know what Mildred wants from him, saying "I take it you do not mean to spend the rest of the morning in silent contemplation of my manly form or the young Saleh's adolescent grace."[81] Barron's choice of a Somali lover is interesting given that he has earlier stated that the Somali are "the Irish of Africa" and "are temperamental, treacherous and cruel, but against this they are the best fighting men throughout Africa."[82] Within the colonial racial hierarchy, the nomadic Somali were considered to be physically superior to agriculturalist Kenyan African groups.[83] The reference to Somalis as being "temperamental, treacherous and cruel" calls to mind the racialization of Arabs as despotic, yet fierce; and indeed the Somali, with their linguistic and cultural connections to the Arabic world, were sometimes considered to be more Asian than African.[84]

It is worth noting that, in the British racial schema, Arabs were also considered to be prone to homosexuality, although Strange depicts Saleh's views on his sexual relationship with Barron in rather ambiguous terms.

Barron is upset when Mildred reacts to the scene on the veranda by reminding him that Saleh "keeps his favourite dancing girl" at a nearby Somali location, the implication being that he only slept with Barron for financial gain.[85] And indeed, Saleh does leave Barron to return to his village, and, by extension, to heterosexuality. Years later, however, when Saleh hears that Barron has had a stroke, he returns to care for him, even though Saleh has by this time contracted tuberculosis. When Barron dies, his Alsatian dog dies the day after, and a week later Saleh follows them into the grave.[86] The juxtaposition with the dog reduces Saleh to a loyal servant, one who would do anything for his master, presumably even sleep with him. Saleh's demise also brings to mind the trope that Africans had the magical ability to will themselves into death.[87]

For Barron, homosexuality seems to be the logical extension of his marital infidelity and his perhaps "excessive" admiration for African masculinity. Saleh, however, remains essentially heterosexual; Strange presents him at times as an opportunistic con artist and at other moments as an excessively loyal and impressionable servant, but she never presents him as a desiring subject who freely chooses to engage in sex with a man. She thus echoes the broader colonial contention that Africans rarely practiced same-sex acts unless contaminated by more "civilized" cultures. Barron must die because his sexuality is essentially unsuited to the settler project, both because his desires are directed away from reproductive heterosexuality and because his homosexuality and cross-racial desire pose a threat to white prestige. Importantly, his sexual degeneracy is innately tied to his class status; his aristocratic background renders him vulnerable to the kinds of sexual deviance that would be anathema to the hearty settler of middle-class stock.

Settlers at either end of the class spectrum, then, fall prey to the eugenic landscape of Kenya. In contrast to the middle-class settler, whose queerness can be solved by reconnecting him/her with innate sexual desires, working- and upper-class queerness calls for eugenic elimination. Settler queerness cannot survive the confrontation with the Kenyan landscape, which provides a Darwinian curative that allows only the fit to survive and reproduce.

Conclusion

"Within the lexicon of bourgeois civility," Stoler writes, "self-control, self-discipline, and self-determination were defining features of bourgeois selves in the colonies. . . . These discourses of self-mastery were productive of racial distinctions, of clarified notions of 'whiteness' and what it meant to be truly European."[88] In both the metropole and colonies, the middle class was defined through its ability to discipline itself. Strange's novels, however, reflect increasing worries in the late nineteenth and early twentieth century that this self-control, while allowing the middle class to attain ever higher levels of civilization, might also produce the kinds of sexual malfunctions that threatened their ability to reproduce. The eugenic landscape of Kenya solves this eugenic dilemma by promoting heterosexual desire in those settlers who are fit to reproduce.

By attending to the dynamics of settler queerness, this chapter presents a more nuanced vision of imperial sexuality. While the "primitivity" of African peoples was consistently used as a rationale for their colonization, the eugenic and sexological discourses of the late nineteenth and twentieth centuries increasingly flirted with the notion that "primitive" sexuality might be healthier than that of repressed middle-class Europeans. This revision of the standard script of European sexual normativity and African sexual pathology did not result in a rejection of the colonial project; rather, experts suggested that "civilized" peoples must get back in touch with their "primitive" sexual roots in order to maintain and extend empire. Contact with "primitive" landscapes and people—and the two were frequently conflated—could cure settler queerness, opening settlers to reproductive futurity, and thus achieving the biopolitical goals of the settler state.

Yet the discourse of settler queerness was not only relevant to settlers but also to those Britons who never made it to the outposts of empire. I would like to suggest that Strange's novels themselves served as a portable eugenic landscape that held the potential to open readers up to heterosexual desire—and thus to provide an antidote to metropolitan queerness. The potential to inspire sexual desire in readers is inherent in the romance novel. Descriptions of the sexual exploits of the characters might be construed, then, as not merely entertainment but as a strategy to provoke erotic feelings. The reader of Strange's novels traversed this eugenic landscape as she turned each page; reading about the (hetero)sexual exploits of Kenyan settlers might instill erotic desires in otherwise frigid and neurotic readers. Thus, Strange's novels should be viewed not only as describing a reproductive project but also as manifesting one; to the degree that the novels awakened desire in their readers, they contributed to a larger project of reinvigorating the sexual drives of the "overcivilized" domestic Briton.

The next chapter brings the book full circle. Having established the discourse of African primitive normativity, settlers and officials were able to use the supposed "deviance" of Mau Mau oathing practices to argue that the rebels were contaminated, mentally unbalanced, and therefore atypical. I focus on narratives of consumption, both the forms of consumption that Mau Mau supposedly partook in and white consumption of oathing mythologies themselves, to show how colonizers used the language of sexuality to discredit the movement for land and freedom.

SIX

Eating the Other

Erotic Consumption in Anti–
Mau Mau Discourse

IN HIS ACCOUNT of the Mau Mau rebellion, the South African writer Stuart Cloete characterized Mau Mau as "a phenomenon of transition" caused by "the impact of the West upon a socially complex, but mechanically simple, iron age-culture."[1] Specifically, Cloete blamed the violence on urbanization, education, and the influence of "older men who have served abroad [in World War II], who have slept with white prostitutes, and have been exposed to influences with which they were psychologically unprepared to deal."[2] While the Mau Mau themselves characterized their actions as a fight for "land and freedom," both popular and official accounts written by whites explained the movement as the result of rapid "detribalization," a force seen as alienating Africans from their own cultures while exposing them to the vices of both Western and Eastern "civilization."

The threat of detribalization had loomed large in white-produced discourses over the long durée of the colony. Almost from the earliest moments of the settler state, officials and settlers simultaneously expressed their duty to bring "civilization" to this second Eden and extolled their fears that this same civilization would contaminate and degrade the original occupants of the garden. Mau Mau brought the discourse of detribalization full circle; for the first five decades of colonial rule, whites deployed the discourse of primitive normativity to present urbanization, education, and political activity as potentially contaminating "threats" to African well-being. And in the sixth decade, when Mau Mau disturbed the illusions of peace and prosperity held by settlers, they blamed detribalization for the "transformation" of supposedly docile, compliant Africans into violent rebels dangerously ungrateful to their white trustees.

In this chapter, I show how the discourse of detribalization deployed during the Mau Mau crisis drew explicitly on narratives of gender and sexuality, and how this discourse built on the foundation already laid by the discourse of primitive normativity. The response to Mau Mau depicted the movement as the long feared/promised result of too-rapid exposure of Africans to the vices of civilization and to disturbances of the normativity that was depicted as the mortar holding together "traditional" African societies and worldviews. The sexual disorder caused by urbanization, Christianization, and Western-style education was portrayed as both the force that created the breeding ground for Mau Mau and the mechanism by which Mau Mau exerted control over an otherwise docile population. The notion that Mau Mau rebels practiced sexually deviant behaviors was a powerful strategy for dismissing the political claims of Mau Mau: if the sexual behaviors of the Mau Mau were essentially un-African, their demands could be dismissed as misguided, ill-informed, and, ultimately, illegitimate. At this moment, when a significant segment of the African population clearly rejected European paternalism, the settler community marked the Mau Mau rebels as sexually deviant *in order to emphasize their abnormality*. Mau Mau could not speak for the average African since their supposed sexual practices implied a level of neurosis unattainable by "primitive" peoples. Whites read Mau Mau through a racial and sexual frame that allowed them to process the rebellion not as a challenge to colonial rule but as an indication of the continuing relevance of the colonial civilizing mission.

I am not the first to point out that white contemporaries explained Mau Mau as a psychopathological response to rapid modernization, or to point to its utility as a narrative device that explained Mau Mau in a manner that did not challenge white pretentions to benevolent rule: as David Anderson explains, the "disease theory" of Mau Mau suggested that "Mau Mau was not provoked by the denial of things to the Kikuyu but by their own inability to grapple with the challenges of modernity."[3] Likewise, Katherine Luongo observes that "many colonial authorities preferred to read Mau Mau abstractly as a primarily supernatural situation in which atavistic black magic was an engine and means of anti-colonial resistance rather than as a socioeconomic and political conflict rooted in tangible concerns, the remedying of which would necessitate the relinquishment of a significant degree of colonial privilege and power."[4] Despite their recognition of the prominence of this narrative, however, historians of Mau Mau have generally not focused on the degree to which the rhetoric of "detribalization" was tied to a much longer history of anxieties about the effects of "civilization" on primitive peoples. Nor have they attempted to explain the central role played by gender and sexuality in such rhetoric. But attending to the omnipresence of sexuality and gender in the responses to Mau Mau is absolutely essential if we are to make sense of this historical moment, or to understand how and when sexual normativity becomes ascribed to colonized peoples. When Cloete listed the causes of Mau Mau, he added to the generic list of education and urbanization the more specific dangers of Gikuyu men exposed to the sexuality of European women. What is distinctive about the narrative of detribalization as deployed during the Mau Mau rebellion is its deep and broad reliance on narratives of gendered and sexual disorder. This, too, is a trope that only makes sense when placed in the broader context of the first five decades of white supremacy. For if (as I hope I have now shown) the discourse of primitive normativity had proved useful for keeping Africans "in their place," when Africans proved uncontainable, the narrative of degenerate Africans helped explain why *certain* Africans seemed to be determined to reject the status quo. In short, the argument went like this: while "real" Africans were sexually conservative, the key characteristic of Mau Mau, along with their violence, was their outlandish rejection of sexual and gendered mores. Therefore, whites argued, Mau Mau weren't real Africans after all—only the psychologically troubled detritus produced by too-rapid progress.

This chapter argues that colonial responses to Mau Mau centered issues of gender and sexuality. I first give some brief historical background about Mau Mau. I then explain how and why the discourse of detribalization became the most prominent explanation for the movement in both official and popular circles. In particular, I highlight the extent to which sexual and gendered disorder were viewed as key markers of detribalization, as well as one of its most nefarious effects. I then discuss the white preoccupation with Mau Mau oathing rituals, which supposedly obtained their power through sexual practices that were deeply contrary to "traditional" African sexual and gendered norms. I conclude the chapter with a discussion of the government's counterinsurgency efforts, which attempted to reimpose "traditional" sexual and gendered norms on the Gikuyu.

What Was Mau Mau?

The answer to this question turns out to be more complicated than it first appears. Mau Mau is one of the most controversial topics in African history; in particular, scholars disagree on how to characterize the movement and its effects. As I discuss at length in this chapter, contemporary accounts characterized the movement as a psychological response to too-rapid progress; Elspeth Huxley infamously described it as "a yell from the swamps."[5] This interpretation prevailed in the British government's official response to the movement, the Corfield Report, which drew heavily on the work of the two "experts on the African mind," Louis Leakey and J. C. Carothers.[6] Clearly, this interpretation was deeply flawed since it was embedded in the same white supremacist logics that governed the colonial project writ large.

However, even later histories of Mau Mau have not been able to reach a consensus on the nature of the movement. One of the first scholarly studies, Nottingham and Rosberg's *The Myth of "Mau Mau"* (1966), argues that Mau Mau was a nationalist movement that grew out of long-standing grievances with the colonial state.[7] Several other studies have followed suit in depicting the Mau Mau as an organic response to discriminatory policies surrounding land, mobility, and political representation.[8] A number of scholars (especially those influenced by Marxist historiographical traditions) have argued that the role of poor African farmers was key to the movement, characterizing it as a peasant rebellion.[9] More recently, David Anderson has classified it as a civil war in which Gikuyu militants targeted those seen as collaborators with the colonial government.[10] Members of the "Nairobi School" have classified it as a "tribalist" movement aimed at gaining more power for the Gikuyu[11]—an argument that reflects the dominance of the Gikuyu in post-independence Kenyan politics. Still others (notably Caroline Elkins) have framed Mau Mau as an explicitly nationalist anticolonial war.[12]

Here's what *is* clear about Mau Mau: by the time the movement broke out in the early 1950s, Kenyan Africans had experienced five decades of exploitative colonial labor policies, political discrimination, and reduced access to land. World War II exacerbated these grievances in two ways: first, the roughly seventy-five thousand Kenyan Africans who served in the war returned home to find that their efforts would not be recognized with any change in political or social status.[13] The war also brought economic changes (including more investment in colonial development and an expansion of the monetary economy) that increased the wealth of whites but did not benefit Africans.[14] Meanwhile, tensions festered within the Gikuyu community between conservative "chiefs" like Chief Waruhiu who had benefitted from colonial rule, Western-educated nationalists like Jomo Kenyatta, and more militant nationalists—frequently also involved in trade unionism—like Fred Kubai and Bildad Kaggia.[15]

By the late 1940s, Gikuyu militants (as well as members of some other groups including the Embu, Meru, and Kamba) began to administer oaths of loyalty and gather weapons and resources. This is the beginning of the movement that came to be known as Mau Mau. As with so many other elements of the movement, the origins of the name "Mau Mau" is a matter of debate. The militants called themselves the "Land and Freedom Army," emphasizing the two major demands. Some scholars, notably Rosberg and Nottingham, have suggested that the name "Mau Mau" was invented by the colonial regime.[16] The Mau Mau leader J. M. Kariuki suggested that it was a reworking of the term "uma, uma" meaning "go, go" and was meant to symbolize the demand that the Europeans leave Kenya.[17] Another Mau Mau rebel, General China, explained that it was a corruption of the Gikuyu word for oath, "mma."[18] The historian David Branch suggests that the word's etymology may describe a term for "greedy eating" that was "sometimes used by mothers to rebuke children who were eating too fast or too much."[19] Regardless of its origins, this term quickly became dominant and is still used to refer to the movement today, in Kenya and elsewhere.

By the early 1950s, Mau Mau came to the attention of the white public as members of the movement began to attack livestock on colonial farms and to kill loyalist Gikuyu. Although Mau Mau is popularly remembered in the West for targeting white settlers, in fact, only thirty-two settlers were killed during the conflict. Meanwhile more than 1,800 African civilians died at the hands of the Mau Mau, most notably in the awful Lari massacre of 1953, during which Mau Mau killed seventy-four people and wounded another fifty.[20] The crisis came to a head in October 1952, when the prominent loyalist Chief Waruhiu was assassinated, prompting the governor, Sir Evelyn Baring, to declare a State of Emergency that allowed the colonial government to conduct mass arrests and detain suspects without trial.

What followed was a massive campaign by the colonial government to repress the movement. The Mau Mau retreated to the forests of central

Kenya, from which they continued to stage attacks. Meanwhile, the Gikuyu were subjected to mass "screenings," in which they were rounded up and interrogated to find out whether they had taken the Mau Mau oath of loyalty. Those who failed such screenings were placed in detention camps; the historian David Anderson estimates that "at least 150,000 Kikuyu, perhaps even more, spent some time behind the wires of a British detention camp over the course of the rebellion."[21] Detainees suffered from disease, overcrowding, and torture. The government also adopted a "villagization" campaign designed to prevent noncombatants from supplying the Mau Mau rebels with food, weapons, and other supplies. Bethwell Ogot and William Ochieng' estimate that roughly 1,077,500 Gikuyu and Embu, mostly women, children, and old men, were put in these villages between May 1954 and August 1956.[22] There they were subjected to both physical and sexual abuse.[23] Meanwhile, their lands and possessions were confiscated by the government and distributed to loyalist Africans.

By 1957, only a few forest rebels continued to resist. The colonial counterinsurgency campaign had wiped out a large number of Mau Mau: David Anderson estimates that twelve to twenty thousand Mau Mau died during the conflict.[24] Meanwhile, the government began to gradually dismantle the detention camps, releasing the 1,600 persons who remained in detention.[25] This step was made all the more necessary as reports about camp conditions had begun to create a scandal in the British press, due largely to the efforts of Labour MPs Barbara Castle and Fenner Brockway.[26] The Hola Massacre of 1959, during which eleven Mau Mau detainees were killed by guards in the Hola Detention Camp, became a particular source of criticism.[27]

The Emergency officially ended in January of 1960. The same year, the two major African nationalist parties, the Kenya African National Union (KANU) and the Kenya African Democratic Union (KADU), were formed. Decolonization followed, with Kenya achieving independence in December of 1963. Jomo Kenyatta, who had been arrested and convicted for his supposed leadership of the Mau Mau rebellion, became president of a new government dominated by KANU. Kenyatta, who (despite the belief of most colonists) was at heart a moderate, chose a path of reconciliation; his Kenya would make room for both the former colonists and the new African elite. The former Mau Mau rebels were never recognized for their part in the overthrow of the colonial government. Kenyatta borrowed from the settler's rhetoric when he declared that "Mau Mau was a disease which has been eradicated and must never be remembered again."[28]

Why Detribalization?

One reason Mau Mau was so consistently portrayed as the result of too-rapid detribalization was that it helped explain how the Gikuyu, previously racialized as loyal and passive, could turn against their colonial mentors. In other words, this was the explanation that allowed white settlers to maintain both their belief that they knew and understood the Gikuyu they lived and worked alongside as well as their belief that colonialism was a benevolent force—even in the face of tremendous evidence to the contrary. Because the Gikuyu were the group most exposed to the "perils" of European civilization, this logic held, they were thus the most vulnerable to the powerful psychological effects of detribalization. In an essay published in the *Sunday Times* in September 1953, the novelist Graham Greene observed that "the Kikuyu were perhaps too close to ourselves."[29] Unlike the aristocratic Maasai, the Gikuyu were well-suited to European civilization: they were viewed as democratic and religious, if disconcertingly acquisitive. Thus, Greene notes, "When the revolt came, it was to the English colonist like a revolt of the domestic staff. The Kikuyu were not savage, they made good clerks and stewards. It was as though Jeeves had taken to the jungle."[30] As in the last two chapters, the domesticity of settler colonialism—both the actual use of domestic servants and the fact that settler colonialism brought empire home in distinctive ways—was a recurring touchstone of anxiety and of meaning-making.

Greene's observations indicate one of the most troubling aspects of the Mau Mau rebellion for settlers: the ways in which it undercut the European pretension to intimate knowledge of "the native." First, it challenged the racialization of Gikuyu as a "nonmartial" race. From the earliest days of the colony, the Gikuyu had been characterized as passive, even helpless. In a statement that would prove deeply ironic, the first ethnography of the Gikuyu people predicted in 1910: "It seems highly improbable that the Akikúyu, even if they desired to do so, would ever achieve sufficient combination for a united attempt to throw off British rule."[31] The construction of Gikuyu identity as passive and loyal was a comforting mythology for the white farmers who surrounded themselves with Gikuyu laborers, relying on them for their survival on a daily basis. Peter Hewitt, a Briton who served in the colonial police force during the rebellion, highlighted this dependence when he characterized one settler as trusting his servants "as he would a barber with a razor."[32]

The Gikuyu were also disproportionately impacted by colonization. As John Lonsdale puts it, "Of all African groups the Kikuyu enjoyed the best opportunities and endured the worst oppression."[33] While other groups, notably the Maasai, were deemed to have a cultural integrity worthy of preservation,[34] the Gikuyu were viewed as particularly suited to serve as servants and farm laborers. Carolyn Martin Shaw has compared the racialization of the Maasai and the Gikuyu in Kenya to that of Native Americans and African Americans in the United States; the Maasai and the Native Americans were deemed "noble savages," while Gikuyu and African Americans were dismissed as "deceitful servants." Thus, "In Kenya, the noble savage was projected onto the majestic, expansive landscape, while the ignoble savage, the ignominious servant, was close by in the cultivated garden . . . Africans who lived in the recently developed Kenyan cities were especially reviled for their association with the corruption of European progress and their distance from the noble landscape."[35] Here we see the double-bind in which colonialism placed the Gikuyu: deemed most suitable to have their "traditional" lifestyles interrupted, they were also reviled for having strayed from that "tradition"—particularly when they wished to engage in practices that threatened white supremacy.

This brings us to the second way in which Mau Mau challenged white claims to "know" the African. Mau Mau revealed that the Gikuyu cooks, "house-boys," farm laborers, and stewards who made life in the Highlands possible for Europeans did not, in fact, view their employers with grateful reverence; rather, they were so dissatisfied that they were willing to assist in the murder of white settler families. One could hardly invent a situation more calculated to inspire anxiety in settler households. Some settlers reacted to the involvement of trusted servants in Mau Mau murders by insisting on their complete knowledge of their own employees. Peter Hewitt recalled attending dinners where "to have made the slightest allusion to the disloyalty of your settler host's Kikuyu house staff would have been a blatant breach of etiquette. A doubtful innuendo on the morals of his wife could not have provoked him half so much."[36] Hewitt's comparison to cuckolding is interesting—it reframes the relationship between domestic servants and their employers as primarily conjugal, emphasizing again the degree to which sexuality became a central analytic for making sense of the threat posed by Mau Mau. As I discuss further in this chapter, one reason the "oathings" that Mau Mau used to ensure loyalty became such a central part of settler mythology is that they provided a convenient explanation for how supposedly loyal, passive Gikuyu could transform into violent rebels. The concept of "transformation," indeed, became a central trope of Mau Mau–era discourse as settlers struggled to align their conceptions of benevolent colonialism with the deep anger revealed by Mau Mau.

This was particularly true of the two predominate "experts" on the origins of the Mau Mau rebellion, Louis Leakey and J. C. Carothers, who served on the Committee to Enquire into the Sociological Causes and Remedies for Mau Mau, an advisory panel that David Anderson has credited with popularizing the "disease theory" of Mau Mau.[37] Louis Leakey grew up in Kenya, the son of two of the first missionaries in East Africa. Unable to return to England for school because of the outbreak of World War I, Louis Leakey remained in Kenya throughout his adolescence. After the war, he received training as an undergraduate at Cambridge under the anthropologist A. C. Haddon, but much of his authority came from his experience growing up among Gikuyu children, and his knowledge of the Gikuyu language. These early interactions with Gikuyu people bolstered Leakey's definition of himself as a "white African" (this was in fact the title of his 1937 memoir[38]) who claimed to "know the Kikuyu better than any white man living," being "in so many ways a Kikuyu myself."[39] In addition to several anthropological studies, Leakey authored two studies on Mau Mau. *Mau Mau and the Kikuyu* was published in 1952, followed by *Defeating Mau Mau* two years later; both were successful sellers in the United States and United Kingdom.[40] These works emphasized the inherent value of rural Gikuyu culture and the troubling effects that European civilization posed to it: as Carolyn Martin Shaw has put it, "Leakey envisioned the Kikuyu as an egalitarian, harmonious, and healthy little community transformed by colonialism into a detribalized urban population and impoverished rural traditionalists."[41]

The second of the major "experts" called on to explain the Mau Mau rebellion was John Colin Carothers. Although Carothers would eventually become one of the most prominent and influential psychiatrists on the African continent, he came to this calling almost by accident. In 1937, the Kenyan medical board chose the young physician to replace Dr. James Cobb as the head of the Mathari Mental Hospital.[42] Carothers, a white South African, had been trained as a medical doctor in Britain. However, he did not specialize in psychology; as McCulloch notes, "Six one-hour lectures on psychology at St Thomas' [Hospital, University of London] constituted his only training in psychological medicine."[43] Yet, by the 1950s, whites both within Kenya and in the metropole considered Carothers to be an expert on "the African psyche."[44]

Both Leakey and Carothers cited detribalization as a major cause of the Mau Mau rebellion. Leakey believed that "the break-down of Kikuyu law, custom, religious beliefs, and training of the young people, and the substitution either of modifications or new ideas has led to a state of affairs in which Mau Mau could operate."[45] Leakey particularly blamed Western-style education and urbanization for alienating the Gikuyu from their culture, complaining that modern Gikuyu children "get little of the education in behaviour, native law and custom, and character training that were all part of the organized tribal education system."[46] Instead, they attended mission schools, government schools, or independent schools (set up by Gikuyu nationalists during the Circumcision Crisis) where they were exposed to book learning but not moral education.[47]

Likewise, Carothers embraced the common discourse of detribalization, warning that contact with European culture was dangerous for Africans. In an article published in the *Journal of Mental Science* in 1947, Carothers maintained that insanity rarely occurred in "primitive life."[48] Yet, he warned, "the East African native has however an immense admiration for European institutions and manner of life, so that contact with this alien culture is rapidly destroying his own," creating "a potent source of mental breakdown."[49] While "traditional" and "tribal" cultures protected Africans from the worst effects of civilization, in the cities, "tribal discipline" would break down, as Africans started drinking, gambling, and stealing. He listed the following factors as contributing to the so-called detribalization of Africans: "Christianization, secular education, working relationships with non-African employers, relationships with Government officials and with shop-keepers (the latter mostly Indian), life in townships, and the introduction of syphilis, spirits and other drugs."[50] Conveniently for the settlers, who relied on African labor, Carothers felt that Africans who lived on white-owned farms "usually carry with them the habits and outlook of the tribal area from which they came, family life is not disrupted, the traditional manner of living is not seriously interfered with, and in general the influence of the alien culture on these people is minimal."[51] Like Leakey, Carothers believed that the Gikuyu were particularly prone to detribalization, since they had experienced earlier and more sustained contact with European and Asian cultures, and because Gikuyu men were disproportionately represented among those who had received mission educations.[52]

Carothers and Leakey also embraced the discourse of primitive normativity. In accounting for the danger of "detribalization," Carothers and

Leakey emphasized its tendency to corrupt the norms of "traditional" African sexual conservatism. Leakey in particular was deeply complimentary of Gikuyu sexual morality. The Gikuyu offered an appropriate sexual outlet for each stage of physical development; he emphasized that for the Gikuyu "the whole of life was marked by a series of *rites de passage*, as the social anthropologist calls them, in other words stages, through which the individual must pass."[53] Moreover, Leakey emphasized the strong social pressure to conform to sexual mores, since any Gikuyu who defied these norms faced severe retribution from his/her age grade. This is in keeping with Leakey's broader contention that the "traditional" mechanism of Gikuyu social control (i.e., the rule of elders) was essential to the well-being of the community.

However, when such social controls broke down through the process of detribalization, Leakey believed that Gikuyu morality also suffered—with particularly stark consequences for Gikuyu women. He lamented growing numbers of unmarried mothers as young Gikuyu began to engage in premarital sex, a factor that he viewed as "playing its part in the rising tempo of insecurity and discontent within the tribe."[54] Leakey also blamed the migration of men to work in cities or as squatted labor for the destabilization of Gikuyu marriages; the absence of available husbands caused Gikuyu women to "join the ever-increasing number of prostitutes in the towns or else make a semipermanent liaison with some man to whom she is not married, either by native law and custom, or by the Christian ceremony, or by ordinary civil marriage."[55] Leakey believed that the destabilization of gendered institutions, including marriage as well as the age-based regulations on sex between men and women, created broader disorder in the Gikuyu community and rendered the Gikuyu vulnerable to the predations of unscrupulous politicians from political organizations like the Kikuyu Central Association. In *Defeating Mau Mau*, written in 1954, Leakey was even more vehement about the dangerous consequences of Gikuyu detribalization. Again, he emphasized the danger of a loss of *sexual* morals: as tribal communities broke down, he claimed, "Dishonestly of all kinds became common and sexual morals degenerated. The old sexual laws were no longer obeyed (they were not even known), but there were no others that had been inculcated in the young."[56] Importantly, Europeans were to be blamed for this transformation, "for we failed to appreciate the demoralising effect of a little book-learning, if it was not accompanied by very careful instruction in moral behaviour and in citizenship."[57] The central trope of Leakey and Carothers' analysis—which in turn directly shaped the government's response to the rebellion—was that the Gikuyu had been corrupted by their contact with "civilization."

Importantly, the sign and symptom of this corruption was to be found in the changes to the gendered and sexual practices of the Gikuyu.

While Carothers and Leakey wrote for a specialized audience, they nevertheless had an enormous influence on attitudes toward Mau Mau in the broader public. As Marouf Hasian points out, "Thousands of readers who may have never read Carothers' analysis or Leakey's texts could nevertheless read other popular novels that came from settlers who either cited their work or wrote about related topics."[58] The public discourse adopted the contention that Mau Mau was the result of a catastrophic confrontation between "primitive" Africans and a level of civilization they were not yet ready for. Even more significantly, the public discourse adopted the argument that gendered and sexual disorder was a central feature of the Mau Mau phenomenon.

For instance, a document titled "The Kikuyu Tribe and Mau Mau" from the papers of the Elector's Union (the most prominent settler's organization in the 1950s) depicts Mau Mau as the result of detribalization, and in particular the loss of traditional mechanisms for demonstrating masculinity. As the Gikuyu detribalized, traditional methods of signifying manhood were no longer available, with the result that the young Gikuyu man was driven to acts of criminality and "spivvery" as a way of asserting masculinity.[59] The Gikuyu blamed the Europeans for their own limitations, the document claimed; Europeans were thus a "whipping horse" for Africans who could not deal with the modern world.[60]

The reference to "spivvery" was a particularly salient one in the public discourse surrounding Mau Mau. In the United Kingdom, "spiv" was a popular slang word which referred to flashy dressers and/or small-time crooks. In Kenyan lingo, the "spiv" was used in a more limited fashion to refer to a detribalized, urban African man who attempted to adopt European modes of dress and behavior.[61] In doing so, the spiv made himself ridiculous—his efforts to perform European masculinity rendered him laughably effeminate and dangerously perverse. As Brett Shadle writes, "It was virtually uncontested [among Kenyan settlers] that western-style clothing erased Africans' sexual morality."[62] Missionaries were partly to blame, since by "encourag[ing] the natives to clothe themselves . . . [they] stimulate[d] the sex consciousness by causing to be hidden the natural functions of the body."[63] Like Adam and Eve before the fall, the nakedness of Africans symbolized their sexual innocence.[64] "Spivs," who not only clothed themselves but invested considerable energy in dressing smartly, were thus viewed as particularly susceptible to the temptations of Mau Mau.

One particularly graphic example of this trope can be found in a Mau Mau "Souvenir book," titled *Shambulia* (Kiswahili for "to attack"), created by the South African cartoonist "Bokkie" who had served in the Security Forces during the repression of the rebellion.[65] The cartoon depicted the transformation of a detribalized urban African—from "City Slicker" to "Mick Hero."[66] (Settlers and officials sometimes referred to Mau Mau as "Mickey Mouse," or "Mick.") The "City Slicker" wears a vest, complete with pocket square, ill-fitting pants, Oxford shoes, and a smart cap. He smokes a cigarette and holds the handlebars of a bicycle—two coveted material objects for the urbanized African. His transformation into a Mau Mau rebel—unclothed except for pair of grubby shorts and with his hair styled into dreadlocks—indicates that he has exchanged the trappings of urban style for the guns and pangas (machetes) of rebel life. Interestingly, he is also depicted as having gained a potbelly. On one level, this belly may signal Mau Mau's reputation as "greedy eaters," as subjects who were demanding to consume resources. However, his rounded belly also makes the "Mick Hero" appear to be pregnant, signaling again the gendered and sexual disorder produced by Mau Mau. In essence, the "spiv's" excessive, effeminate attention to dress primes him for the more profound gendered disorder of Mau Mau.

If Mau Mau involved a revision of African masculinity, it was also viewed as transforming African femininity. Popular accounts stressed that women were among those most susceptible to Mau Mau because the movement offered them a form of emancipation from the oppression and drudgery that supposedly characterized the lives of African women. The concern expressed by settlers about the role played by Gikuyu women in Mau Mau was not entirely misplaced—they were, in fact, essential to the movement. While women were a minority among the rebels fighting in the forests of the Kenyan highlands, many more women supported Mau Mau as part of the "passive wing," passing food, weapons, and information to the rebels. Yet, as Cora Presley notes, government and settler propaganda depicted female supporters of Mau Mau as prostitutes. Such propaganda was useful because it suggested "that women were attracted to Mau Mau for reasons other than rational political ones and that only those women who were pariahs in European and African society were liable to be seduced by Mau Mau."[67]

A document from papers of the Elector's Union emphasized this point: it claimed that women, resentful of the "progress" of Gikuyu men, were exploiting the Mau Mau rebellion to bring men back to a more "primitive" state.[68] Another document from the Elector's Union claimed that female prostitutes were withholding sex until their clients joined the rebellion—directly tying illicit, "nontraditional" forms of sexuality to the production of Mau Mau.[69] The notion that women gained power and authority through Mau Mau was itself an indication that the movement had profoundly disrupted "traditional" Gikuyu gendered norms, since settlers and officials consistently adopted the view that African women were treated as "chattel" by their husbands and fathers. It also connects interestingly to the debates surrounding the Silberrad Scandal discussed in chapter 2: in the earliest days of colonialism, the specter of African women left to prostitute themselves in urban spaces was held up as the disastrous future that might befall detribalized societies, those who let women slip out of the tight control exercised by "traditional" African social systems. Here, five decades later, powerful, martial women were characterized as prostitutes and displayed as the ultimate symbol of Mau Mau's degeneracy and of the movement's distance from "authentic" African values.

Some sources went even further in their efforts to present Mau Mau as a corruption of normative African gender roles. In his history of the Kikuyu Guard,[70] an organization of "loyal" Gikuyu used in the suppression of the rebellion, Anthony Lavers proclaimed that Mau Mau had such a transformative effect on women that it even caused them to reject their maternal roles, seen as a key attribute of African womanhood:

> The extent to which the women have been affected by the Mau Mau virus can be gauged from a story related in a captured terrorist diary. It told how a gang, hurrying back to the forests after a raid, was accompanied by a young woman with her newly born child. The woman found it hard to keep up with the terrorists, so she threw her child into the bush, to die slowly from starvation or more quickly from being devoured by ants or wild animals. For this extraordinary act—Kikuyu are generally devoted to their children—the woman received high praise form the terrorist hierarchy.[71]

Given the importance of motherhood in African cosmologies—an importance recognized by Lavers—the notion that the Mau Mau "virus" caused women to abandon their children signaled its transformative power.[72]

The cartoonist Bokkie echoes this notion that Mau Mau corrupted African women's "innate" devotion to motherhood—but with a twist. *Shambulia* features an image of a female "ayah" (nanny) pushing a (presumably white) infant in a pram. This "Virtuous Virgin" is transformed into a "Howling Harpy," heavily pregnant and fingering a panga menacingly. The implicit message is that Mau Mau has routed African women away from appropriate maternity—that is, a maternity that involved caring for the children of white settlers—and toward their own reproduction. Ironically, this shift toward prioritizing her own reproductive ambitions is depicted as an emasculating force—while the "virtuous virgin" has long lashes, a tidy dress, and hair neatly tied back in a headscarf, the "howling harpy" wears a dirty cloth that reveals one sagging breast, with dreadlocked hair and scowling eyes that are indistinguishable from the depictions of Mau Mau men. Even her pregnancy does not mark her as female, since it so closely echoes the distended belly of the "Mick Hero" discussed earlier. Bokkie's cartoon extends the white reluctance to allow Africans to consume resources to the bodies of African women themselves—suggesting that their desire to devote their reproductive labor to their own children renders them profoundly unfeminine.

White descriptions of Mau Mau oathing rituals also maintained that women—or more specifically, women's bodies—played a central role in generating the power of the oath. Crucially, sexual and gendered "depravities" were *the central organizing feature* of oathing mythologies. The argument went like this—the Mau Mau oaths required oath takers to engage in behaviors that were deeply anathema to Gikuyu sexual and gendered norms. Therefore, once someone had taken the oath, they were placed so far outside the pale of "traditional" African sexual conservatism that they became capable of any form of monstrosity. In the next section, I explore the narratives that circulated around Mau Mau oathing practices, arguing that it is impossible to understand either the meaning of these discourses or the desires that ensured their circulation without attending to the key dimension of sexuality—and more specifically, how sexuality was tied to race throughout the Kenyan colonial era.

Eating the Other: Consumption of and in Mau Mau Oathing Mythologies

In bell hooks's canonical essay "Eating the Other," she discusses the eroticization of the racial Other, which leads to a kind of consumption of difference through sexual contact and consumerism. As she puts it, "The 'real fun' is to be had by bringing to the surface all those 'nasty' unconscious fantasies and longings about contact with the Other embedded in the secret (not so secret) deep structure of white supremacy."[73] This section looks at how the Otherness of Mau Mau militants was consumed by whites through the mythology surrounding oathings. Oathing mythologies, published widely at the time in both local papers and sources as ubiquitous as *Time* magazine, both emphasized Mau Mau as men and women who engaged in deviant forms of (literal) consumption, and allowed whites to consume erotic fantasies about the sexual disorder of Mau Mau rebels.

Mau Mau oathing operated on two distinct levels. On the material level, oathings were used by the Mau Mau to ensure loyalty and solidarity among troops. Mau Mau leader Bildad Kaggia explained the function of the oath thus: "We decided that the movement could not succeed unless it was a mass organization. We ordered the oath to be administered to as many peoples as possible. *All means were to be used to get people to come over; persuasion, bribes, even force.*"[74] As the italicized sentence indicates, oathing could be a coercive practice: David Anderson has shown that oathing was used as a method to ensure that civilians would provision the forest rebels with food and supplies, and to intimidate these civilians into silence.[75]

The question of what actually happened during Mau Mau oathings is an extremely controversial and politically loaded one. Mau Mau oathing practices seem to have varied considerably among different groups of rebels, and at different moments in the crisis. As another Mau Mau leader Josiah Mwangi Kariuki describes them, Mau Mau oaths built on Gikuyu traditions, in which goat meat was "a prominent feature of [Gikuyu] social life," and in which oaths were taken prior to raids "to give those participating a feeling of mutual respect, unity, and shared love, to strengthen our relationship, to keep away any bad feelings and to prevent any disputes."[76] However, Mau Mau oaths differed from older Gikuyu oaths, perhaps most notably in that they were sometimes administered by force or coercion. Due to the secrecy of Mau Mau oathing practices, the use of torture to elicit descriptions of the oaths, and European attempts to distort popular perceptions of those practices, it is extraordinarily difficult to determine what Mau Mau oathings actually looked like.

For our purposes in this chapter, however, knowing what "really" happened is not particularly important. I am much more interested in understanding how oathings operated at the *discursive* level. In other words, Mau Mau oaths took on an entirely separate life when they became a central and reoccurring feature of anti–Mau Mau propaganda. I am interested in exploring this second domain: just as I have eschewed the question of how people "really" had sex in favor of exploring the social meanings produced through a discursive deployment of sexuality, I am now jettisoning the question of what "really" happened in Mau Mau oathings to focus instead on how whites used oathings as a heuristic device. In this section, I look at "oathing mythologies," the set of narratives about the oaths produced and consumed by white audiences. In referring to these as mythologies, I want to emphasize that descriptions of oathing practices should not be taken as accurate or truthful; accounts of Mau Mau oathings were a product of white imaginaries rather than a reflection of actual practices. Second, by describing these as mythologies, I want to point to how descriptions of oathing took on a narrative life of their own, emerging into a tight discursive formation complete with generic rules and literary form. My contention is that oathing mythologies can tell us a great deal about how whiteness processed the trauma of Mau Mau, and very little about the actual operations of Mau Mau rebels.

Oathing mythologies highlighted several deviant practices that Mau Mau rebels supposedly engaged in during oathing rituals—almost all of them invoking sexual or gendered barrier crossings or contaminations. The first, and most centrally featured in oathing mythologies, was the consumption of materials that were supposedly thathu, contaminating substances that, if consumed, would endanger life and thus necessitated ritual cleansing. Significantly, the substances in question were highly sexual in nature. The most infamous was known as the "Kaberichia Cocktail," a mixture of menstrual blood, sheep's blood, and semen, to which urine and feces might be added.[77] The "cocktail" represented a compounded transgression in which the male body was sullied by contact with female, animal, and autoerotic contamination; sources also emphasized that the semen was most often "produced in public"—that is, that it was sourced through public masturbation.[78] The consumption of sexual materials thus also necessitated deviant sexual activities, including bestiality and public sex.

Oathing mythologies also sometimes emphasized the inappropriateness of the bodies from which cannibalized materials were sourced. Sometimes the sourced body was inappropriate because it was either too old or too young to be deemed sexual within "traditional" Gikuyu beliefs—oathing mythologies include accusations that both girls and old women were incorporated into sexualized rituals. The notion that oath takers either engaged in sex with menstruating women, or consumed menstrual blood, also appeared frequently.[79] Such discourses emphasized the degree to which such practices violated "traditional" Gikuyu sexuality, which forbade sex with a partner outside one's age group, or contact with bleeding women.[80] As such, it emphasized the normativity of "traditional" African codes of sexual conduct while simultaneously pathologizing Mau Mau through the mechanism of sexuality. The focus on contamination, on the crossing of barriers, also develops quite logically from the discourse of primitive normativity. The threat of "contamination" by more "advanced" cultures was deployed throughout the first five decades of rule to ensure the social, and sometimes physical, separation of racial groups; therefore, describing oathings as occasions where contaminated and dangerously "mixed" substances were consumed emphasizes that this perceived threat had at last manifested in monstrous fashion.

The centrality of prostitutes in oathing mythologies also supported the contention that Mau Mau emerged from detribalized Africans. Prostitution was consistently portrayed in colonial rhetoric as the unfortunate product of urbanization of African women, and the breakdown of "traditional" forms of social control within Kenyan African communities— both the result of detribalization.[81] Likewise, the accusation that Mau Mau leaders took adolescent boys as lovers indicated the extent to which they had deviated from African sexual and moral values. For example, *A History of the Kikuyu Guard*, written during the rebellion for private circulation, captions a picture of Mau Mau leader General Matenjagwo thus: "One of his concubines sits next to him [Matenjagwo], while his 'Adjutant', Brigadier Gakure Karuri, brings his catamite boy."[82] (The boy in the picture is merely sitting next to the other rebels.)

The profound deviance of sex between African men was highlighted by the fact that oathing mythologies maintained that it was included in only the highest levels of the oath. A description of the Mau Mau oaths, marked "confidential" but found in the papers of the Elector's Union, suggested that the fifth oath required men to have sex with a virgin girl, but the sixth oath required the oath taker to have sex with a young boy.[83] The seventh (and highest) oath mandated that the child be killed, and parts of him be eaten, after this sexual contact.[84] The increasing power of each oath was correlated to the inappropriateness of the bodies with which the oath taker was required to have intercourse, with the child's body being deemed more thathu than the adult's, and the male child's body more thathu than the female child's. Given that colonial rhetoric consistently emphasized that homosexuality was not only absent from "traditional" African societies but essentially *impossible* prior to the attainment of a high level of civilization, the charge that oathings involved same-sex contact forcefully drove home the notion that the Mau Mau were, at their very core, un-African.

In fact, the idea that the sexual/alimentary practices involved in the oaths were a profound violation of African sexual mores was essential to the argument of colonial commentators. Precisely because they required the oath taker to violate his or her traditional values, the oaths supposedly separated Mau Mau from other Africans and bound them together as moral outlaws. Louis Leakey was especially preoccupied with Mau Mau oathings as a violation of Gikuyu tradition. He cited four violations in particular: Mau Mau performed oathing rituals at night, in secret, and administered them by force and to women. The oath was thus "utterly and completely contrary to native law and custom."[85] Leakey opened his discussion of the oaths by emphasizing their vulgarity and unspeakableness: "It is not possible in this book to give full details of the horrible, filthy, and degrading acts which are involved in the more advanced Mau Mau oaths. To do so would be to ensure that this book was never published, or if it was, that it would probably be banned."[86] Despite his claim that he could not describe the content of the oath, he listed examples of the "acts of defilement" undertaken during oathing ceremonies: "For instance," he noted, "in Native Law and Custom incest with one's own mother was an act for which there was no purification. It resulted in the person concerned being outlawed for all time. Similarly, an unnatural sexual offence, committed with a ewe, rendered the person concerned uncleansable. Both these crimes were regarded by law just as within the orbit of what might be done by very degenerate persons."[87] Leakey's use of the word "degenerate" here is significant, since it implies that the subject had reached a high stage of evolution and then declined. The Gikuyu people's exposure to "civilization" had not only isolated them from the traditional mechanisms of social control that had previously regulated sexual behaviors but also created the potential for psychopathology. The sexually deviant practices that oathing supposedly involved were thus both a sign of the madness of the Mau Mau and an explanation for the power of the oath to transform ordinary Gikuyu into monsters: oath takers were rendered "so abnormal and unnatural that, after what they have gone through, no act of arson or massacre, or disemboweling of victims, can seem to be anything but mild."[88]

The notion that the oaths became increasingly depraved as an individual climbed the ranks of Mau Mau was also emphasized in oathing mythologies. Oathing mythologies thus echoed and inverted the logic of both evolutionary anthropology and Freudian frameworks of sexual development. Evolutionary anthropology proposed that groups progressed through predetermined stages from primitivity to civilization. Freud borrowed this schema to develop a theory of sexual development where each individual progressed from a "primitive" stage of sexuality to "healthy" heterosexuality, hitting a number of landmarks along the way. The notion that Mau Mau progressed through various "levels" of the oath borrowed from these frameworks but reversed the directionality of Freudian thought—instead of an orderly progression through sexual stages toward the end goal of "civilized" sexuality, Mau Mau oathings represented a progressive degeneration. The significance of this narrative can be seen only when Mau Mau is placed within the larger context of the narrative of African primitive normativity. If "true" Africans were considered to be too primitive to engage in sexually deviant practices, the notion that the oaths involved a progression toward ever more deviant sexual behaviors signaled the exceptionality of the Mau Mau rebels, their distance from the conservative sexual values of the Gikuyu, and the state of madness that supposedly inspired their movement.

Robert Edgerton has noted that the elaboration and circulation of oathing mythologies became a central focus of government efforts to vilify the insurgents: "Throughout the Emergency," he writes, "the Kenya Government prepared press releases describing graphic details of oathing ceremonies that included bestiality, orgiastic group sexual melees, drinking the menstrual blood of prostitutes, and cannibalistic frenzies that involved killing traitors, drinking their blood, and eating their brains."[89] Edgerton is correct that oathing mythologies helped to discredit Mau Mau—specifically by portraying them as "contaminated" Africans who did not represent the opinions of the "authentic" African subject. But oathing mythologies also served an additional purpose: they provided an opportunity for white consumption of pornographic materials, under cover of "research" about the Other.

This is especially apparent when we examine the consistent framing of descriptions of Mau Mau oaths as restricted reading, even while descriptions of oathings appeared widely in newspapers and official accounts in East Africa, Britain, and beyond. Texts describing oaths took pains to warn the reader of the appalling contents found within; the result, of course, was to make the reader all the more eager to continue. As John Lonsdale notes, "Many writers left the details unsaid and readers' imagination free to range in fascinated self-disgust. Others adopted a formula which withheld 'the full details' but then gave specifics which one could scarcely bear to think of as less than complete."[90] A special issue of *Candour* magazine, which described the oaths at some length, published the following warning signed by the publisher:

IT SHOULD **NOT** BE READ BY SUBSCRIBERS, ESPECIALLY WOMEN SUBSCRIBERS, WHO LACK STRONG NERVES AND TOUGH MINDS.

WHAT IS PUBLISHED HERE IS A TERRIFYING DOCUMENT, A HOR-
RIFYING DOCUMENT, AN OBSCENE DOCUMENT, BUT AN OFFICIAL
DOCUMENT . . .

WHAT FOLLOWS SHOULD NOT BE JUDGED BY THE FIRST HALF
OF IT. THE DOCUMENT BECOMES INCREASINGLY HORRIBLE TO
READ . . .

SUBSCRIBERS CAN NOW BURN THE SUPPLEMENT OR READ ON.[91]

Such a warning almost guaranteed a page-turner—not only was the document unsuitable for those without "strong nerves and tough minds" but
it also promised to get juicier with each paragraph. Yet, the publisher was
careful to remind the reader that this was an "official document." These
warnings set up a dynamic in which the reader was lured in by the promise
of salacious materials, and then reassured that his/her interest in the documents was of a purely informative nature. Authors delighted in explaining
that the details of oaths were "unmentionable," and then describing them
in loving detail a page or two later. The tension implied by the publication of the unknowable, unsayable, and unimaginable clearly indicates the
erotic importance of "knowing" Mau Mau.

This dynamic appears in an interesting way in Peter Hewitt's memoir
Kenya Cowboy. In one section, Hewitt is having dinner at the home of
an Anglo-Kenyan couple. After dinner, the men retreat to the lounge for
brandy and a smoke, while Hewitt presses his host for details about the
Mau Mau oath. His host complies, feeding Hewitt the standard story of
orgiastic oaths full of blood-drinking and pagan rites, and what Hewitt
calls the "pièce de résistance"—cannibalism. The conversation is structured as its own sexual encounter between the two men; having retreated
to an all-male space, they indulge in their fantasies of oathings until they
reach a sort of climax with the supposed revelation of Mau Mau cannibalism.[92] Their own cannibalistic consumption of Mau Mau lore is obscured
by the focus on cannibalistic content.[93] At precisely the moment when
Mau Mau was rejecting white claims to knowledge about and control over
Black bodies, oathing mythologies offered white readers an opportunity
to consume an eroticized formation of Blackness at will.

In her study of British counterinsurgency tactics, Susan Carruthers
observes, "Becoming obsessed with Mau Mau's psychological origins and
with the depravity of its actions, many colonial officials (and authorities
on Mau Mau) appear to have overlooked Mau Mau's ends, or insisted that
the movement had none other than perversion itself. Believing that Mau

Mau members themselves made a fetish of their means, many fell victim to their own myth of Mau Mau."[94] Carruthers is clearly right to point out that the focus on the "depravity" of Mau Mau oathings allowed colonial officials to craft an alternative explanation of Mau Mau that privileged psychological rather than economic or political explanations. Yet this was not, as Carruthers seems to suggest, an accident; rather, the oathing mythologies were useful precisely because they offered an explanation of Mau Mau that negated the need to take seriously Mau Mau's demand for the access to land and freedom. Instead, white consumption of oathing mythologies offered both an explanatory framework that built convincingly on much older rhetoric of the threat of detribalization and provided a methodology of consumption that enabled readers to "know" Mau Mau through an erotic engagement with sensational(ized) texts.

Retribalization

As evidenced in the previous section, narratives of sexual and gendered disorder were central to white understandings of the power of the oath. Thus, it is unsurprising that government attempts to suppress the rebellion emphasized two goals: to undo the transformative power of the oath and to restore "traditional" norms of Gikuyu sexual and gendered conservatism. As Luise White notes, "The complicated and seemingly inappropriate nature of the British 'cure' for Mau Mau had little do with resuscitating colonial values . . . but with reconstructing men and women, through the process of domestic work, for a social order created and compromised by a British vision of calm and productive African families."[95] This process of "gender reconstruction" is particularly apparent in the "villagization" campaign adopted by the colonial government in 1954.[96]

"Villagization" targeted noncombatant Gikuyu, who were rounded up and moved into 804 villages.[97] The idea of villagization had been promoted by Carothers, who saw it as a solution to Mau Mau—"and to many other psychological problems of Kikuyu-land."[98] As envisioned by Carothers, this policy would move Gikuyu men and women into government-formed and controlled "villages," where their activities could be monitored and corrected by European administrators. Such villages would be easier to defend from Mau Mau incursions, but more importantly, they would "help solve the problem of family disruption and flatten out the cultural diversity between the men and women which seems to have played such a part in giving rise to *Mau Mau*."[99] (It is not entirely clear what Carothers means by "cultural diversity between the men and women"—most likely, he is pointing to the supposed dominance of men over their beleaguered wives and daughters, as well as the long-term separation of men from their families necessitated by work in the cities or some isolated farms.) As he envisioned it, villagization would provide opportunities for Africans to be instructed in cleanliness, health and diet, and infant welfare.[100] The colonial "civilizing mission" could thus be administered to a literally captive audience.

Leakey, too, viewed the reestablishment of "traditional" sexual and gendered norms as essential to the counterinsurgency.[101] Leakey recommended a combination of legitimate responses to Gikuyu grievances—providing land, improving employment prospects, and ending segregation—and biopolitical efforts designed to reestablish domestic/rural space as the center of Gikuyu life. The latter included the establishment of birth control clinics to prevent the overpopulation of Gikuyu on limited land, the establishment of small villages from which workers could commute to European-owned farms, and the lowering of the price of bridewealth, the money or livestock paid to a Gikuyu bride's family.[102] Each of these solutions sought to reduce Gikuyu mobility and reinscribe "traditional" Gikuyu gender norms: a smaller Gikuyu population would reduce overcrowding in the Native Reserves, thus reducing the need for Gikuyu to migrate to cities. Likewise, commuting villages would allow agricultural workers to keep in touch with rural "traditions." Finally, reducing bridewealth would enable men to marry at a younger age, preventing unmarried women from turning to prostitution for a livelihood, and discouraging young men from seeking sexual satisfaction outside of the prescribed lines of Gikuyu sexual morals. Leakey believed that the feminized space of the household would be a powerful restraint on young activist Gikuyu men.[103] The official solution proposed to the Mau Mau crisis was thus to reverse the temporal thrust of colonialism and forcibly "retribalize" Gikuyu people.

Although based on the recommendations of Carothers and Leakey,[104] in practice, the villages resembled them in little other than name; the "villages" were, according to David Anderson, "little more than concentration camps to punish Mau Mau sympathizers."[105] Placing Gikuyu into these heavily policed camps prevented the "passive wing" of Mau Mau—those who sympathized with Mau Mau but did not actually fight with them—from passing food, weapons, and information to the forest rebels. The program also, however, had ideological import: Berman explains that the villages were viewed as an opportunity to "reconstruc[t] Kikuyu society on a stable tri-class basis consisting of the wealthy elite, a solid and numerically dominant middle class of 'yeoman' farmers, and lower class of landless artisans and labourers."[106] In addition to reasserting "traditional" Gikuyu social classes, Caroline Elkins maintains that the villages were "intended as a punitive strategy to contain, control, and discipline Mau Mau women."[107] The notion that villages could reinstate "traditional" gender roles was fundamentally flawed since so many Gikuyu men were far away in detention camps. Far from being spaces that recreated the idyllic space of the rural African homestead, villages concentrated women with children and old men, and exposed them to the sexual predations of Loyalist Guards and white officers.

Sexual and gendered language were absolutely ubiquitous in contemporary accounts of Mau Mau, in both official and popular explanations of its power, and solutions proposed. Given this fact, it is perhaps surprising that historians have largely avoided discussing this language in their accounts of Mau Mau. In part, this may be due to a sense that the icky sexual stuff is less important or salient than the material impacts of the rebellion, of the material deprivations that helped bring it about, and the incredibly violent repressions that followed it. It may also be due to a very valid concern that discussing these sexual libels would also mean recirculating them. However, I think that the role of sexuality must be discussed if we are to understand not only the events of the 1950s but also how Mau Mau fits into the larger discursive history of colonial Kenya. The discourse of primitive normativity enabled the anti–Mau Mau propaganda discussed in this book. Tracing the genealogy of this discourse from its birth in the earliest days of the British East African Protectorate and seeing it through to its culmination in the response to the Mau Mau threat to white supremacy allows us to see how not only sexuality but the concept of sexual normativity itself operated as an alibi of empire.

Conclusion

THIS BOOK HAS argued that a distinctive narrative about race and sexuality developed in colonial Kenya. Rather than the standard discourse of the sexual deviance of the colonized, Kenyan Africans were characterized as practicing an essentially normative sexuality, one absent of aberrations like rape, prostitution, homosexuality, or frigidity. I show how settlers and officials both adopted a discourse of "primitive normativity," which suggested that Kenyan Africans were not yet sufficiently developed to engage in particular kinds of "deviance." Further, I've shown how this narrative served the interests of white supremacy by shoring up policies that restricted African mobility, political participation, and mission education.

I have also shown how various historical actors deployed, intervened in, and/or reworked the discourse of primitive normativity to serve their own ends. Jomo Kenyatta repurposed the idea of African sexual normativity to argue for the superiority of the Gikuyu people; Hubert Silberrad used it to ensure his sexual access to African girls; Sitaram Achariar argued that Kenyan Indians were the appropriate guardians of African sexual propriety; and Nora Strange presented Kenya as a eugenic landscape that would weed out those settlers who were unable or unfit to reproduce. The discourse of primitive normativity was effective in part because it was highly malleable, able to be deployed by all these figures to serve their own ends.

The narrative of African sexual normativity lives on today, most obviously in the antigay rhetoric espoused by several African political and religious leaders, including in Kenya. The following anecdote is a case in point. In 2015, the US president Barack Obama took his first state visit to Kenya. During this trip, Obama chastised Kenyan president Uhuru Kenyatta for Kenya's record on gay rights. Drawing a parallel to the legacy of institutionalized racism in the United States, Obama remarked "When a government gets in a habit of treating people differently, those habits can spread. As an African-American, I am painfully aware of what happens when people are treated differently under the law, and there were all sorts of rationalizations that were provided by the power structure for decades in the United States for segregation and Jim Crow and slavery, and they were wrong. So I'm unequivocal on this."[1] Kenyatta replied by asserting that, while Kenyans and Americans shared many common values, "there are some things that we must admit we don't share. Our culture, our societies don't accept."[2] Half a century after Jomo Kenyatta had argued that homosexuality was entirely absent from Gikuyu culture, his son made a similar case about Kenyan culture writ large.

This exchange between two presidents highlights some of the difficulties of thinking through the politics of sexuality and race in Kenya. In analogizing between racism and homophobia, President Obama erased the intersections of the two. Yet, as I have shown here, the notion that homosexuality was un-African was produced alongside narratives that racialized Kenyans, positioning them as temporally backward and unfit for self-rule. Obama's well-meaning comments entrenched a divide between powerful nations with the privilege to ignore their own civil rights violations and the poorer nations who are the frequent targets of such lecturing. Kenyatta's reply—that homosexuality is simply unacceptable for most Kenyans—presents homophobia as populism and, in the context of such lecturing, as an assertion of the rights of Kenyans to self-determination. Unfortunately, through this exchange, antigay sentiment becomes a marker of anti-imperial rhetoric.

This contention that homosexuality is un-African has deeply shaped queer African studies. Scholars have responded to this assertion in two primary ways. The first trend has sought to prove that queer folks existed in precolonial Africa, and further that they were accepted or even celebrated in their communities.[3] While this scholarship has provided valuable insights, it also trucks in a logic whereby only acts and identities that predated colonialism can be considered valid or legitimate.[4] In doing so, it reiterates the idea of an unchanging Africa where only the rural, traditional, and precolonial is valid. It also runs the risk of imposing terminologies and identities with Western genealogies on African contexts.

The other major trend in queer African studies has been the assertion that homophobia—not homosexuality—is the colonial import. Scholarship by Marc Epprecht in particular has made this case, which has been adopted by many LGBTQ rights activists on the African continent.[5] However, as Keguro Macharia points out, this idea has become canonized to a degree not yet supported by historical studies.[6] The assertion that homophobia was universally absent across all spaces and times in the immense and diverse continent of Africa is just as generalizing and ahistorical as the assertion that homosexuality never existed. Furthermore, as Rahul Rao notes, it represents a sort of "pinkwashing" of African homophobia that presents Africans as hapless dupes of an overwhelming colonial culture.[7] Reflecting on this impasse in the literature, Macharia argues that "a deeply genealogical method is needed to understand how certain figures become imbued with, and represent, the intimate anxieties of their geo-histories."[8]

This book attempts to provide such a genealogy of race and sexuality and offers a potential way out of this impasse. By moving away from homosexuality, away from acts and subjectivities altogether, and instead focusing on the concepts of normativity and deviance writ large, we can temporarily put aside questions of what people actually did in the precolonial era. Instead, we can see how the very concept of normativity itself is deeply raced and gendered. By showing that normativity is not always ascribed to those with the most power, I've sought to offer a new way of looking at concepts of deviance and normativity as they intersect with race and colonialism. In offering the terminology of "primitive normativity," I try to make visible the strictures that tied together narratives about evolutionary time and stadial sexuality. In other words, normativity was not a one-size-fits-all model. Instead, within nineteenth- and early twentieth-century regimes of knowledge, particular patterns of sexual desires, behaviors, and moralities were deemed appropriate to each stage of development—whether the development of an individual or the evolution of a racial group. By attending to the competing timescapes of settler colonialism, which contrasted the pure/primitive with the degenerate/civilized, we can understand how Africans could be constructed both as *more normative* and as *less evolved* than their colonizers—and how this discourse facilitated the goals of the settler state. In short, by maintaining that the "raw native" possessed a normative sexuality, settlers could argue against processes like urbanization, mission education, and political participation on the basis that these "detribalizing" forces would corrupt African sexual morality. Settlers thus presented themselves as the proper custodians of African morality *precisely because* they understood themselves to practice a more evolved, and hence more queerly problematic, sexuality.

While this project is deeply rooted in a particular space and time, I think it also has potential to speak to queer studies more generally—in particular, to encourage scholars in this area to look beyond the United States. The groundbreaking work on normativity by folks like Michael Warner remains largely focused on the context of the United States.[9] Even studies that take a more transnational approach, like Jasbir Puar's work on homonormativity, are often still focused on US empire.[10] What could we gain by looking at other empires, at other times and spaces? Historical examples from spaces beyond the US empire can offer queer studies a strategy for looking at the great diversity of how race and sexuality are constructed in relation to each other.

I am also curious about the degree to which this phenomenon shows up in other colonial spaces and times. The malleability of the narrative of "primitive normativity" makes it a potent force for constructing and enforcing ideas about race and sexuality. Where else might this discourse have taken shape? Are there other ways it was used to shore up colonial regimes? Are there other ways that the discourse was coopted and reworked by colonized peoples?

As I conclude this study, I'm also very aware of some of its limitations. Most glaringly, in pursuing a history of a discourse, I've left aside questions of reception and resistance. In part, this is a reflection of my archival approach. By rooting my approach in archival documentation, I am able to prove the existence of a narrative that seems profoundly counterintuitive. At the same time, however, staying "true to the archive" means that I miss other opportunities. Scholars like Saidiya Hartman, Tiya Miles, and Marisa Fuentes have productively engaged with speculative histories.[11] How might engaging with such speculative approaches facilitate those questions of resistance and reception that are largely neglected in this study? How might refusing the authority of the archive present its own challenge to colonial ways of knowing?

Despite these limitations, I believe that this project has the potential to open up new ways of thinking through the intersections of race and sexuality in colonized spaces. I hope, too, that this study of the past can help us find new ways to approach the future. In *The Intimacies of Four Continents*, Lisa Lowe describes her work as "A history of the present." Such a history "refuses the simple recovery of the past and troubles the givenness of the present formation. It is not a historical reconstruction that explains or justifies our present, but a critical project that would both expose the constructedness of the past, and release the present from the dictates of that former construction."[12] This, I think, is the ultimate goal of anticolonial history: to allow us to imagine new ways of being and knowing and, by doing so, to alter the continuing conditions of coloniality in the spaces we research, as well as the spaces from which we write. Perhaps in some small way this study can contribute to this ongoing project of rejecting the colonial past and present in favor of a more liberatory future.

NOTES

Introduction

Epigraph: Anonymous, "East Africa Prot: Cont," memo or report, Kenya National Archives [KNA]: AM/1/5 (or 1/1/5), Indecent Assaults, 1920–1944, Room 1, Shelf 269, Box 1, n.d.

1   Shaw, *Colonial Inscriptions*; Kennedy, *Islands of White*; Shadle, *Souls of White Folk*; Anderson, "Sexual Threat and Settler Society"; Anderson, "Master and Servant"; Anderson, "Punishment, Race"; Anderson, *Histories of the Hanged*; Jackson, *Madness and Marginality*; Kanogo, *African Womanhood*; Ocobock, *Uncertain Age*.
2   Macharia, *Frottage*.
3   Carotenuto, "Repatriation in Colonial Kenya," 11. See also Ocobock, *Uncertain Age*, 105–12.
4   E. B. Hosking, *Memorandum on the Native Locations of Nairobi*, Oxford: Rhodes House Library [RH]: MSS Afr. s. 633 [Sir Robert Coryndon], Box 5, File 1, c. 1930, p. 10.
5   Vaughan, *Curing Their Ills*, 109.
6   The Gikuyu are one of the largest ethnic groups in Kenya and, along with the Embu and Meru, the group most involved in the Mau Mau rebellion.
7   Davin, "Imperialism and Motherhood."
8   Shadle, *Souls of White Folk*; Jackson, *Madness and Marginality*.
9   Rifkin, *Settler Common Sense*; Morgensen, *Spaces between Us*.
10 Tallie, *Queering Colonial Natal*, 7.
11 Jackson, *Becoming Human*.
12 Rao, *Out of Time*.
13 Macharia, *Frottage*, 5.
14 Cohen, "Punks, Bulldaggers, and Welfare Queens," 438.
15 Cohen, "Punks, Bulldaggers, and Welfare Queens," 442.
16 Cohen, "Punks, Bulldaggers, and Welfare Queens," 452.
17 Epprecht, *Heterosexual Africa?*
18 Hoad, *African Intimacies*, xxiv.
19 Hoad, "Arrested Development," 137.
20 Macharia, "African Queer Studies."
21 Rubin, "Thinking Sex."

22 Stoler, *Race and the Education*, 6–7; Macharia, "African Queer Studies."

23 Macharia, *Frottage*, 27.

24 Arondekar, "Queering Archives," 211.

25 Foucault, "Lives of Infamous Men," 76–91.

26 See, for instance, Kanogo, *African Womanhood*; Davison, *Voices from Mutira.*

27 Stoler, *Along the Archival Grain.*

28 Stoler, *Along the Archival Grain*, 20.

29 Arondekar, *For the Record*, 1.

30 Arondekar, *For the Record*, 3.

31 Arondekar, *For the Record*, 4.

32 Lonsdale, "Kenya," 75.

33 Sorrenson, *Origins of European Settlement*, 1.

34 Gregory, *India and East Africa*, 51.

35 Gregory, *India and East Africa*, 54.

36 Sorrenson, *Origins of European Settlement*, 24.

37 Gupta, "South Asians in East Africa," 110.

38 Aiyar, "Anticolonial Homelands," 989.

39 Sorrenson, *Origins of European Settlement*, 65.

40 Kennedy, *Islands of White*, 184.

41 Kennedy, *Islands of White*, 184.

42 Kennedy, *Islands of White*, 186.

43 Kennedy, *Islands of White*, 43.

44 Kennedy, *Islands of White*, 50.

45 For more on the Soldier Settlement Scheme, see Duder, "'Men of the Officer Class.'"

46 Kennedy, *Islands of White*, 56.

47 Kennedy notes that 550 of the 685 nonlocal participants in the scheme were officers and had or subsequently inherited peerages. Kennedy, *Islands of White*, 56.

48 Kennedy, *Islands of White*, 71.

49 Shadle, *Souls of White Folk*, 66.

50 Kennedy, *Islands of White*, 48.

51 Kennedy notes that in Rhodesia, too, Afrikaners "were commonly regarded as the main candidates for poor white status." Kennedy, *Islands of White*, 173.

52 Duder and Youé, "Paice's Place," 269.

53 Shadle, *Souls of White Folk*, 65.

54 Shadle, *Souls of White Folk*, 15.

55 Shadle, *Souls of White Folk*, 4.

56 Ghai and McAuslan, *Public Law and Political Change*, 27.

57 White, *Comforts of Home*, 32.

58 Shadle, "Bridewealth and Female Consent," 241–62. See also Lonsdale, "When Did the Gusii (or Any Other Group) Become a Tribe?"

59 Gregory, *India and East Africa*, 180. Although not explicitly banning Indian ownership of land in the highlands, in practice the ordinance ensured that the highlands would remain in white hands.

60 The ten-mile coastal strip owned by the Sultan of Zanzibar continued as a protectorate.

61 The relevant laws are the Resident Native (Squatters) Ordinance of 1918 and the Resident Native Labourers Ordinance 1937. For a more detailed discussion of this legislation, see Anderson, "Masters and Servants," 465–66; Berman and Lonsdale, *Unhappy Valley*, 104–22.

62 The legislation established that squatters must work for 180 days out of the year for the land owner in exchange for the right to live and farm on his/her property (later raised to up to 270 days). Ghai and McAuslan, *Public Law and Political Change*, 83.

63 Berman and Lonsdale, *Unhappy Valley*, 108–10.

64 Anderson, *Histories of the Hanged*, 24.

65 The hut tax was also imposed on widows. As Fiona Mackenzie notes in her study of African women's collective organizing, this fact caused much consternation in 1937 when widows in the Murang'a District began to refuse to pay it. In just three months, 550 women in the district were prosecuted for nonpayment of taxes. Mackenzie, "Political Economy of the Environment, Gender, and Resistance under Colonialism," 249.

66 In her study of the social meanings of currency in Kenya, Wambui Mwangi argues that the hut tax helped establish the notion of an African individual, as opposed to a member of a (tribal) collective: "The hut, then" she writes "was the space of African individuation—the generative place of the subject." Mwangi, "Of Coins and Conquest," 780.

67 Anderson, "Master and Servant."

68 After 1923, however, a court ruled that resident laborers (squatters) were not servants and could therefore not be penalized for desertion. Anderson, "Master and Servant," 465.

69 Berman and Lonsdale, *Unhappy Valley*, 113.

70 Anderson, "Master and Servant," 464.

71 Anderson, "Master and Servant," 465.

72 The Native Authority Amendment Ordinance of 1920 expanded compulsory labor, making it legal for chiefs/headmen to require another sixty days of labor with minimal compensation. Berman and Lonsdale, *Unhappy Valley*, 110.

73 Quoted in Gregory, *Sidney Webb and East Africa*, 28.

74 Macharia, *Frottage*, 98.

75 Carina Ray has also used this term, although in a slightly different register: she discusses how prominent West African men mobilized the notion that African women were being abused by white men as a way to reject colonialism. Ray, "Decrying White Peril."

One. The Intellectual Roots of Primitive Normativity

1   Torgovnick, *Gone Primitive*, 9.

2   Epprecht, *Heterosexual Africa?*, 40.

3   It was not until 1884 that the first university post in anthropology was created for Sir Edward Tylor at Oxford. Henrika Kuklick notes that the amateur archaeologist General Pitt-Rivers had made his donation of his collection of anthropological objects to Oxford conditional on Tylor's appointment. Kuklick, *Savage Within*, 52.

4   Brickman, *Aboriginal Populations*, 47.

5   Kuklick, *Savage Within*, 75.

6   Lyons and Lyons, *Irregular Connections*, 104.

7   For more on the cultural effects of the Great War, see Fussell, *Great War and Modern Memory*.

8   Kuklick, *Savage Within*, 23.

9   Even during the eighteenth and nineteenth centuries, however, there were some nuances within the discourse of primitive promiscuity. Native Americans were, for instance, sometimes portrayed as sexually excessive, but also sometimes seen as lacking "sexual ardor." Lyons and Lyons, *Irregular Connections*, 20.

10 Lyons and Lyons, *Irregular Connections*, 103.

11 Quoted in Lyons and Lyons, *Irregular Connections*, 111.

12 This is evidenced by the belief, embraced by all three thinkers, in the hypothesis of sexual "periodicity," that is, the idea that "primitive" women experienced a period of "heat" in which they were fertile. Abstention from sex outside of these periods of "heat" indicated sexual restraint, but also the animalistic nature of less "evolved" peoples. Lyons and Lyons, *Irregular Connections*, 114.

13 Lyons and Lyons, *Irregular Connections*, 166.

14 Quoted from Malinowski's notes on Ellis's work. This idea that "civilized" societies needed to learn from the healthier sexual mores of "primitive" peoples was also reflected in the work of the American anthropologist Margaret Mead, who argued that Samoans benefited from the sexual freedom and openness of their society. Lyons and Lyons note that Mead was "only too delighted to draw lessons for her own milieu from the cultures she studied" and that her work was "full of diagnostic and prescriptive asides." Lyons and Lyons, *Irregular Connections*, 166, 190–91.

15 Torgovnick, *Gone Primitive*, 7.

16 Lyons and Lyons, *Irregular Connections*, 175.

17 Lyons and Lyons, *Irregular Connections*, 176.

18 Stocking, *After Tylor*, 266.

19 Kuklick, *Savage Within*, 183.

20 Kuklick, *Savage Within*, 222.

21 Seligman, *Races of Africa*, 64. Seligman believed that this danger was caused by basic differences in the brain structures of "civilized" and "primitive" peoples. To support this point about the racial differences in brain function, he cited works including F. W. Vint's 1934 article "The Brain of the Kenya Native." Vint was a Kenyan doctor and one of the most prominent eugenicists in the colony. Campbell, "Juvenile Delinquency in Colonial Kenya," 129–51. Vint also served as the medical examiner in the Hilda Stumpf case, the infamous rape and/or circumcision of an American at the Kijabe mission in 1930. KNA: AG/52/395.

22 Quoted in Kuklick, *Savage Within*, 265–66.

23 Pick, *Faces of Degeneration*, 3.

24 Pick, *Faces of Degeneration*, 11.

25 Notably Wallace, *Freud and Anthropology*; Brickman, *Aboriginal Populations*.

26 Quoted in Hodgen, "Doctrine of Survivals," 307.

27 Brickman, *Aboriginal Populations*, 45.

28 Brickman, *Aboriginal Populations*, 67.

29 Brickman, *Aboriginal Populations*, 87 (emphasis mine).

30 Freud, "'Civilized' Sexual Morality," 189 (emphasis in original).

31 Freud, "'Civilized' Sexual Morality," 190.

32 Freud, "'Civilized' Sexual Morality," 184.

33 Freud, "'Civilized' Sexual Morality," 197.

34 Freud, "'Civilized' Sexual Morality," 182.

35 Epprecht, *Heterosexual Africa?*.

36 Epprecht, *Heterosexual Africa?*, 74–75.

37 Frederiksen, "Jomo Kenyatta," 23–48.

38 Frederiksen, "Jomo Kenyatta," 28.

39 Kenyatta was born as Kamau s/o Ngengi and later baptized as Johnstone Kamau at the Church of Scotland Mission. He chose to publish *Facing Mount Kenya* under the more Afrocentric name Jomo. He subsequently went by Jomo for the rest of his life—although he was given the affectionate nickname Mzee (old man) as president.

40 Frederiksen, "Jomo Kenyatta," 26.

41 Frederiksen, "Jomo Kenyatta," 39.

42 Torgovnick, *Gone Primitive*.

43 Luongo, *Witchcraft and Colonial Rule*, 11.

44 Huxley, *Red Strangers*; Perham, *Native Administration in Nigeria*; Perham, "A Re-Statement of Indirect Rule"; Perham, "Supplement."

45 Berman, "Ethnography as Politics," 333.

46 Berman and Lonsdale, *Unhappy Valley*, 386.

47 Berman and Lonsdale, *Unhappy Valley*, 387–88.

48 Malinowski had pulled some strings to get Kenyatta, who had no college or secondary school diploma, enrolled as a graduate student. Kenyatta

did, however, have a certificate in English composition from Quaker Woodbrooke College; the prominent liberals Norman Leys, William McGregor Ross, and the MP C. R. Buxton paid for his tuition. Berman, "Ethnography as Politics," 314, 320.

49 Stocking, *After Tylor*, 413.

50 Quoted in Berman, "Ethnography as Politics," 328–29.

51 Berman, "Ethnography as Politics."

52 Gikandi, "Pan-Africanism and Cosmopolitanism," 11.

53 Kenyatta, *Facing Mount Kenya*, 128.

54 Berman, "Ethnography as Politics," 334.

55 Kenyatta, *Facing Mount Kenya*, 149.

56 Kenyatta, *Facing Mount Kenya*, 149.

57 Macharia, "Queer Natives," 243.

58 However, he seems to contradict this belief a few pages later when he asserts that, while some may experience "sexual relief" through ngweko, the primary purpose is "the enjoyment of the warmth of the breast." Kenyatta, *Facing Mount Kenya*, 152.

59 Macharia, *Frottage*, 125.

60 Kenyatta, *Facing Mount Kenya*, 152–53.

61 Kenyatta, *Facing Mount Kenya*, 153.

62 Kenyatta, *Facing Mount Kenya*, 155–56.

63 Kenyatta, *Facing Mount Kenya*, 155–56.

64 Macharia also points out that Kenyatta's gendered and aged description of masturbation neutralizes any potentially homosexual taint, focusing "on the ritually imposed distinction between boyhood and manhood to remove group masturbation from a homosexual economy." Similarly (unlike his rival Leakey), he avoids mention of the practice of ngweko between girls. Macharia, "Queer Natives," 249, 238–39.

65 Kenyatta, *Facing Mount Kenya*, 156.

66 Jesse Kariuki, the vice chairman of the KCA, claimed that uncircumcised girls were more likely to become prostitutes, echoing the negative moral and sexual consequences of both "detribalization" and, possibly, female sexual desire. Peterson, *Creative Writing*, 109. However, in his earlier discussion of irua, Kenyatta noted that before the clitoridectomy, a girl was "closely questioned to verify that she never had sexual intercourse or indulged in masturbation"—if she admitted to such practices, she had to be purified. Read against the grain, this is an admission that Gikuyu women did sometimes engage in masturbation despite the cultural disapprobation. Kenyatta, *Facing Mount Kenya*, 131.

67 Epprecht, *Heterosexual Africa?*, 102.

68 Kenyatta, *Facing Mount Kenya*, 155 (emphasis mine).

69 Kenyatta, *Facing Mount Kenya*, 156. Macharia has pointed out that this explanation of homosexuality as a product of isolation from female sexual

partners was borrowed from the work of Ellis and Malinowksi. Macharia, "Queer Natives," 251.

70 Kenyatta, *Facing Mount Kenya*, 157.

71 Kenyatta, *Facing Mount Kenya*, 158.

72 Kenyatta, *Facing Mount Kenya*, 168.

73 Kenyatta, *Facing Mount Kenya*, 167–68.

74 He noted, for instance, that the "system of mutual help and tribal solidarity" had declined "among those Gikuyu who have been Europeanised or detribalised. The rest of the community look upon these people as mischief-makers and breakers of tribal traditions, and the general disgusted cry is heard: '*Mothongo ne athogonjire borori*,' i.e. the white man had spoiled and disgraced our country." Kenyatta, *Facing Mount Kenya*, 116.

75 Sylvia Tamale, "OPINION: Homosexuality Is Not Un-African." *Al Jazeera*, April 26, 2014, http://america.aljazeera.com/opinions/2014/4/homosexuality-africamuseveniugandanigeriaethiopia.html.

Two. Sleeping Dictionaries and Mobile Metropoles

1 The East African Protectorate became the colony of Kenya in 1920.

2 W. Scoresby Routledge, "An East African Official and Native Women," *The Times* (London), December 3, 1908, 10.

3 The names of the Africans involved in this scandal were transcribed by colonial officials and may be inaccurate.

4 Routledge, "East African Official," 10.

5 Parliamentary Papers [PP]: July 27, 1909, p. 1054.

6 Shadle, *The Souls of White Folk*, 101.

7 Spillers, "Mama's Baby, Papa's Maybe."

8 Spillers, "Mama's Baby, Papa's Maybe," 76.

9 Allen, *Tales from the Dark Continent*, 14.

10 The 1911 census gives the figure of 3,175 for the total white population. Ghai and McAuslan, *Public Law and Political Change*, 36.

11 Henrika Kuklick cites the Crewe Circular as prompting a major shift in colonial cultures, stating that "it is possible to mark the emergence of self-contained colonial societies by an official act: on January 11, 1909, the colonial secretary, Lord Crewe, warned all of the colonial employees within his jurisdiction that any of them who had sexual relationships with local women would suffer 'disgrace and official ruin.'" Kuklick, *Savage Within*, 285. This is, however, something of an overstatement; the Crewe Circular certainly did not end all relationships between officers and colonized women, nor did it prevent settler men from engaging in such relationships.

12 Thomas, *Politics of the Womb*, 13.

13 The distinction was based on the notion that existing officers would likely have already established sexual relationships with colonized women, and thus could probably not be convinced to abandon the practice entirely. In fact, the circular was not sent to some colonies where interracial sex was deemed to be too common a practice; these included the West Indies, Mauritius, and the Seychelles. A note in the Colonial Office papers stated that "There is a very strong feeling in the West Indian Department that to send it to those Colonies where black and white live together and often intermarry, and where you have every shade of colour living side by side in social union, would be a great blunder." British National Archives [BNA]: CO 533/52/44293, Colonial Office: Kenya Original Correspondence: Note to Antrobus from Macnaughton, January 6, 1908.

14 The case is also very briefly discussed in Jeremy Paxman's popular history. Paxman, *Empire*, 144.

15 Hyam, "Empire and Sexual Opportunity."

16 Hyam, *Empire and Sexuality*.

17 Hyam, *Empire and Sexuality*, 51.

18 Hyam, *Empire and Sexuality*, 53.

19 Hyam, *Empire and Sexuality*, 75.

20 Hyam, "Concubinage and the Colonial Service."

21 Berger, "Imperialism and Sexual Exploitation"; Strobel, *European Women*. More recently, Carina Ray has critiqued Hyam in her comparative study of interracial sex across multiple empires: see her chapter "Interracial Sex and the Making of Empire," 190–91.

22 Voeltz, "The British Empire."

23 Hyam's response to these criticisms is also telling. In a response to Mark Berger, he asked, with apparent sincerity, "Is it 'exploitation' if the white man is offered 'sexual hospitality' in accordance with traditional custom? Is it exploitation if he negotiates with the father or headman, presents the expected gift, and pays the requisite bridewealth for a temporary wife? Is it exploitation if Afghan or Maori women throw themselves at British soldiers or sailors and demand sex?" Hyam, "'Imperialism and Sexual Exploitation,'" 94.

24 Gartrell, "Colonial Wives," 165.

25 Stoler, "Making Empire Respectable," 638.

26 Brownfoot, "Memsahibs in Colonial Malaya," 190.

27 For more on this, see chapter 4.

28 Stoler, "Sexual Affronts and Racial Frontiers," 514. Of course, interracial sex did not cease with the development of a segregated settler culture.

29 Ghose, "Memsahib Myth," 122.

30 The phrase is borrowed from Stoler, "Making Empire Respectable," 645.

31 Routledge had trained as a medical doctor but never received a degree: he had already visited Kenya in 1902 and conducted preliminary ethnographic research on the Gikuyu. His wife, Katherine, was herself an

amateur ethnographer and a graduate of Somerville Hall (later a College of Oxford). Her cousin, Sir Alfred Edward Pease, was a world-renowned big-game hunter who owned land in the East African Protectorate. Van Tilburg, *Among Stone Giants*, 54–65.

32   Routledge and Routledge, *Prehistoric People*.

33   BNA: CO/533/43/21793, Kenya Original Correspondence, Despatches, May 14–June 19, 1908: Letter from W. Scoresby Routledge to Sir James Hayes-Sadler, February 29, 1908.

34   I have given much consideration to whether to use pseudonyms for these three girls, particularly since (as I show later in this chapter) the archival record seems to make it clear that they were victims of sexual abuse. I have ultimately decided to include their names for three reasons. First, their names appear in Hyam's piece and hence have already been entered into the historical record. Second, first names in Kenya often convey important information about the ethnic/linguistic background of the person in question. But most importantly, naming these girls seems important given the ways that their experiences and perspectives have been erased from the historical record. By not only naming them but also reinserting their own testimony into this analysis, I mean to pay respect to their personhood and to honor the strength and solidarity they displayed throughout this crisis.

35   BNA: CO/533/43/21793, Kenya Original Correspondence, Despatches, May 14–June 19, 1908: Report on evidence from enquiry by Judge J. W. Barth, April 13, 1908.

36   BNA: CO/533/43/21793, Kenya Original Correspondence, Despatches, May 14–June 19, 1908: Report on evidence from enquiry by Judge J. W. Barth, April 13, 1908. The evaluations of the girls' ages, which come from a report written by Judge Barth, were most likely based on his own visual assessment as his consistent use of the phrase "she appears to be ___ years old" would indicate. Judge Barth's inability to accurately state the girls' ages is probably not reflective of a lack of oversight or interest; rather, it is unlikely that the girls themselves or their families would have an accurate idea of their age in years, as East Africans more generally understood age in terms of age grades, groups of peers who underwent certain developmental rites (particularly circumcision) at the same time. Individuals were understood to be members of a certain age cohort, but were not generally described in terms of years of age.

37   The third girl had already returned home.

38   BNA: CO/533/43/21793, Kenya Original Correspondence, Despatches, May 14–June 19, 1908: Intra-office memo, June 26, 1908.

39   This privileging of supposed "tribal traditions" over individual experiences is in keeping with the philosophy of British rule in colonial Africa, which colonized Africans "in their capacity as collections of people and not as individuals." Mwangi, "Order of Money," 85. For other descriptions

of this phenomenon, see Mamdani, *Citizen and Subject*; Vaughan, *Curing Their Ills*, 11.

40 Shadle, "Debating 'Early Marriage,'" 92.

41 Ocobock, *An Uncertain Age*, 32.

42 See for instance Wipper, "Kikuyu Women," 300; Kanogo, *African Womanhood in Colonial Kenya*, 43.

43 White, *Comforts of Home*, 29.

44 As White notes, "mortality estimates for central Kenya ranged from 10 to 70 percent of the population." White, *Comforts of Home*, 32.

45 Ambler, *Kenyan Communities*, 1–2.

46 Kanogo, *African Womanhood in Colonial Kenya*, 45.

47 Kanogo, *African Womanhood in Colonial Kenya*, 47.

48 White, *Comforts of Home*, 32–37.

49 White, *Comforts of Home*, 35.

50 Kanogo, *African Womanhood in Colonial Kenya*, 9.

51 KNA: PC/Coast/1/3/130: "Native Women Leaving this Reserve: Desertion of Women from Nyika Reserve," 1920–1927.

52 RH: MSS Afr. s. 382: "General Political and Domestic Conditions NATIVES," by Ainsworth, February 6, 1917.

53 Strange, *Kenya Today*, 77, 102.

54 Kanogo, *African Womanhood in Colonial Kenya*, 63.

55 Kenyatta, *Facing Mount Kenya*, 167–68.

56 This is borne out by the fact that urban African women were consistently "repatriated" back to rural homesteads. Carotenuto, "Repatriation in Colonial Kenya"; Peterson, *Ethnic Patriotism*, 127–51; Shadle, *Girl Cases*.

57 The hut tax was also imposed on widows. As Fiona Mackenzie notes in her study of African women's collective organizing, this fact caused much consternation in 1937 when widows in the Murang'a District began to refuse to pay it. In just three months, 550 women in the district were prosecuted for nonpayment of taxes. Mackenzie, "Political Economy of the Environment," 249.

58 BNA: CO 533/396/5.

59 BNA: CO 533/396/5.

60 RH: MSS Brit. Emp. s. 22/G132: Anti-Slavery Society, no date but likely in the teens.

61 Thomas, *Politics of the Womb*, 30.

62 BNA: CO/533/43/21793, Kenya Original Correspondence, Despatches, May 14–June 19, 1908: Note from Mr. Harris to Mr. Cox, June 26, 1908.

63 BNA: CO/533/43/21793, Kenya Original Correspondence, Despatches, May 14–June 19, 1908: Report by the Committee of the Executive Council appointed to enquire into charges against Mr. Haywood.

64 BNA: CO/533/43/21793, Kenya Original Correspondence, Despatches, May 14–June 19, 1908: Report by the Committee of the Executive Council appointed to enquire into charges against Mr. Haywood.

65 Interestingly, in their ethnography the Routledges acknowledge this fact, stating "though only six years have elapsed since the English conquest, the new order has already laid its hand on the old . . . The student looks sadly at the pages of his notebook, filled with information seriously given, about the power and position of the chief, when he realises that the chieftainship itself in its present form is an English creation." Routledge and Routledge, *Prehistoric People*, 195.

66 Lonsdale and Berman, "Coping with the Contradictions," 497.

67 BNA: CO/533/43/21793, Kenya Original Correspondence, Despatches, May 14–June 19, 1908: Testimony from enquiry.

68 In her testimony, it is sometimes unclear whether Wameisa is referring to Silberrad or his predecessor Haywood; it appears that she was taken by local headmen to live with both officials on separate occasions.

69 BNA: CO/533/43/21793, Kenya Original Correspondence, Despatches, May 14–June 19, 1908: Testimony from enquiry.

70 BNA: CO/533/43/21793, Kenya Original Correspondence, Despatches, May 14–June 19, 1908: Testimony from enquiry. The language in which Wameisa's testimony is recorded is significant. The document is written in English, except for certain Kiswahili words, for example, boma, shauri, and mzungu. What may not be apparent to a reader unfamiliar with materials from colonial Kenya is that these words are part of the lexicon of "Ki-Setla" used by officials and settlers to communicate with Africans, especially employees. It is not likely that Wameisa would have been a native speaker of Kiswahili; she probably spoke the Gikuyu language. Wameisa's testimony was likely filtered through a translator; the use of these Swahili terms may have been introduced by her, or by her interlocutor. What is significant about their use is that Ki-Setla was a Creolized language native to neither whites nor Africans; even native Swahili speakers would have had to adapt to the peculiar grammar of Ki-Setla, which applied English-language plurals and often dropped letters that proved troublesome to pronounce. (For example, settlers almost universally refer to African children as "totos," an Anglicization of the Swahili mtoto/watoto, meaning child/children.) The use of Ki-Setla in this testimony may indicate that either the translator or Wameisa was attempting to describe her experiences in words that white observers would understand. The retention of these words in the translation indicates that local whites like Judge Barth and Governor Sadler took a certain pride in their comprehension of the colonial lingo. Their status as insiders with special knowledge of the conditions on the ground is indicated by these unglossed words. For more on Ki-Setla, see Williams, "Recipes for Disaster."

71 Gikuyu women seem to have been aware of this discourse presenting them as abused chattel, and were critical of it: when Katherine Routledge

asked her female informants what she should tell white folks about, they made two points: "One is, that we never marry any one we do not want to; and the other is, that we like our husbands to have as many wives as possible." Routledge and Routledge, *Prehistoric People*, 124.

72   BNA: CO/533/43/21793: Letter from Silberrad to governor, May 14, 1908.

73   BNA: CO/533/43/21793, Kenya Original Correspondence, Despatches, May 14–June 19, 1908: Testimony from enquiry.

74   BNA: CO/533/43/21793, Kenya Original Correspondence, Despatches, May 14–June 19, 1908: Testimony from enquiry. Again, the characteristically British phrasing used here ("had connection") seems to indicate the heavy hand of a translator or interlocutor.

75   BNA: CO/533/43/21793, Kenya Original Correspondence, Despatches, May 14–June 19, 1908: Testimony from enquiry.

76   It is not clear whether these are biological or adopted brothers.

77   Hyam, *Empire and Sexuality*, 161. This discourse also closely resembles the discussions of the psychosexual motivations of Shaka Zulu in the 1920s that Marc Epprecht has analyzed. These discourses proposed that the Zulu rebellion was prompted by Shaka Zulu's anxiety over a too-small penis, and his repression of homosexual tendencies. See Epprecht, *Heterosexual Africa?*, 65–99.

78   BNA: CO/533/43/21793, Kenya Original Correspondence, Despatches, May 14–June 19, 1908: Silberrad's statement to inquiry.

79   BNA: CO/533/43/21793, Kenya Original Correspondence, Despatches, May 14–June 19, 1908: Silberrad's statement to inquiry.

80   BNA: CO/533/43/21793, Kenya Original Correspondence, Despatches, May 14–June 19, 1908: Silberrad's statement to inquiry.

81   The Executive Council consisted of members nominated by the local government to advise the governor. They were separate from the Legislative Council, which included both appointed and elected members.

82   BNA: CO/533/43/21793, Kenya Original Correspondence, Despatches, May 14–June 19, 1908: Report on evidence from enquiry by Judge J. W. Barth, April 13, 1908.

83   BNA: CO/533/43/21793, Kenya Original Correspondence, Despatches, May 14–June 19, 1908: Minutes of the proceedings of a meeting of the Executive Council, held on May 18, 1908 at Nairobi.

84   BNA: CO/533/43/21793, Kenya Original Correspondence, Despatches, May 14–June 19, 1908: Minutes of the proceedings of a meeting of the Executive Council, held on May 18, 1908 at Nairobi.

85   BNA: CO/533/43/21793, Kenya Original Correspondence, Despatches, May 14–June 19, 1908: Letter from Hayes-Sadler to Lord Crewe, May 21, 1908. This reading is, of course, directly contradicted by the girls' testimony.

86   Even Routledge agreed to some extent with this point of view, writing to the governor that "you should not deal further with the case of Mr. Silberrad until I have had the opportunity of showing you how much he

has been led into doing what he has done by common official thought and custom." BNA: CO/533/43/21793, Kenya Original Correspondence, Despatches, May 14–June 19, 1908: Letter from W. Scoresby Routledge to Sir James Sadler, February 29, 1908.

87 BNA: CO/533/43/21793, Kenya Original Correspondence, Despatches, May 14–June 19, 1908: Intra-office memo, June 26, 1908.

88 We know that K. Routledge wrote to at least one of these cousins, as a letter from MP Joseph Alfred "Jack" Pease to Colonel Seely (an under-secretary in the Colonial Office) appears in the Colonial Office papers. Jack Pease referred to a letter he had received from his cousin Katherine, "alleging indecent behaviour by officials in East Africa to native women." BNA: CO/533/56/25633, Colonial Office: Kenya Original Correspon-dence, Individuals, R–Z, Letter from Joseph Pease to Colonel Seely, July 16, 1908; PP: 1127.

89 The eight MPs in question were Sir C. Hill, Sir G. S. Robertson, Mr. Cath-cart Wason, Mr. Pike Pease (another of Mrs. Routledge's cousins), Mr. Wedgwood, Mr. Fell, Mr. Bennett, and Sir H. Cotton. Mr. Cathcart Wason's question was notable in being explicitly sympathetic to Silberrad and the colonial government.

90 PP: July 27, 1909, p. 1079.

91 PP: July 27, 1909, p. 1119. Mr. Pike Pease disputed Colonel Seely's claim that the girls ages could not be determined, stating that, from reading Judge Barth's report, "it is perfectly plain that one of the girls was 13 and the other 12." The girls' ages, however, were not particularly relevant since "age in that part of the world is different to similar age in this"; the real offense was that Silberrad "took advantage of his official position to procure these women." PP: July 27, 1909, p. 1036.

92 PP: July 27, 1909, p. 1036.

93 Katherine Routledge, "Letter to the Editor of *The Spectator*," *The Spectator* (London), December 26, 1908.

94 "A Canker in Imperial Administration," *The Spectator* (London), Decem-ber 12, 1908, 980.

95 "A Canker in Imperial Administration," *The Spectator* (London), Decem-ber 12, 1908, 980.

96 "A Canker in Imperial Administration," *The Spectator* (London), Decem-ber 12, 1908, 980.

97 Letter to the Editor from "One Who Knows," *The Spectator* (London), December 19, 1908, 1053.

98 Letter to the Editor from "One Who Knows," *The Spectator* (London), December 19, 1908, 1052.

99 Letter to the Editor from "One Who Knows," *The Spectator* (London), December 19, 1908, 1052.

100 Letter to the Editor from "One Who Knows," *The Spectator* (London), December 19, 1908, 980.

101 By 1926, every cadet in the Colonial Service was required to undergo a year of training at Oxford or Cambridge. Allen, *Tales from the Dark Continent*, 41.

102 "Letter to the Editor signed 'Nyasaland,'" *The Spectator* (London), December 26, 1908, 1094.

103 "Letter to the Editor signed 'Nyasaland,'" *The Spectator* (London), December 26, 1908, 1094.

104 "Letter to the Editor signed 'Nyasaland,'" *The Spectator* (London), December 26, 1908, 1094.

105 BNA: CO 533/52/45005, Colonial Office: Kenya Original Correspondence, 1908: Letter from T. F. Victor Buxton to the editor of *The Times* (London), January 9, 1909.

106 BNA: CO 533/52/45005, Colonial Office: Kenya Original Correspondence, 1908: Letter from T. F. Victor Buxton to the editor of *The Times* (London), January 9, 1909.

107 "Letter to the Editor from D.S.S.," *The Spectator* (London), December 19, 1908, 1053. The paper's editor appended a note to this letter, asserting "We do not think that there are any signs of unwillingness on the part of Englishwomen to do their share of Imperial work by going out to distant parts of the Empire as the wives of officials. The pluck with which delicately nurtured girls face hardships, solitude, and the risk of life in dangerous climates is beyond all praise" but salaries needed to be raised so that officers could afford them.

108 PP: July 27, 1909, p. 1038.

109 PP: December 7, 1908, p. 71.

110 PP: July 27, 1909, p. 1055.

111 PP: July 27, 1909, p. 1122.

112 Mr. Morrow and Mr. Harris of the Colonial Office both argued in favor of reducing Silberrad's punishment, stating that "It must be borne in mind that the practice of cohabitation with native women has been and is extremely common throughout the Colonies and Protectorates of West and East Africa; indeed I am informed that of the unmarried white officials there is only a small percentage who have abstained entirely from the practice. Mr. Monson tells me that he is satisfied that there are many officers in the E.A.P., who have lived more loosely than Messrs Silberrad and Haywood, and he urges that it is hard that they should be made scapegoats." Although Silberrad's decision to lock up Mgulla had "brought about a most awkward situation, and one pre-eminently calculated to bring the Gov't into discredit," Harris nevertheless believed that his actions were not motivated by malice, and that Silberrad should merely be censured and passed over twice for promotion. Now that a "better class of white official is being introduced" to the colonies, Harris expected that morals would tighten and the practice of concubinage would decline. BNA: CO/533/43/21793, Kenya Original Correspondence, Despatches, May 14–June 19, 1908: Colonial Office intra-office memo.

113 Sir Clement Hill, "Letter to Editor of the Spectator," *The Spectator* (London), January 2, 1909, 13.

114 W. Scoresby Routledge, "Letter to the Editor of The Spectator," *The Spectator* (London), February 6, 1909, 218.

115 "Town and Personal," *The Advertiser of East Africa* (Nairobi), July 16, 1909.

116 *Nyasaland Times* (Blantyre, Nyasaland), February 22, 1912.

117 Leys, *Kenya*, 207.

Three. "Stoop Low to Conquer"

An earlier version of this chapter appeared as Williams, Elizabeth. "'Stoop Low to Conquer': Race and Sexual Trusteeship in the Kenyan 'Indian Crisis' of 1923." *Journal of Colonialism and Colonial History* 19, no. 3 (2018).

1 For an excellent study of the racial politics of Kenyan newspapers, see Frederiksen, "Print, Newspapers and Audiences in Colonial Kenya," 155–72.

2 RH: MSS Afr. s. 633 [Sir Robert Coryndon], Box 3, File 4, Indian Questions: *The Democrat*, edited by Sitaram Achariar, Mombasa, Friday, February 16, 1923, no. 14: "Stoop Low to Conquer!"

3 Shadle, *Souls of White Folk*, 30–31.

4 Youé, "Threat of Settler Rebellion"; Gregory, *Sidney Webb and East Africa*; Kennedy, *Islands of White*; Berman and Lonsdale, *Unhappy Valley*; Aiyar, *Indians in Kenya*; Aiyar, "Empire, Race and the Indians."

5 Aiyar, *Indians in Kenya*, 16. One exception to this rule is Brett Shadle, whose recent book contains a brief discussion of the Achariar article. He characterizes the white reaction to Achariar's article as an extension of white "chivalry," the protection of white women from assaults, real or imagined, by nonwhite men. Shadle, *Souls of White Folk*, 89–90.

6 Sinha, *Colonial Masculinity*.

7 The local African populations, who existed largely outside of a waged economy and showed little desire for Western trade goods, could not be induced to join up. Even those few Africans who did agree to work on the railroad insisted on leaving periodically to cultivate their fields. Gregory, *India and East Africa*, 51.

8 Sorrenson, *Origins of European Settlement*, 24.

9 Aiyar, "Anticolonial Homelands."

10 In 1919, there were about fifteen thousand Indians living in Kenya. Sana Aiyar provides a breakdown of their occupations "3,942 were large-scale merchants and petty shopkeepers, while 3,024 were skilled workers, particularly artisans, carpenters, masons, drivers, and mechanics, and 2,500 were government employees in low-level jobs, serving predominately as clerks and policemen." Indian clerks were paid less than Europeans. However, once Africans were allowed to join the civil service (beginning in

the early 1920s), *they* were paid less than the Indians. Aiyar, "Anticolonial Homelands," 58, 222, 231.

11   The figures for Europeans and Asians (the latter included both Indians and Goans) are taken from Ghai and McAuslan, *Public Law and Political Change*, 36. The estimates of Arab and African populations are from Kuczynski, *Demographic Survey*, 156.

12   For the most part, Arabs were not actively involved in the agitation surrounding the Indian Crisis. Robert Gregory has noted that the two Arab representatives who testified in front of the Joint Committee on Closer Union in 1930 opposed the establishment of a common electoral roll "because of fear of being swamped by other communities." Presumably, they had also opposed the common roll in 1923. Gregory, *India and East Africa*, 365.

13   Ghai and McAuslan, *Public Law and Political Change*, 27.

14   The Resident Native (Squatters) Ordinance of 1918 required squatters to perform 180 days of labor per annum, and the Resident Native Labourers Ordinance of 1937 expanded the requirement to up to 270 days in 1937. For a more detailed discussion of this legislation, see Anderson, "Master and Servant," 465–66; Berman and Lonsdale, *Unhappy Valley*, 104–22.

15   Gregory, *India and East Africa*, 180. Although not explicitly banning Indian ownership of land in the highlands, in practice, the ordinance ensured that the highlands would remain in white hands.

16   Aiyar, *Indians in Kenya*, 54.

17   Aiyar, *Indians in Kenya*, 59.

18   This phrase is attributed to Cecil Rhodes and was repeated by Winston Churchill in his speech at London's East African Dinner in January 1922. In his speech, he also urged East African governments not to adopt policies that would cause them "needlessly to inflict an invidious distinction upon those who may be held in some way to represent the enormous mass of subjects of the British Crown in the land of Hindustan." RH: MSS Afr. s. 594 [Convention of Associations], Box 1, File 14. Churchill's words would often be repeated by Kenyan Indians as they sought to legitimize their struggle for civic inclusion.

19   RH: MSS Afr. s. 633 [Sir Robert Coryndon], Box 3, File 1: Memo from meeting between governor and Indian representatives, January 10, 1923.

20   In fact, Kenyan Indians advocated a very limited enfranchisement—the correspondent of the London *Daily News* H. Wilson Harris estimated that the Churchill Memorandum (which had proposed the vote for all "civilized" peoples) would have enfranchised only 3,500 Indians. They would therefore be easily outnumbered by white voters. Furthermore, as Harris noted, "since the vote itself is merely for an unofficial minority which could be beaten on any division by the nominated official majority; and since the whole Council is merely advisory, the charge that the Indians are scheming to control the Government through an inflated electorate collapses at

sight." RH: MSS Brit. Emp. s. 22/G135 [Indians in East Africa, Antislavery and Aboriginal Protection Society]: *Daily News* (London), May 7, 1923.

21 Sinha, *Specters of Mother India*, 29.

22 Sinha, *Specters of Mother India*, 32.

23 For an excellent summary of the international context of the Indian Crisis, see Aiyar, *Indians in Kenya*, 76–87.

24 Gandhi's anticolonial activism was famously sparked by his distaste for being treated like African "natives" during his time in South Africa. For more on how Gandhi's time in South Africa shaped his anticolonial politics, see Bhana, *The Making*; Guha, *Gandhi before India*.

25 The phrase is from Edwin Samuel Montagu, the secretary of state for India, in a speech given to the House of Commons in 1919. This philosophy was subsequently adopted as part of the Government of India Act of 1919. Danzig, "Announcement."

26 KNA: MAC/EAI/29/7 [Murumbi Papers]: Indian Delegations from Kenya to London, document published by Kenya Indian Delegates, London, July 18, 1923.

27 The settlers crafted this plan with considerable attention to detail. In a letter to the governor of Kenya summarizing the colonists' position from a military perspective, the author notes that white women would be recruited to look after "purdah women" and serve as nurses. RH: MSS Afr. s. 633 [Sir Robert Coryndon], Box 3, File 2. For a detailed analysis of the plan, and some of its leaders, see Duder, "Settler Response."

28 Youé, "Threat of Settler Rebellion," 347. Interestingly, in a letter to the undersecretary of state of the India Office in February of 1924, the Colonial Office declined a request for the release of materials related to the Indian Crisis in East Africa, on the basis that "Their publication would tend to confirm the impression already existing in some quarters that the settlement was a surrender to the threats of violence on the part of Europeans in Kenya, and that the standpoint of native interests was adopted as an expedient to justify that surrender." Colonial Office [CO]: CO 533/322 [Records of the Colonial Office, Commonwealth and Foreign and Commonwealth Offices, Empire Marketing Board, and related bodies]: Letter from the CO to the undersecretary of state, India Office, February 8, 1924.

29 *The Kenya Gazette*, August 17, 1923.

30 Gregory, *Sidney Webb and East Africa*, 44.

31 Gregory, *Sidney Webb and East Africa*, 37.

32 Mwangi, "Of Coins and Conquest," 763–87.

33 Mwangi, "Of Coins and Conquest," 774.

34 Mwangi, "Of Coins and Conquest," 774.

35 See Anagol-McGinn, *Age of Consent Act*; Sinha, *Specters of Mother India*; Burton, "From Child Bride"; Sarkar, "A Prehistory of Rights"; Sarkar, "Rhetoric against Age of Consent."

36 Sinha, *Specters of Mother India*, 5.

37 Leopold, "British Applications," 578–603.

38 Sinha, *Colonial Masculinity*, 20.

39 This remained the case until Partition, when a separate Muslim Indian organization was founded in Kenya. For more on Kenyan Indian politics during the post-partition period, see Aiyar, "Anticolonial Homelands."

40 RH: MSS Afr. s. 382 [John Ainsworth], File 2: *Report of the Economic Commission*, 1918, Ch. 7, General Native Policy.

41 *Mombasa Times*, February 24, 1923, 2.

42 *East African Standard* [EAS] (Nairobi), April 26, 1923.

43 Elizabeth Coxoni, "Indian Women. Three Questions on the Franchise. Knotty Points to Consider." Letter to the editor, EAS, February 26, 1923, 1.

44 For more on the role of the EAWL in Kenyan politics, see van Tol, "Women of Kenya Speak."

45 RH: MSS Brit. Emp. s. 22/G135 [Anti-Slavery and Aborigines Protection Society: Indians in East Africa]: East Africa Women's League, "The Indian Question in Kenya: The Kenya Women's Point of View" (Nairobi: Swift Press, 1923).

46 The remainder of the quote, however, brought the focus back to the threat posed to white womanhood: "How could white women continue to reside here under such conditions? How could they attempt to rear and educate their children in a British Colony where the British were no longer the ruling race? It is unthinkable. The attitude of the average Indian towards women is too well known to require comment here." RH: MSS Brit. Emp. s. 22/G135 [Anti-Slavery and Aborigines Protection Society: Indians in East Africa]: East Africa Women's League, "The Indian Question in Kenya: The Kenya Women's Point of View" (Nairobi: Swift Press, 1923).

47 RH: MSS Brit. Emp. s. 22/G135 [Anti-Slavery and Aborigines Protection Society: Indians in East Africa]: East Africa Women's League, "The Indian Question in Kenya: The Kenya Women's Point of View" (Nairobi: Swift Press, 1923).

48 Similar sentiments were expressed by a meeting of white women in the town of Ruiru: a cable sent to the governor's office opposed the inclusion of Indians in the government on the basis that they were unfit to treat sick Africans, both because of a lack of skill and a surfeit of "humanity." RH: MSS Brit. Emp. s. 22/G135 [Anti-Slavery and Aborigines Protection Society: Indians in East Africa]: Cable to governor from meeting at Ruiru, August 25, 1921.

49 Steinem, "If Men Could Menstruate," 367.

50 RH: MSS Afr. s. 594 [Convention of Associations], Box 1, File 18: *Memorandum on the Case Against the Claims of Indians in Kenya* (Nairobi: Swift Press, September 1921), 8 (emphasis mine).

51 RH: MSS Afr. s. 594 [Convention of Associations], Box 1, File 18: *Memorandum on the Case Against the Claims of Indians in Kenya* (Nairobi: Swift Press, September 1921), 8.

52 Letter to the editor, "The White Man's Burden," from Lionel Lawford, commander, R.N., EAS, February 21, 1923, 7.

53 Letter to the editor, "The White Man's Burden," from Lionel Lawford, commander, R.N., EAS, February 21, 1923, 7.

54 Letter to the editor, "The White Man's Burden," from Lionel Lawford, commander, R.N., EAS, February 21, 1923, 7.

55 The copy in the archives of the Colonists' Association has no author, but a review of "Thermopylae of Africa" in the *Mombasa Times*, July 17, 1923, lists the author as E. Powys Cobb. RH: MSS Afr. s. 594 [Convention of Associations], Box 1, File 18: "The Thermopolyae of Africa: Kenya's Responsibility in the Conflict of the Primary Races," 31.

56 RH: MSS Afr. s. 594 [Convention of Associations], Box 1, File 18: "The Thermopolyae of Africa: Kenya's Responsibility in the Conflict of the Primary Races," 31 (emphasis in original).

57 RH: MSS Afr. s. 594 [Convention of Associations], Box 1, File 18: "The Thermopolyae of Africa: Kenya's Responsibility in the Conflict of the Primary Races," 31.

58 Aiyar, *Indians in Kenya*, 4.

59 Banerjee, *Politics of Time*, 54.

60 Quoted in RH: MSS Afr. s. 633 [Sir Robert Coryndon], Box 3, File 4, Indian Questions: *The Democrat*, edited by Sitaram Achariar, Mombasa, Friday, February 16, 1923, no. 14: "Stoop Low to Conquer!" Shaw also created great controversy in the colony in February of 1923 when he wrote a letter to the EAS comparing the prophet Muhammad to the devil. The letter prompted outcry from the Indian, Arab, and Swahili communities. Indians were blamed for exploiting this situation for their own interests: a note in the files of then governor Robert Coryndon laments that "One meeting of 10,000 Swahilis was held at which Indians took pains to inflame their already angry feelings." RH: MSS Afr. s. 633 [Sir Robert Coryndon], Box 3, File 5.

61 RH: MSS Afr. s. 633 [Sir Robert Coryndon], Box 3, File 4, Indian Questions: *The Democrat*, edited by Sitaram Achariar, Mombasa, Friday, February 16, 1923, no. 14: "Stoop Low to Conquer!"

62 RH: MSS Afr. s. 633 [Sir Robert Coryndon], Box 3, File 4, Indian Questions: *The Democrat*, edited by Sitaram Achariar, Mombasa, Friday, February 16, 1923, no. 14: "Stoop Low to Conquer!"

63 RH: MSS Afr. s. 633 [Sir Robert Coryndon], Box 3, File 4, Indian Questions: *The Democrat*, edited by Sitaram Achariar, Mombasa, Friday, February 16, 1923, no. 14: "Stoop Low to Conquer!"

64 RH: MSS Afr. s. 633 [Sir Robert Coryndon], Box 3, File 4, Indian Questions: *The Democrat*, edited by Sitaram Achariar, Mombasa, Friday, February 16, 1923, no. 14: "Stoop Low to Conquer!"

65 RH: MSS Afr. s. 633 [Sir Robert Coryndon], Box 3, File 4, Indian Questions: *The Democrat*, edited by Sitaram Achariar, Mombasa, Friday, February 16, 1923, no. 14: "Stoop Low to Conquer!"

66 Shadle, *The Souls of White Folk*, 89–90.

67 "Poisonous Literature," EAS, February 23, 1923.

68 Letter to editor from Barrister K. S. Chowdhury in Nairobi, EAS, February 23, 1923.

69 Letter to editor from Barrister K. S. Chowdhury in Nairobi, EAS, February 23, 1923.

70 "Poisonous Literature," EAS, February 23, 1923.

71 RH: MSS Afr. s. 633 [Sir Robert Coryndon], Box 3, File 1, Letters 1923, Jan.–Nov.: Letter E. A. T. Dutton to Mr. Leftwich, March 8, 1923.

72 *Mombasa Times*, March 15, 1923, 2.

73 "Indian Lies," EAS, February 21, 1923, 6.

74 Achariar later served as editor of a Bombay-based paper called the *Sun*. Gregory, *Quest for Equality*, 170.

75 I offer a more extended discussion of African-authored sources elsewhere. Williams, "'Stoop Low to Conquer.'"

76 Twaddle, "Z. K. Sentongo and the Indian Question in East Africa," 313.

77 RH: MSS Afr. s. 633 [Sir Robert Coryndon], Box 3, File 1: Supplement to *Sekanyolya*, July 1, 1921. Twaddle suggests that this was in response to a call from the Convention of Associations asking Africans to help defeat the Indian platform. Twaddle, "Z. K. Sentongo," 321.

78 RH: MSS Afr. s. 633 [Sir Robert Coryndon], Box 3, File 1: Supplement to *Sekanyolya*, July 1, 1921.

79 RH: MSS Afr. s. 633 [Sir Robert Coryndon], Box 3, File 1: Supplement to *Sekanyolya*, July 1, 1921.

80 Baganda expatriates were in direct economic competition with Indian merchants and artisans both at home and in Nairobi. Additionally, Twaddle notes that Sentongo was educated at King's College, Budo, by the Church Missionary Society, where he would have imbibed negative opinions about Indians in Africa. "Indian traders," he notes, "were frequently considered by Christian missionaries, as well as by other Europeans, also to have been responsible for introducing a wide range of illnesses, including syphilis" and for "moral ruin to the unsophisticated Baganda women and girls." Twaddle, "Z. K. Sentongo," 323–24.

81 Letter from Jalou Obner Owyo son of Obiero, EAS, Wednesday, February 7, 1923.

82 RH: MSS Afr. s. 633 [Sir Robert Coryndon], Box 3, File 3: Copy of
    telegram of May 25, 1923, from the East African Association to Colonial
    Office. Aiyar notes that the statement was also printed in the *East African
    Standard*.

83 RH: MSS Afr. s. 2304 [C. K. Archer], Box 3, File 3: Translation of cable
    received from Nairobi, June 8, 1923.

84 RH: MSS Afr. s. 2304 [C. K. Archer], Box 3, File 3: Translation of cable
    received from Nairobi, June 8, 1923.

85 "The Voice of Africa," EAS, February 7, 1923, 6.

Four. White Peril

Portions of this chapter appeared in Elizabeth Williams, "Recipes for
Disaster: Cookery Books and the Management of Intimacy in Colonial
Kenyan Settler Homes 1919–1944," *Gender & History* 35, no. 2 (2023):
511–27.

1   The Special Committee was composed of the Chief Native Commis-
    sioner, the Principal Medical Officer, the Commissioner of Police and
    three members of the colony's Legislative Council, Sir. Northrup Mac-
    Millan, Mr. W. J. Moynagh, Mr. T. A. Wood, MBE, and the Chairman,
    Mr. H. W. B. Blackall.

2   KNA: AM/1/5 (or 1/1/5), Indecent Assaults, 1920–1944: "Report of the
    Special Committee on Sexual Assaults of Natives upon Europeans,"
    July 22, 1920.

3   KNA: AM/1/5 (or 1/1/5), Indecent Assaults, 1920–1944: "Report of the
    Special Committee on Sexual Assaults of Natives upon Europeans,"
    July 22, 1920.

4   To this point: when the eight-and-a-half-year-old daughter of a promi-
    nent Kenyan settler was allegedly assaulted by an African domestic
    servant in 1924, the police report noted that the accused "had that night
    tried to prevail upon a native woman named Mera to sleep with him and
    that she had refused," the implication being that he was driven to commit
    his crime when his access to "free love" was restricted. BNA: CO 533/612:
    Precis of Criminal Case no. 38 of 1924, Crime in Nakuru, January 16, 1924.

5   A decade later, the opinion that Kenya was relatively safe from Black Peril
    was also expressed in an exchange between J. H. F. Murray, Lieutenant-
    Governor of Papua New Guinea and Nairobi's Commissioner of Police in
    July of 1930. Murray explained that "We have been much troubled of late
    years by offenses, mostly trivial but at the same time very exasperating
    against white women" and asked for advice on how rape was deterred in
    Kenya. The commissioner's reply stated that "serious indecent assault[s]
    on white women by Africans have been comparatively rare in this coun-

try, and with the exception of one pending case, the accused have been detected and convicted." He recommended that white women in Papua should be advised not to live by themselves or walk alone at night, and that domestic servants should be registered. KNA: AM/1/5 (or 1/1/5), Indecent Assaults, 1920–1944: Letter from J. H. F. Murray to Nairobi's Commissioner of Police, July 3, 1930.

6   Carina Ray has also written about "White Perils" on the Gold Coast, although she uses the term to refer to sexual assaults committed by European men upon African women. Ray, "Decrying White Peril." The term "White Peril" was also used in a report from Rhodesia in 1915 to refer to sex between white men and "coloured" women. McCulloch, *Black Peril, White Virtue*, 70.

7   Lucy Delap notes, however, that supplies of domestic servants picked up again in the 1930s, due to the decreased employment options created by the depression. Delap, *Knowing Their Place*, 13.

8   Kennedy, *Islands of White*, 140.

9   Stoler, *Carnal Knowledge and Imperial Power*, 6.

10 Haskins and Lowrie, *Colonization and Domestic Service*, 2.

11 Haskins and Lowrie, *Colonization and Domestic Service*, 41.

12 Lowrie, "White Mistresses and Chinese 'Houseboys,'" 210–34.

13 Tranberg Hansen, *Distant Companions*, 30.

14 Tranberg Hansen, *Distant Companions*, 67.

15 Feimster, *Southern Horrors*, 5.

16 Feimster, *Southern Horrors*, 5.

17 Feimster, *Southern Horrors*, 5.

18 Dorr, *White Women*, 5.

19 Dorr, *White Women*, 11.

20 Hyslop, "White Working-Class Women," 60.

21 McCulloch, *Black Peril, White Virtue*, 12.

22 Martens, "Settler Homes, Manhood and 'Houseboys,'" 397. Likewise, Norman Etherington has argued that an 1870s rape scare in Natal was tied to fears about a loss of economic control over white women. Etherington, "Natal's Black Rape Scare," 36–53.

23 Martens, "Settler Homes, Manhood and 'Houseboys,'" 380–81.

24 Martens, "Settler Homes, Manhood and 'Houseboys,'" 395.

25 Jeater, *Marriage, Perversion, and Power*, 89.

26 Anderson, "Sexual Threat and Settler Society," 47–74.

27 Anderson, "Sexual Threat and Settler Society," 48.

28 "While whites in other times and places often portrayed black women as hypersexualized," he notes, "white stereotypes of African women in Kenya focused more on their exploitation by African men. Rather than a temptress of loose morals, the African woman in Kenya was a slave sold off as a girl to some toothless old man, the rest of her life a monotony of childrearing and field work." Shadle, *Souls of White Folk*, 102.

29 Vaughan, *Curing Their Ills*, 22.

30 Kennedy's book predated much of the other work on Black Peril in Africa. As Jock McCulloch notes, Kennedy was writing in the 1980s when "the history of settler societies was an unfashionable subject." McCulloch, *Black Peril, White Virtue*, 7. One exception is the work of Charles van Onselen, whose 1982 work *Studies in the Social and Economic History of the Witswatersland* touched on the subject.

31 Kennedy, *Islands of White*, 138, 141.

32 For instance, as early as 1903, Rhodesia passed a law that made even attempted rape punishable by capital punishment (which, as McCulloch notes may well have been the most severe law of its kind anywhere in the British empire). McCulloch, *Black Peril, White Virtue*, 4. Meanwhile, the legislation making rape a capital offense in Kenya was not passed until 1926 and did not extend to cases of attempted rape. McCulloch notes that "the major Black Peril panics [in Southern Rhodesia] occurred between 1902 to 1905 and 1908–1911"—at a time when the Kenyan settler community had not yet been fully established. McCulloch, *Black Peril, White Virtue*, 20.

33 Kennedy, *Islands of White*, 146.

34 Kennedy's research is also limited by his almost exclusive focus on the Grogan incident of 1907 as an example of "Black Peril"—apart from a brief mention of the Semini case, this is the only Kenyan case that Kennedy discusses. The Grogan incident was atypical both because it took place at a very early date of settlement, when the settler culture of Kenya had not yet been solidified, and because it was a case that did not actually involve sex—Grogan accused three rickshaw drivers of insulting the prestige of two white women passengers by jostling them excessively.

35 Shadle, *The Souls of White Folk*, 96–108.

36 Shadle, *The Souls of White Folk*, 5.

37 Hinde was also the mother of General W. R. N. Hinde, who would later be placed in charge of the Mau Mau counterinsurgency efforts.

38 Hildegarde Hinde, "The 'Black Peril' in British East Africa. A Frank Talk to Women Settlers," *The Empire Review and Journal of British Trade*, vol. 35, edited by Sir Clement Kinloch-Cooke, London: Macmillan, 1921. Brett Shadle also discusses this source in *The Souls of White Folk*, 106–8.

39 He borrowed this name for the title of his memoir: *From the Cape to Cairo: The First Traverse of Africa from South to North*.

40 *EAS*, "From the African World," May 4, 1907, 10.

41 Anderson, "Sexual Threat and Settler Society," 50.

42 Kennedy, *Islands of White*, 143.

43 Hinde, "The 'Black Peril,'" 193.

44 Hinde, "The 'Black Peril,'" 196.

45 Hinde, "The 'Black Peril,'" 196.

46 Hinde, "The 'Black Peril,'" 197.

47 Hinde, "The 'Black Peril,'" 197.

48 KNA: AM/1/5 (or 1/1/5), Indecent Assaults, 1920–1944: "Report of the Special Committee on Sexual Assaults of Natives upon Europeans," July 22, 1920.

49 KNA: AM/1/5 (or 1/1/5), Indecent Assaults, 1920–1944, Room 1, Shelf 269, Box 1: Anonymous, "East Africa Prot: Cont," memo or report, n.d., possibly from Major, General Staff Officer Intelligence KAR for inclusion in Intelligence Report circa April–May 1920. Interestingly, the author proposed that in order to prevent assaults Europeans should be educated "in the correct methods of dealing with natives and the advantages of learning at least one native language properly and something of their manners and customs."

50 RH: MSS Afr. s. 382: Ainsworth Extract from Ainsworth's Record of Service.

51 KNA: AM/1/5 (or 1/1/5), Indecent Assaults, 1920–1944: Article, July 1, 1920, "The Recent Rape Trial," unnamed paper.

52 KNA: AM/1/5 (or 1/1/5), Indecent Assaults, 1920–1944, Room 1, Shelf 269, Box 1: Anonymous, "East Africa Prot: Cont," memo or report, n.d., possibly from Major, General Staff Officer Intelligence KAR for inclusion in Intelligence Report circa April–May 1920 (emphasis mine).

53 KNA: AM/1/5 (or 1/1/5), Indecent Assaults, 1920–1944, Room 1, Shelf 269, Box 1: Anonymous, "East Africa Prot: Cont," memo or report, n.d., possibly from Major, General Staff Officer Intelligence KAR for inclusion in Intelligence Report circa April–May 1920.

54 KNA: AG/52/393, Rape Supreme Court Criminal Case no. 60 of 1926, Kijabe Outrage Case 1926, Room 2, Shelf 214, Box 197, *Daily Standard*, June 18, 1926.

55 Williams, "Recipes for Disaster."

56 Davin, "Imperialism and Motherhood," 12.

57 KNA AM/1/5 (or 1/1/5), Indecent Assaults, 1920–1944: "Report of the Special Committee on Sexual Assaults of Natives upon Europeans," July 22, 1920.

58 KNA AM/1/5 (or 1/1/5), Indecent Assaults, 1920–1944: "Report of the Special Committee on Sexual Assaults of Natives upon Europeans," July 22, 1920.

59 KNA: AM/1/5 (or 1/1/5): Letter to Editor of *The Leader*, June 12, 1920, "A Woman's View," signed Maramuki Kidogo.

60 KNA: AM/1/5 (or 1/1/5), Indecent Assaults,1920–1944: Letter to Mr. Maxwell from Kisumu, June 17, 1926, unsigned.

61 Jiggers are an insect that burrows under the skin and lays eggs. As Brett Shadle points out, white settlers believed that Africans had special expertise in the difficult task of removing the egg sack from the skin without bursting it. Shadle, *The Souls of White Folk*, 43.

62 KNA: AM/1/5 (or 1/1/5), Indecent Assaults, 1920–1944: Letter to Mr. Maxwell from Kisumu, June 17, 1926, unsigned.

63 KNA: AM/1/5 (or 1/1/5), Indecent Assaults, 1920–1944: Letter to Mr. Maxwell from Kisumu, June 17, 1926, unsigned.

64 KNA: AM/1/5 (or 1/1/5), Indecent Assaults, 1920–1944, Room 1, Shelf 269, Box 1: Anonymous, "East Africa Prot: Cont," memo or report, n.d., possibly from Major, General Staff Officer Intelligence KAR for inclusion in Intelligence Report circa April–May 1920.

65 KNA: AM/1/5 (or 1/1/5), Indecent Assaults, 1920–1944, Room 1, Shelf 269, Box 1: Anonymous, "East Africa Prot: Cont," memo or report, n.d., possibly from Major, General Staff Officer Intelligence KAR for inclusion in Intelligence Report circa April–May 1920.

66 KNA: AM/1/5 (or 1/1/5), Indecent Assaults, 1920–1944, Room 1, Shelf 269, Box 1: Anonymous, "East Africa Prot: Cont," memo or report, n.d., possibly from Major, General Staff Officer Intelligence KAR for inclusion in Intelligence Report circa April–May 1920.

67 Delap, *Knowing Their Place*, 13.

68 For more on class and whiteness in colonial Kenya, see Jackson, "Dangers to the Colony" and "Bad Blood."

69 Shadle, *Souls of White Folk*, 69.

70 Shadle, *Souls of White Folk*, 127.

71 Shadle, *Souls of White Folk*, 127.

72 Quoted in Campbell, *Race and Empire*, 124.

73 Jackson, "Bad Blood."

74 Jackson, "Bad Blood," 76.

75 Jackson, *Madness and Marginality*, 15.

76 Jackson, *Madness and Marginality*, 7.

77 KNA: AM/1/5 (or 1/1/5), Indecent Assaults. 1920–1944: Manifesto on Criminal Law Amendment Ordinance Circulated by Mission and Senior Commissioners, August 1926.

78 KNA: PC/NZA 3/17/18/2: Letter to Mr. Maxwell from Kisumu, June 17, 1926, unsigned.

79 KNA: PC/NZA 3/17/18/2: Letter to Mr. Maxwell from Kisumu, June 17, 1926, unsigned.

80 KNA: AM/1/5 (or 1/1/5), Indecent Assaults, 1920–1944, Room 1, Shelf 269, Box 1: Anonymous, "East Africa Prot: Cont," memo or report, n.d., possibly from Major, General Staff Officer Intelligence KAR for inclusion in Intelligence Report circa April–May 1920.

81 For more on the role of "native assessors" see Shadle, "Rape in the Courts of Gusiiland," 27–50; Shadle, "African Court Elders in Nyanza Province, Kenya," 180–201.

82 KNA: AM/1/5 (or 1/1/5), Indecent Assaults, 1920–1944: "Report of the Special Committee on Sexual Assaults of Natives upon Europeans."

83 KNA: AM1/1/5: Article, July 1, 1920, "The Recent Rape Trial," unnamed paper. This concern about the use of "native assessors" in cases of sexual

assault can be usefully compared to the outrage over the Ilbert Bill in colonial India in the years 1883–1884. The Ilbert Bill proposed to amend the
IPC so that Indian civil servants would have jurisdiction over European
subjects. As Mrinalina Sinha writes, "the Anglo-Indian opposition [to the
bill] received its momentum from capitalizing on the notion that the bill
was a blow to the prestige and security of the 'pure and defenceless white
woman in India.'" Sinha, "'Chathams, Pitts,'" 99. Anglo-Indians claimed
that Indians were unfit to try Europeans due to their supposed effeminacy and barbaric treatment of women. Additionally, they suggested that
Indian magistrates might exploit their power to coerce white women into
sexual relationships. Sinha, "'Chathams, Pitts,'" 100–101. Furthermore,
as Fae Dussart has shown, the Ilbert Bill controversy also focused on
the relationship between memsahibs and their Indian (male) domestic
servants; "some women argued that the passage of the Bill would damage
the prestige of English rule, claiming that servants would trump false
charges against, in particular, their female employers. They would thus
challenge their vulnerable mistresses' authority and force them into an
unnaturally public position, tainted with the possibility of humiliation
at the hands of an Indian judge." Dussart, "'To Glut a Menial's Grudge,'"
n.p. The crisis ended with a compromise that granted Indian civil servants limited jurisdiction but also gave Europeans the right to a trial by a
jury composed of at least half European members.

84   KNA: AG/52/393: *Daily Standard*, August 30, 1926, signed Wambugu wa
      Mathangai, paramount chief, Gideon Gatere, headman, Musa Muruthi,
      CMS, and Arthur M. Champion, President and DC.

85   KNA: AM/1/5 (or 1/1/5), Indecent Assaults, 1920–1944, Room 1, Shelf
      269, Box 1: *The Daily Leader of British East Africa*, April 9, 1920.

86   KNA: AM/1/5 (or 1/1/5), Indecent Assaults, 1920–1944, Room 1, Shelf
      269, Box 1: *The Daily Leader of British East Africa*, April 9, 1920.

87   KNA: AM/1/5 (or 1/1/5), Indecent Assaults, 1920–1944, Room 1, Shelf
      269, Box 1: *The Daily Leader of British East Africa*, April 9, 1920.

88   KNA: AM/1/5 (or 1/1/5), Indecent Assaults, 1920–1944, Room 1, Shelf
      269, Box 1: *The Daily Leader of British East Africa*, April 9, 1920.

89   BNA: CO 533/612: Extract from Debate of Kenya Legislative Council,
      June 30, 1926.

90   BNA: CO 533/612: Extract from Debate of Kenya Legislative Council,
      June 30, 1926.

91   BNA: CO 533/612: Extract from Debates of Kenya Legislative Council,
      June 30, 1926. There is disagreement among scholars about how rape cases
      were understood within indigenous Kenyan communities. In her study
      of gender in colonial Kenya, Tabitha Kanogo explains that cases of sexual
      assault were, in fact, viewed through a distinct framework in many East
      African societies. "Sexual relations," she explains, "were not private or
      personal in traditional Kenyan societies. Having intercourse affected the

welfare of the families and clans of the parties doing it. Sexual misconduct of all categories was perceived as a transgression against the clan members of either one or the other of the parties involved." Therefore, among certain groups like the Kamba, "it was the clan that was perceived to be the aggrieved party to be appeased, for the woman had no individual standing in the matter, cultural or legal. . . . Social responsibility was gendered, which, while sparing women the social anguish of culpability, also robbed them of agency. Meanwhile their personal suffering was irrelevant." Kanogo, *African Womanhood in Colonial Kenya*, 55. Brett Shadle, meanwhile, found that Gusii court elders understood rape to be a crime committed against women, not against their guardians. Shadle, "Rape in the Courts," 28. Regardless, in describing sexual assaults as a crime against property, Kenealy reinforced paternalistic ideas about African misogyny while missing the nuances of a worldview that centered around the community rather than the individual.

92 KNA: AM/1/5 (or 1/1/5), Indecent Assaults, 1920–1944, Room 1, Shelf 269, Box 1: Anonymous, "East Africa Prot: Cont," memo or report, n.d., possibly from Major, General Staff Officer Intelligence KAR for inclusion in Intelligence Report circa April–May 1920.

93 KNA: AM/1/5 (or 1/1/5), Indecent Assaults, 1920–1944, Room 1, Shelf 269, Box 1: Article sent by author, M[?] Cross to John Ainsworth, written February 17, 1920.

94 KNA: AM/1/5 (or 1/1/5), Indecent Assaults, 1920–1944, Room 1, Shelf 269, Box 1: Article sent by author, M[?] Cross to John Ainsworth, written February 17, 1920.

95 KNA: AM/1/5 (or 1/1/5), Indecent Assaults, 1920–1944, Room 1, Shelf 269, Box 1: Article sent by author, M[?] Cross to John Ainsworth, written February 17, 1920.

96 BNA: CO 533/612, Native Offences Against European Women Criminal Law Ordinance: Letter from Gov. Grigg to Amery, July 13, 1926.

97 BNA: CO 533/612, Native Offences Against European Women Criminal Law Ordinance: Letter from Gov. Grigg to Amery, July 13, 1926.

98 BNA: CO 533/612: Telegram, Grigg to Amery, June 5, 1926.

99 David Anderson mistakenly states that the law criminalized only the rape of white women in his article "Sexual Threat and Settler Society"; however, my research has shown that there was no racial distinction, as is stated in a more recent study by Brett Shadle, *The Souls of White Folk*, 136. The first rape case to be tried under the revised legislation did not occur until 1928. The victim was a twenty-four-year-old white woman from Nairobi, and her alleged assailant, a Luo man, was convicted and hanged. KNA: AG/52/392.

100 RH: MSS Afr. s. 594 [Convention of Associations], Box 1A: "Report of the Session of the Convention of Associations Held in the Memorial Hall, Nairobi, on October 25th, 26th, 27th, 28th, & 29th, 1926," 469.

101 Indeed, the London *Times* described the legislation as a "drastic bill." "Kenya Penalties for Outrages on Women," *Times* (London), July 2, 1926, 13.

102 RH: MSS Afr. s. 594 [Convention of Associations], Box 1A: "Report of the Session of the Convention of Associations Held in the Memorial Hall, Nairobi, on October 25th, 26th, 27th, 28th, & 29th, 1926," 471–72.

103 RH: MSS Afr. s. 594 [Convention of Associations], Box 1A: "Report of the Session of the Convention of Associations Held in the Memorial Hall, Nairobi, on October 25th, 26th, 27th, 28th, & 29th, 1926," 471–72.

104 The Devonshire Declaration of 1923 established that the Legislative Council would include five elected Indian unofficial (i.e., non–civil servant) members, one elected Arab member, one nominated Arab official member, and eleven Europeans members, with nominated officials maintaining the majority, and one nominated missionary member to represent Africans. RH: MSS Afr. s. 594 [Convention of Associations], Box 1, File 14: *Official Gazette*, August 17, 1923.

105 BNA: CO 533/612: Extract from Debates of Kenya LegCo, June 30, 1926.

106 BNA: CO 533/612: Extract from Debates of Kenya LegCo, June 30, 1926.

107 BNA: CO 533/612: Extract from Debates of Kenya LegCo, June 30, 1926.

108 BNA: CO 533/612: Extract from Debates of Kenya LegCo, June 30, 1926.

109 Anderson, "Master and Servant," 466.

110 KNA: PC/NZA/3/13/54, Domestic Servants, 1932–1948, Room 3, Shelf 1600, B 72.

Five. Queering Settler Romance

A shorter version of this chapter appeared as Elizabeth W. Williams, "Queering Settler Romance: The Reparative Eugenic Landscape in Nora Strange's Kenyan Novels," in *Archiving Settler Colonialism: Culture, Space, and Race*, ed. Yuting Huang and Rebecca Weaver-Hightower (London: Routledge, 2019), 190–204.

1 Strange, *Kenya Noon*, 201.

2 Shadle, *Souls of White Folk*, 97. Similarly, John Lonsdale has blamed the colony's bad reputation on the "'Kenya novel', pulp fiction of its day, in which native gossip turned white adultery into racial treachery." Lonsdale, "The History of Swahili," 89. Strange herself rejected this characterization, writing "The well-known cliché, 'Are they married or living in Kenya?' was neither the invention of a novelist nor a journalist, but the Colony's own easy tolerance and acceptance of the evaders of the seventh commandment, which has tended to make it a dumping ground for lost matrimonial causes. The woman novelist, in particular, comes in for an avalanche of indiscriminate criticism, which a business man or a settler would not tolerate for an instant." Strange, *Kenya Today*, 167–68.

3   Ann Laura Stoler critiques this approach in the historiography of
    imperialism, noting that "the writing of colonial history has often been
    predicated on just the assumption that Foucault attacked; the premise
    that colonial power relations can be accounted for and explained as a subli-
    mated expression of repressed desires in the West, of desires that resurface
    in moralizing missions, myths of the 'wild woman,' in a romance with the
    rural 'primitive,' or in other more violent, virile, substitute form." Such his-
    tories operate from an "implicitly Freudian" perspective, which envisions
    colonialism as the result of white sexual repression. Stoler, *Race*, 167–68.

4   Stanley Paul was purchased by Hutchinson & Co in 1928. https://www
    .austlit.edu.au/austlit/page/A37360.

5   Strange, *Kenya Today*.

6   The Cobbald Family History Trust, https://www.cobboldfht.com/.

7   Strange, *Kenya Today*, 129.

8   *Cyclopedia of India*, 201.

9   A significant exception is Patricia Lorcin's book *Historicizing Colonial
    Nostalgia*, which devotes a large portion of the fourth chapter to a study
    of Strange and her literary rival Florence Riddell.

10 Davin, "Imperialism and Motherhood."

11 Morgensen, "Theorising Gender," 11.

12 For instance, in 1926 (just two years after the publication of Strange's
    first novel) the white settler population was 12,529, compared to 29,324
    Asians and more than 2.5 million Africans. Ghai and McAuslan, *Public
    Law*, 36; Kuczynski, *Demographic Survey*, 145.

13 She did, however, author one novel set in colonial India—1928's *Mistress
    of Ceremonies*.

14 Veracini, "'Settler Colonialism,'" 313.

15 There was also a much larger population of Indian settlers; colonial prop-
    erty laws, however, prevented them from owning land in the most desir-
    able farming areas of the colony. Hence, they tended to hold positions as
    artisans, shopkeepers, clerks, and so on rather than as farmers reliant on
    African labor. For more on Kenyan Indians, see Aiyar, *Indians in Kenya*.

16 Quoted in Veracini, "'Settler Colonialism,'" 320.

17 Quoted in Morgensen, "Theorising Gender," 9.

18 Veracini, "'Settler Colonialism,'" 315.

19 The scheme, which allowed veterans of the Great War to purchase land in
    Kenya, nearly doubled the white population in the colony. However, the
    requirement that settlers possess £5,000 in capital largely restricted par-
    ticipation to officers. Londsale, "Home Country and African Frontier,"
    75. For more on the scheme, see Duder, "'Men of the Officer Class.'"

20 Pick, *Faces of Degeneration*, 15.

21 The Boer War raised concerns "that the urban conditions in which most
    Britons lived fostered physical and moral degeneration—for the army
    rejected many potential recruits as physically unfit, and those it selected

were hard pressed to defeat an Afrikaner population they outnumbered." Kuklick, *Savage Within*, 22. On the impact of the Boer War, see also Davin, "Imperialism and Motherhood."

22 Morgensen, "Settler Homonationalism," 106.

23 Strange, *Kenya Today*, 102. Lyons and Lyons note a similar discourse about the lack of prostitution among Indigenous Australians: in his study of *London Labour and the London Poor* (1861–62), Henry Mayhew stated that prostitutes "as a class" did not exist among the Australians "for prostitution of this kind implies some advance towards the forms of regular society." Quoted in Lyons and Lyons, *Irregular Connections*, 45.

24 Strange, *Kenya Today*, 102. It is not clear what specific "hygienic practices" she was referring to, although there was a general belief that Indians practiced poor sanitation, thus leading to the spread of disease.

25 As Megan Vaughan has shown, "detribalized natives" were also viewed as the most likely to develop mental illness: "African society was portrayed as encouraging gratification and sexual promiscuity. At the same time it was said that the emphasis on social conformitivity in African culture led to the excessive dependence of the individual on the collectivity. There was both too much and too little restraint in African society, the end result being that the African lacked a clearly defined personality, was emotionally unstable and might easily become insane if subjected to the stress which accompanied 'deculturation.'" Vaughan, *Curing Their Ills*, 118.

26 Strange, *Kenya Today*, 102–3.

27 As literary scholar Pamela Regis has pointed out, "a marriage—promised or actually dramatized—ends every romance novel." Regis, *Natural History*, 9.

28 Brickman, *Aboriginal Populations in the Mind*, 18.

29 Mwangi, "The Order of Money," 189. Physical anthropologists did not, however, reach consensus on this issue until the 1950s, when they determined that East Africa, not Asia, was indeed the home of the oldest human ancestors. For more on the history of this debate, see Meredith, *Born in Africa*.

30 This term is often used to describe the rape of queer/lesbian women and gender nonconforming people as a method of "curing" them of their sexual and gendered deviance. I use the term here to underscore how rape is being used to "cure" a different kind of queerness, one whose deviance lies not in object choice or gender presentation, but rather an aversion to sexuality altogether.

31 Radway, *Reading the Romance*, 143.

32 Strange, *Latticed Windows*.

33 Strange, *Latticed Windows*, 76.

34 Strange, *Latticed Windows*, 77.

35 Strange, *Latticed Windows*, 81–82.

36 Strange, *Latticed Windows*, 93.

37 Van Doorne turns out to be the former German spy who betrayed Roger's best friend Guy Fraser. Fraser "had fallen victim to German propaganda in its oldest form since Adam—a woman German prisoner of war, who had extracted from him in a moment of madness, valuable information regarding the movements of a certain convoy, which had been subsequently blown to pieces." Strange, *Latticed Windows*, 21.

38 Strange, *Latticed Windows*, 197.

39 Strange, *Latticed Windows*, 231.

40 Regis, *Natural History*, 35.

41 Strange, *Kenya Dawn*.

42 Strange, *Kenya Dawn*, 186.

43 Strange, *Kenya Dawn*, 178.

44 Strange, *Kenya Dawn*, 144.

45 Strange, *Kenya Dawn*, 153–54.

46 Blixen (who wrote under the pen name Isak Dinesen) claimed that the story of the victim "with his firm will to die . . . stands out with a beauty of its own. In it is embodied the fugitiveness of wild things who are, in the hour of need, conscious of a refuge somewhere in existence; who go when they like; of whom we can never get hold." Dinesen, *Out of Africa*, 287–91. For more on the Abraham case, see Anderson, "Punishment, Race," 485–89.

47 Chief Native Commissioner John Ainsworth, for instance, was frustrated by the demands of many settlers, "including all the South Africans," to "have the country governed with the idea of making it absolutely a white man's country, and making all the laws to suit the white man; they wish that all natives should be of no particular account, except in so far as they are useful to further the white Colonists' ends. This I know is the South African ideal." Quoted in Sorrensen, *Origins of European Settlement*, 242. Sorrenson provides an extensive discussion of white immigration patterns in the early years of Kenyan settlement—up to 1915. Despite the fact that most of these migrants were British South Africans, they were sometimes lumped in with Boers. Dane Kennedy quotes a colonial administrator's summary of the situation "English people think that the majority of the lower class Afrikanders [British South Africans] have all the vices of the Dutch without any of their redeeming qualities." Kennedy, *Islands of White*, 48.

48 Strange, *Kenya Dawn*, 305.

49 Strange, *Kenya Dawn*, 305.

50 Strange, *Kenya Dawn*, 305.

51 Stoler, *Race*, 109–10.

52 Lessing, *Grass Is Singing*; Oyono, *Houseboy*.

53 Kennedy, *Islands of White*, 168.

54 Jackson, "Bad Blood," 76. Elsewhere, Jackson has shown that women who were seen as being too familiar with Africans, or those who bore illegitimate children, were particularly liable to be deported as "Distressed

British Subjects," those who lacked sufficiently financial means to prosper in the colony. Jackson, "Dangers to the Colony," n.p.

55 Strange, *Kenya Calling.*

56 Strange, *Kenya Calling,* 52.

57 Strange, *Kenya Calling,* 52.

58 Strange, *Kenya Calling,* 54.

59 Strange, *Kenya Calling,* 55.

60 Strange, *Kenya Calling,* 56.

61 Strange, *Kenya Calling,* 59.

62 Strange, *Kenya Calling,* 59.

63 Strange, *Kenya Calling,* 77.

64 Like several of Strange's novels, *The Sheik* depicts rape as a method of female sexual awakening. As Hsu-Ming Teo points out in her discussion of the novel, in *The Sheik,* "rape performs the function of permitting Diana [the heroine] to experience sex while absolving her from all responsibility, thus maintaining her status as a virtuous and virginal heroine. Not only does Diana endure rape, she actually comes to enjoy sex and to participate in it, thus transforming rape into consensual sex and even the suggestion of a modern, companionate relationship with the Sheik." Teo, "Historicizing the Sheik," 14.

65 Strange, *Kenya Calling,* 77.

66 Strange, *Kenya Calling,* 77.

67 Strange, *Kenya Calling,* 77.

68 Strange, *Kenya Calling,* 88.

69 Strange, *Kenya Calling,* 185.

70 Strange, *Wife in Kenya,* 32.

71 Strange, *Wife in Kenya,* 32.

72 Strange, *Wife in Kenya,* 184.

73 "Napier" calls to mind Sir Charles James Napier, the general who conquered Sindh for the British in 1842 and later served as Governor of the Bombay Presidency and as Commander-in-Chief of India. Pierce's wife "Beryl" is perhaps intended as a reference to Beryl Markham, a female aviator who lived in Kenya and was famously involved with Denys Finch Hatton, previously the lover of the writer Karen Blixen, although Markham's most famous exploits took place after the novel was written. Strange was fond of using character names to wink at the most famous personalities of colonial Kenya.

74 Strange, *Wife in Kenya,* 185.

75 Strange, *Wife in Kenya,* 185.

76 Strange, *The Clinton Heritage.*

77 My thanks to Ruth Mazo Karras for pointing out the significance of this name.

78 Delamere, who also claimed to be a "blood-brother" of the Maasai, was one of the largest landholders in Kenya and the unofficial leader of white

settlers. The Maasai were considered by many to be the "aristocrats of Kenya," a martial race with Nilotic (rather than Bantu) roots: as Strange puts it, "the most arresting features of these tall, lithe warriors were their enigmatic, slightly contemptuous expression which showed that they were well aware that they represented the aristocratic element amongst East African tribes and had not forgotten that in the heyday of their power lesser breeds, such as the Kikuyu, had fled to the forests for safety at the beat of their war-drums." Strange, *Clinton Heritage*, 36.

79 The fact that Barron has a Somali servant also marks him as upper class, since they cost more to employ and were hence considered particularly fashionable.

80 Strange, *Clinton Heritage*, 159, 160.

81 Strange, *Clinton Heritage*, 161.

82 Strange, *Clinton Heritage*, 146.

83 In his study of the "races of Africa," the anthropologist C. G. Seligman classified the Somali as Hamitic—and thus superior to "Negroid" races—and suggested they were "comparatively recent migrants from across the sea." Seligman, *Races of Africa*, 124.

84 For example, the Somali Exemption Ordinance of 1919 established that government officials could grant a certificate of exemption from payment of the Native Hut and Poll Tax "to any Somali who is able to prove that on the grounds of education and birth it is undesirable that such Somali should be included in the definition of native." *Kenya Gazette*, June 18, 1919, 8.

85 Strange, *Clinton Heritage*, 161.

86 Strange, *Clinton Heritage*, 193.

87 The use of this trope by another novelist of Kenya, Karen Blixen, has been criticized by Ngũgĩ wa Thiong'o in *Detained*, 35–36.

88 Stoler, *Race*, 8.

Six. Eating the Other

1 Cloete, *A Storm over Africa*, 5. Cloete was born in France of South African and Dutch parentage. He migrated to Pretoria at the age of twenty to become a farmer and wrote his study of Mau Mau "after a long journey through Kenya." He is probably related to C. J. Cloete, a South African settler who led a large migration to the Uasin Gishu district of Kenya in 1911. Nicholls, *Red Strangers*, 63.

2 Cloete, *A Storm over Africa*, 7. The contention that service in World War II had exposed African men to sexual vice was echoed by Mrs. E. C. Palmes, who complained that soldiers who served in Egypt and the Levant had been "contaminated" by their contact with working-class soldiers. RH: MSS Afr. s. 946 [Mrs. E. C. Palmes]: "The Scene Changes," 115.

3 Anderson, *Histories of the Hanged*, 280.

4 Luongo, *Witchcraft and Colonial Rule*, 160.

5 Quoted in Anderson, *Histories of the Hanged*, 1.

6 Corfield, *The Origins and Growth of Mau Mau*. As Mickie Mwanzia Koster has noted, the Corfield Report "distinguish[ed] Mau Mau from other revolutionary movements in Africa based on three characteristics: it was considered tribal in nature; it was based on primitive superstition that was practiced primarily through oath taking; and it was anti-Christian." Koster, "Mau Mau Inventions and Reinventions," 30.

7 Rosberg and Nottingham, *The Myth of "Mau Mau."*

8 Berman and Lonsdale, *Unhappy Valley*; Berman, *Control and Crisis*.

9 Kanogo, *Squatters*; Bates, "The Agrarian Origins"; Barnett and Njama, *Mau Mau from Within*.

10 Anderson, *Histories of the Hanged*.

11 The most prominent proponents of this view are William Ochieng' and B. E. Kipkorir. For a summary of this school of thought, see Kinyatti, "Mau Mau," 303–4.

12 Elkins, *Imperial Reckoning*; Rosberg, *The Myth of "Mau Mau."*

13 Anderson, *Histories of the Hanged*, 3.

14 In fact, the economic situation of Kenyan Africans grew more dire during this period. As white farmers increasingly abandoned old crops like coffee, tea, and pyrethrum in favor of cattle and dairy farming, they employed fewer African laborers. Those who remained were not allowed to keep their own livestock, as it was believed that "native" cattle would spread disease to the expensive imported breeds farmed by whites. Berman and Lonsdale, *Unhappy Valley*, 256–57. For more on the connection between squatted labor and Mau Mau, see Kanogo, *Squatters*; Bates, "The Agrarian Origins"; and Throup, *Economic & Social Origins*.

15 Anderson, *Histories of the Hanged*, 11–13.

16 Rosberg and Nottingham, *The Myth of "Mau Mau."*

17 Kariuki, *"Mau Mau" Detainee*, 23.

18 He provides this explanation: "that word was said when one man, a Masai by tribe, was being given the oath at Naivasha and he told the Europeans that he was given Mumau. In Kikuyu the word for oath is Mma, but because of its pronunciation the Europeans wrote it as Mau Mau." Itote, *Mau Mau in Action*, 167.

19 Branch, *Defeating Mau Mau, Creating Kenya*, 23. Carolyn Martin Shaw also encountered this explanation during her ethnographical fieldwork. Shaw, *Colonial Inscriptions*, 154.

20 Anderson, *Histories of the Hanged*, 128.

21 Anderson, *Histories of the Hanged*, 5.

22 Ogot and Ochieng', *Decolonization & Independence in Kenya*, 50.

23 Elkins, *Imperial Reckoning*. Elkins has been criticized by a number of scholars, most of whom suggest that she vastly overestimates the number of victims of imperial repression in detention camps and government-

run "villages." She has also been accused (mostly outside of the official record) of making up facts, particularly those related to torture and violence. However, many of her assertions about torture and violence are backed up by evidence in Robert Edgerton's earlier study, *Mau Mau: An African Crucible*; his work also relies on oral histories to provide most of this information. The British government was recently forced to release a huge number of documents relating to the torture of Mau Mau detainees, which corroborate Elkins' evidence. Both Elkins and Anderson testified as expert witness in a court case in which five Kenyans detained in Mau Mau camps sued for reparations; in 2013, the British government agreed to pay almost £20 million in compensation to more than five thousand victims. "UK to Compensate Kenya's Mau Mau Torture Victims," *The Guardian*, June 6, 2013. For more on the circumstances surrounding the release of documents, see Anderson, "Mau Mau in the High Court," 699–716.

24 Anderson, *Histories of the Hanged*, 4–5, 128.

25 Anderson, *Histories of the Hanged*, 330.

26 For more on metropolitan opposition to the repression of Mau Mau, see chapter 10 in Elkins, *Imperial Reckoning*.

27 The eleven detainees refused to perform hard labor. They were subsequently "clubbed to death by their African guards whilst European warders looked on." The Labour MP Barbara Castle subsequently led a debate in the House of Commons, decrying the massacre. Ironically, Enoch Powell, the nativist Tory who would later become infamous for his prediction that "rivers of blood" would flow in the streets of England if immigration was not stopped, denounced the abuse of the Kenyan prisoners during the debate. As Anderson writes, "If Powell and his like were wavering, then the game of empire really was up in Kenya." Anderson, *Histories of the Hanged*, 327.

28 Anderson, *Histories of the Hanged*, 336. For more on Kenyatta's policies, see Anderson, *Histories of the Hanged*, 333–36.

29 *The Sunday Times*, September 17, 1953, 4. The essay was later reprinted in Greene, *Ways of Escape*, 195.

30 *The Sunday Times*, September 17, 1953, 4.

31 They did however presciently predict that "it is quite conceivable that, if unwisely dealt with from headquarters, the native might be inspired to make trial of strength in a way that would issue in terrible tragedy in the case of isolated settlers." Routledge and Routledge, *With a Prehistoric People*, 332.

32 Hewitt, *Kenya Cowboy*, 137.

33 Berman and Lonsdale, *Unhappy Valley*, 274.

34 British colonists made efforts to preserve the cultural integrity of groups, notably the Maasai, that they considered to be superior to other East African ethnic groups. A pastoral people believed to have "Hamitic" roots, the Maasai were considered racially superior to "Bantu" Africans like the Gikuyu. Hodgson, *Once Intrepid Warriors*.

35 Shaw, *Colonial Inscriptions*, 183.

36 Hewitt, *Kenya Cowboy*, 89.

37 The chair of the committee was the liberal Tom Askwith, head of the colony's community development program. Two officials, H. E. Lambert and Sidney Fazan, served on the committee, as well as two African representatives, David Waruhiu and Harry Thuku. Warahiu was the son of a loyalist chief who had been murdered by Mau Mau, while Harry Thuku, at one time a prominent nationalist, had by this time been coopted by the colonial government. But Anderson notes that Leakey and Carothers were "by far the most influential members of the committee." Anderson, *Histories of the Hanged*, 281–82.

38 Leakey, *White African*.

39 Leakey, *Defeating Mau Mau*, 7. As Carolyn Martin Shaw points out, Leakey's attempt to situate himself as a professional friend of the Africans also meant that "Leakey expected, and often received, praise and adulation from Africans for his patronage, knowledge, and competence." Shaw, *Colonial Inscriptions*, 98.

40 Berman and Lonsdale, "Louis Leakey's Mau Mau," 144.

41 Shaw, *Colonial Inscriptions*, 143.

42 Cobb appears to have been an eccentric alcoholic—Carothers claimed that Cobb had been having sex with the two lion cubs that he kept at Mathari. The rumor was probably not true, but it echoes the contention that sexual deviance could be interpreted as a sign of madness. McCulloch, *Colonial Psychiatry*, 23.

43 McCulloch, *Colonial Psychiatry*, 50. At Mathari, Africans made up the great majority of Carothers's patients, a fact that did not dislodge white assumptions about the rarity of mental illness in African patients but seems to have helped ensure that mental health would remain a relatively low priority for the Kenyan state. In 1948, for example, Mathari treated 750 people; all were African with the exception of sixty-eight Europeans and sixty-two Asians. McCulloch, *Colonial Psychiatry*, 25.

44 For instance, his first book, *The African Mind in Health and Disease*, was written at the request of the World Health Organization.

45 Leakey, *Mau Mau and the Kikuyu*, x.

46 Leakey, *Mau Mau and the Kikuyu*, 76.

47 Leakey, *Mau Mau and the Kikuyu*, 76.

48 Carothers, "A Study of Mental Derangement," 587.

49 Carothers, "A Study of Mental Derangement," 560.

50 Carothers, "A Study of Mental Derangement," 560.

51 Carothers, "A Study of Mental Derangement," 561.

52 Carothers, *The Psychology of Mau Mau*, 9.

53 Leakey, *Mau Mau and the Kikuyu*, 26. Leakey's concern with the progression of humans through stages of development was also reflected in his approach to physical anthropology. As J. E. G. Sutton puts it, Leakey's

"driving ambition—barely disguised in his writings, popular as well as academic, of the 1930s—was to trace the evolution of mankind in a linear way through a succession of stages, or progressively advancing 'races,' each to be demonstrated by finds of skulls, if not whole skeletons." The use of different tools would show "an advance from each culture or phase to the next." Sutton, "Denying History in Colonial Kenya," 316. Leakey did, however, believe that the artifacts he was looking at came from prehistoric Africans; he therefore was not making an argument that *modern* Africans represented a "missing link" in human evolution. Leakey was also among a minority of physical anthropologists who believed that the human species originated in Africa rather than Asia; the scientific consensus did not shift to the former view until the 1950s. For more on this shift, see Meredith, *Born in Africa*.

54 Leakey, *Mau Mau and the Kikuyu*, 25.

55 Leakey, *Mau Mau and the Kikuyu*, 75.

56 Leakey, *Defeating Mau Mau*, 133.

57 Leakey, *Defeating Mau Mau*, 133.

58 Hasian, "Deployment of Ethnographic Sciences," 340.

59 For a discussion of gendered performances among Mau Mau men (rather than just representations of Mau Mau masculinity), see White, "Separating the Men," 1–25.

60 RH: MSS Afr. s. 596 [Elector's Union EEMO], Box 38A, File 1: "The Kikuyu Tribe and Mau Mau."

61 Katherine Luongo has defined a "spiv" as a "gangster," but the use of the word in Kenya also had strong gendered connotations. Luongo, *Witchcraft and Colonial Rule*, 161. The Oxford English Dictionary defines a "spiv" as "A man who lives by his wits and has no regular employment; one engaging in petty blackmarket dealings and freq. characterized by flashy dress." The emphasis on flashy dress was particularly prominent in Kenyan discourse.

62 Shadle, *Souls of White Folk*, 32.

63 Vaughan, *Curing Their Ills*, 109. Another explanation for the detrimental effect of clothing was that it taught Africans to desire material objects, and hence provided temptation to steal. In her unpublished memoir, the settler Mrs. E. C. Palmes records her husband's opinion on the subject. When she questioned whether her African employee's wages were too low, her husband explained that Africans did not need much money because they had nothing to spend it on. However, the missionaries were likely to change this since they were encouraging Africans to wear European clothing. She believed that dressing Africans in European clothes was both unsanitary and bred "snobbishness" in Africans. RH: MSS Afr. s. 946 [Mrs. E. C. Palmes]: "The Scene Changes, Experiences of Life in Kenya," 14. Of course, the African desire for material goods might also encourage Africans to demand higher wages from their European employers.

64 A settler echoed this point in a letter to Chief Native Commissioner John Ainsworth in 1920, comparing the uncontaminated African to Adam and Eve, who were unaware they were naked until they ate the apple. The author, however, was advocating that Africans in cities be required to wear more clothes, which would have the duel benefit of protecting white women from the sight of nude African male bodies, and of forcing Africans to work for wages in order to purchase clothes. KNA: AM/1/5 (or 1/1/5), Indecent Assaults, 1920–1944, Room 1, Shelf 269, Box 1: Article sent by author M[?] Cross to John Ainsworth, "A Black Peril: Wanted a Curfew Hooter; and Decency in our Streets," February 17, 1920.

65 Because of the intensely racist iconography of these cartoons, I've chosen not to reproduce them here. While I have not been able to find much biographical information about "Bokkie," an article from the *East African Standard* in 1944 noted that a "Bokkie" von Maltitz had conducted the burial service of Anna Magdelana Cloete, wife of the early Afrikaner settler Christian Cloete. The article notes that Bokkie was "himself the son of a pioneer." "A Valiant Old Kenya Settler," *East African Standard*, June 16, 1944.

66 Bokkie, *Shambulia*.

67 Presley, *Kikuyu Women*, 158.

68 RH: MSS Afr. s. 596 [Elector's Union/EEMO], Box 38A, File 4: "The Emergency in Kenya," signed J. M. Foxley Norris, January 17, 1954, Mweiga.

69 The document was produced just prior to the institution of the villagization campaign, hence the anxiety about women's mobility. RH: MSS Afr. s. 596 [Elector's Union/EEMO], Box 38A, File 1: "A Review of The Present Emergency in Kenya. August 1953," 5.

70 There were Kikuyu, Meru, and Embu Home Guards, formed to protect chiefs and headmen. As the Emergency progressed, they began to conduct patrols in the Native Reserves. Bennett, *Fighting the Mau Mau*, 16–17.

71 Lavers, *Kikuyu Who Fight*, 34–36.

72 Similar claims are made in Cloete, *Storm Over Africa*, 21, and Stoneham, *Out of Barbarism*, 133.

73 bell hooks, *Black Looks*, 21.

74 Quoted in Berman, *Control and Crisis*, 335 (emphasis in original).

75 Anderson, *Histories of the Hanged*, 42–45.

76 Kariuki, *"Mau Mau" Detainee*, 31.

77 It's described, for example, in Holman and Drummond, *Bwana Drum*, 22; in "Kenya: The Oath Takers," *Time* (June 13, 1960); and in Corfield, *The Origins and Growth of Mau Mau*, 167.

78 Holman and Drummond, *Bwana Drum*, 22.

79 Luise White observed that "prostitutes, menstrual blood, and genitalia" appeared frequently in descriptions of Mau Mau oaths, noting that settlers may have "associated uncontrolled sexuality with uncontrolled politics." White, *The Comforts of Home*, 206.

80 We could of course question to what extent such strictures were followed even in the precolonial era. As discussed in chapter 1, those who conducted the most influential anthropological accounts of Gikuyu sexuality had particular investments in the narrative of primitive normativity and/or in the idea that Gikuyu sexual behaviors were strictly governed through a series of "traditional" social controls. We should read this aspect of oathing mythologies (as indeed the phenomenon of oathing mythologies more generally) as evidence about the mindset and perspectives of those who consumed it rather than as reflective of any "facts" about Gikuyu life.

81 Marc Epprecht notes that prostitution among women, along with masturbation and sex between men, were frequently cited as dangerous effects of detribalization. Epprecht, *Heterosexual Africa?*, 72–73. Interestingly, Ann Stoler has observed that this same triad of behaviors was viewed as evidence of the sexual disorder bred among lower-class whites in the colonies; this susceptibility to sexual desire signified the unsuitability of nonbourgeois or multiracial subjects for the responsibilities of colonial rule. Stoler, *Race*, 179, 182–83. The parallel underscores the broader conflation of lower-class and nonwhite peoples as evolutionarily junior to the European middle class, and hence less able to practice sexual self-control in "civilized" spaces. Tabitha Kanogo also found the association between urbanization/Westernization and sexual immorality to be prevalent among African interlocutors, who interpreted a woman's travel to the cities or her purchase and wearing of Western-style clothes as evidence that she had become a prostitute. Kanogo, *African Womanhood in Colonial Kenya*, 6–7. As Derek Peterson has shown, in the 1940s and 1950s, Luo men used a similar rhetoric to compel the "repatriation" of urban women to rural "tribal" areas. Peterson, *Ethnic Patriotism*, 127–51. In her study of prostitution in colonial Nairobi, Luise White seems to concede that prostitution did not exist in Kenya prior to colonization, at least to the extent that she strongly associates prostitution with the emergence of a capitalist economy. However, she also notes that colonial officials viewed prostitution as a "service" that must be provided to keep Kenya's (male) migrant laborers happy, and thus officials approved of prostitution in the 1920s on the basis that it was "essential to the smooth running of a migrant labor economy." White, *The Comforts of Home*, 76.

82 Rutherford, *A History*, 37.

83 Many documents marked "confidential" appear in the private papers of settlers or settler organizations. Susan Carruthers explains that during the Emergency, "Access to secret material was used as a reward for editorial good behavior [on the part of newspaper editors], and for some time before the publication of the White Paper selected editors had been privy to confidential material on Mau Mau oaths." Carruthers, *Winning Hearts and Minds*, 160. Once the government's White Paper on Mau Mau (the Corfield Report) was published, the "confidential" details of the oaths

were available to the public at large, and disseminated enthusiastically by media outlets. In 1960, for example, the very popular US publication *Time* magazine published an expose (loosely based on the White Paper) titled "The Oath Takers," which reproduced the most graphic accusations regarding Mau Mau oaths—including the infamous "Kaberichia cocktail." "Kenya: The Oath Takers," *Time*, June 13, 1960.

84 RH: MSS Afr. s. 596 [Elector's Union]. Box 38A, File 1: "Mau Mau Oaths."

85 Leakey did not, however, believe that the oaths were entirely new: rather, he noted a "remarkable similarity" between the old KCA oath and the Mau Mau oath. This was further evidence of the atypical nature of the oaths, since to Leakey the KCA represented the younger generation grabbing power from the elders in whom power was legitimately vested. Leakey, *Mau Mau and the Kikuyu*, 99, 96.

86 Leakey, *Mau Mau and the Kikuyu*, 84.

87 Leakey, *Mau Mau and the Kikuyu*, 86.

88 Leakey, *Mau Mau and the Kikuyu*, 99. David Anderson's claim that Leakey "never laid stress on bestiality or perversion" is thus somewhat overstated. Anderson, *Histories of the Hanged*, 283.

89 Edgerton, *Mau Mau*, 135.

90 Lonsdale, "Constructing Mau Mau," 243.

91 British Library [BL]: Cup. 363 ff7: *Candour*, supplement, July 22, 1960 (Surrey, UK: Candour Publishing Company).

92 Hewitt, *Kenya Cowboy*, 176.

93 Susan Carruthers has also observed that during the Emergency, "There was also something of a 'black market' in Mau Mau atrocity photographs"—indicating that the pornographic consumption of anti–Mau Mau propaganda extended beyond the genre of the literary to the visual. Carruthers, *Winning Hearts and Minds*, 168.

94 Carruthers, *Winning Hearts and Minds*, 142.

95 White, "Separating the Men," 25.

96 White, "Separating the Men," 23.

97 Elkins, *Imperial Reckoning*, 235. A similar strategy, known as "resettlement," was used in Malaysia during the 1950s. See Stubbs, *Hearts and Minds*, 100–107.

98 Carothers, *The Psychology of Mau Mau*, 22.

99 Carothers, *The Psychology of Mau Mau*, 22–23.

100 Carothers, *The Psychology of Mau Mau*, 25.

101 Leakey, *Mau Mau and the Kikuyu*, 107–14.

102 Leakey, *Mau Mau and the Kikuyu*, 111–12.

103 Interestingly, Leakey also proposed that single Gikuyu women living in urban spaces be trained as domestic workers—this would prevent them from "wander[ing] about aimlessly, get[ting] into trouble and hav[ing] illegitimate babies long before they marry." It would also discourage them

from joining Mau Mau as a way of alleviating "sheer boredom at having nothing to do all day." Ironically, given his concerns about the threat of detribalization, in this case Leakey saw the space of the European household as a useful tool for reinstating Gikuyu cultural norms. Leakey, *Defeating Mau Mau*, 145.

104 Lonsdale has argued that scholars have misinterpreted Carothers, forgetting that he ended his proposals with "a call for planned modernisation." "The forgotten part of Carothers' report on Mau Mau psychology," he maintains, "argued that it was futile to remake Kikuyu in the individualist English image unless they were given the chance to exercise responsibility, which meant power. Rehabilitation would be complete only with democracy." Lonsdale, "Constructing Mau Mau," 255.

105 Anderson, *Histories of the Hanged*, 294.

106 Berman, *Control and Crisis*, 366.

107 Elkins, *Imperial Reckoning*, 240.

Conclusion

1 David Smith, "Barack Obama Tells African States to Abandon Anti-Gay Discrimination," *The Observer*, July 25, 2015, sec. US news, https://www .theguardian.com/us-news/2015/jul/25/barack-obama-african-states -abandon-anti-gay-discrimination.

2 Kristen Holmes Scott Eugene, "Obama Lectures Kenyan President on Gay Rights | CNN Politics," CNN, July 25, 2015, https://www.cnn.com /2015/07/25/politics/obama-kenya-kenyatta/index.html.

3 Roscoe and Murray, *Boy-Wives and Female Husbands*; Morgan and Wieringa, *Tommy Boys*.

4 Rao, *Out of Time*, 19.

5 Epprecht, *Heterosexual Africa?*

6 Macharia, "African Queer Studies."

7 Rao, *Out of Time*, 19.

8 Macharia, "African Queer Studies."

9 Warner, *Trouble with Normal*.

10 Puar, *Terrorist Assemblages*.

11 Miles, *Ties That Bind*; Fuentes, "Power and Historical Figuring"; Hartman, *Lose Your Mother*.

12 Lowe, *Intimacies of Four Continents*, 136.

BIBLIOGRAPHY

Aiyar, Sana. "Anticolonial Homelands across the Indian Ocean: The Politics of the Indian Diaspora in Kenya, ca. 1930–1950." *American Historical Review* 116, no. 4 (October 2011): 987–1013.

Aiyar, Sana. "Empire, Race and the Indians in Colonial Kenya's Contested Public Political Sphere, 1919–1923." *Africa* 81, no. 1 (2011): 132–54.

Aiyar, Sana. *Indians in Kenya: The Politics of Diaspora.* Cambridge, MA: Harvard University Press, 2015.

Allen, Charles. *Tales from the Dark Continent.* London: Futura Publishing, 1981.

Ambler, Charles. *Kenyan Communities in the Age of Imperialism: The Central Region in the Late 19th Century.* New Haven, CT: Yale University Press, 1988.

Anagol-McGinn, Padma. "The Age of Consent Act (1891) Reconsidered: Women's Perspectives and Participation in the Child-Marriage Controversy in India." *South Asia Research* 12, no. 2 (1992): 100–118.

Anderson, David. *Histories of the Hanged: The Dirty War in Kenya and the End of Empire.* New York: W. W. Norton, 2005.

Anderson, David. "Master and Servant in Colonial Kenya, 1895–1939." *Journal of African History* 41, no. 3 (November 2000): 459–85.

Anderson, David. "Mau Mau in the High Court and the 'Lost' British Empire Archives: Colonial Conspiracy or Bureaucratic Bungle?" *Journal of Imperial and Commonwealth History* 39, no. 5 (2011): 699–716.

Anderson, David. "Punishment, Race and 'The Raw Native': Settler Society and Kenya's Flogging Scandals, 1895–1930." *Journal of Southern African Studies* 37, no. 3 (September 2011): 479–97.

Anderson, David. "Sexual Threat and Settler Society: 'Black Perils' in Kenya, c. 1907–30." *Journal of Imperial & Commonwealth History* 38, no. 1 (March 2010): 47–74.

Arondekar, Anjali. *For the Record: On Sexuality and the Colonial Archive in India.* Durham, NC: Duke University Press, 2009.

Arondekar, Anjali. "Queering Archives: A Roundtable Discussion." *Radical History Review* 2015, no. 122 (2015): 211.

Banerjee, Prathama. *Politics of Time: "Primitives" and History-Writing in a Colonial Society.* New Delhi: Oxford University Press, 2006.

Barnett, Don, and Karari Njama. *Mau Mau from Within: Autobiography and Analysis of Kenya's Peasant Revolt.* London: Macgibbon & Kee, 1966.

Bates, Robert. "The Agrarian Origins of Mau Mau: A Structural Account." *Agricultural History* 61, no. 1 (1987): 1.

Bennett, Huw. *Fighting the Mau Mau: The British Army and Counter-Insurgency in the Kenya Emergency*. Cambridge: Cambridge University Press, 2013.

Berger, Mark T. "Imperialism and Sexual Exploitation: A Response to Ronald Hyam's 'Empire and Sexual Opportunity.'" *Journal of Imperial & Commonwealth History* 17, no. 1 (October 1988): 83–89.

Berman, Bruce. *Control and Crisis in Colonial Kenya: The Dialectic of Domination*. Athens: Ohio University Press, 1990.

Berman, Bruce. "Ethnography as Politics, Politics as Ethnography: Kenyatta, Malinowski, and the Making of Facing Mount Kenya." *Canadian Journal of African Studies / La Revue Canadienne Des Études Africaines* 30, no. 3 (January 1, 1996): 313–44.

Berman, Bruce, and John Lonsdale. "Louis Leakey's Mau Mau: A Study in the Politics of Knowledge." *History and Anthropology* 5, no. 2 (1991): 143–204.

Berman, Bruce, and John Lonsdale. *Unhappy Valley: Conflict in Kenya & Africa*. Eastern African Studies. Athens: Ohio University Press, 1992.

Bhana, Surendra. *The Making of a Political Reformer: Gandhi in South Africa, 1893–1914*. New Delhi: Manohar; Distributed in South Asia by Foundation Books, 2005.

Bokkie. *Shambulia: Emergency Humour Souvenir*. Nairobi: English Press Limited, 1955.

Branch, Daniel. *Defeating Mau Mau, Creating Kenya: Counterinsurgency, Civil War, and Decolonization*. Cambridge: Cambridge University Press, 2009.

Brickman, Celia. *Aboriginal Populations in the Mind: Race and Primitivity in Psychoanalysis*. New York: Columbia University Press, 2003.

Brownfoot, Janice. "Memsahibs in Colonial Malaya: A Study of European Wives in a British Colony and Protectorate." In *The Incorporated Wife*, edited by Hilary Callan and Shirley Ardener, 186–210. London: Routledge, Kegan & Paul, 1984.

Burton, Antoinette. "From Child Bride to 'Hindoo Lady': Rukhmabai and the Debate on Sexual Respectability in Imperial Britain." *The American Historical Review* 103, no. 4 (1998): 1119–46.

Campbell, Chloe. "Juvenile Delinquency in Colonial Kenya, 1900–1939." *The Historical Journal* 45, no. 1 (2002): 129–51.

Campbell, Chloe. *Race and Empire: Eugenics in Colonial Kenya*. Studies in Imperialism. Manchester, UK: Manchester University Press, 2007.

Carotenuto, Matthew. "Repatriation in Colonial Kenya: African Institutions and Gendered Violence." *International Journal of African Historical Studies* 45, no. 1 (February 2012): 9–28.

Carothers, John Colin. *The African Mind in Health and Disease*. World Health Organization Monograph Series no. 17. Geneva: World Health Organization, 1953.

Carothers, John Colin. *The Psychology of Mau Mau*. Nairobi: Government Printer, 1954.

Carothers, John Colin. "A Study of Mental Derangement in Africans, and an Attempt to Explain Its Peculiarities, More Especially in Relation to the African Attitude to Life." *Journal of Mental Science* 93, no. 392 (July 1947): 548–97.

Carruthers, Susan L. *Winning Hearts and Minds: British Governments, the Media, and Colonial Counter-Insurgency, 1944–1960*. London: Leicester University Press, 1995.

Cloete, Stuart. *Storm Over Africa: A Study of the Mau Mau Rebellion, Its Causes, Effects and Implications in Africa South of the Sahara*. Cape Town: Culemborg Publishers, 1956.

Cohen, Cathy J. "Punks, Bulldaggers, and Welfare Queens: The Radical Potential of Queer Politics?" *GLQ: A Journal of Lesbian and Gay Studies* 3, no. 4 (May 1, 1997): 437–65.

Corfield, F. D. *The Origins and Growth of Mau Mau: An Historical Survey*. Cmd. 1030 and Kenya Sessional Paper no. 5. 1959–1960.

The Cyclopedia of India: Biographical, Historical, Administrative, Commercial. Cyclopedia Publishing Company, 1907.

Danzig, Richard. "The Announcement of August 20th, 1917." *Journal of Asian Studies* 28, no. 1 (1968): 19–37.

Davin, Anna. "Imperialism and Motherhood." *History Workshop*, no. 5 (1978): 9–65.

Davison, Jean. *Voices from Mutira: Change in the Lives of Rural Gikuyu Women, 1910–1995*. Boulder, CO: Rienner, 1996.

Delap, Lucy. *Knowing Their Place: Domestic Service in Twentieth-Century Britain*. Oxford: Oxford University Press, 2011.

Dinesen, Isak. *Out of Africa*. New York: Modern Library, 1937.

Dorr, Lisa Lindquist. *White Women, Rape, and the Power of Race in Virginia, 1900–1960*. Chapel Hill: University of North Carolina Press, 2004.

Duder, C. J. D. "'Men of the Officer Class': The Participants in the 1919 Soldier Settlement Scheme in Kenya." *African Affairs* 92, no. 366 (January 1, 1993): 69–87.

Duder, C. J. D. "The Settler Response to the Indian Crisis of 1923 in Kenya: Brigadier General Philip Wheatley and 'Direct Action.'" *Journal of Imperial & Commonwealth History* XVII, no. 3 (May 1989): 349–73.

Duder, C. J. D., and C. P. Youé. "Paice's Place: Race and Politics in Nanyuki District, Kenya, in the 1920s." *African Affairs* 93, no. 371 (April 1, 1994): 253–78.

Dussart, Fae. "'To Glut a Menial's Grudge': Domestic Servants and the Ilbert Bill Controversy of 1883." *Journal of Colonialism and Colonial History* 14, no. 1 (2013): n.p.

Edgerton, Robert. *Mau Mau: An African Crucible*. New York: Free Press, 1989.

Elkins, Caroline. *Imperial Reckoning: The Untold Story of Britain's Gulag in Kenya*. New York: Henry Holt, 2005.

Epprecht, Marc. *Heterosexual Africa? The History of an Idea from the Age of Exploration to the Age of AIDS*. Athens: Ohio University Press, 2008.

Etherington, Norman. "Natal's Black Rape Scare of the 1870s." *Journal of Southern African Studies* 15, no. 1 (1988): 36–53.

Feimster, Crystal Nicole. *Southern Horrors: Women and the Politics of Rape and Lynching*. Cambridge, MA: Harvard University Press, 2009.

Foucault, Michel. "The Lives of Infamous Men." In *Power, Truth, Strategy*, edited by Meaghan Morris and Paul Patton, 76–91. Sydney: Prometheus Books, 1979.

Frederiksen, Bodil Folke. "Jomo Kenyatta, Marie Bonaparte and Bronislaw Malinowski on Clitoridectomy and Female Sexuality." *History Workshop Journal* 65, no. 1 (2008): 23–48.

Frederiksen, Bodil Folke. "Print, Newspapers and Audiences in Colonial Kenya: African and Indian Improvement, Protest and Connections." *Africa* 81, no. 1 (2011): 155–72.

Freud, Sigmund. "'Civilized' Sexual Morality and Modern Nervous Illness." In *Collected Works of Sigmund Freud*, vol. 9, 181–204. Charleston, SC: BiblioBazaar, 2007.

Fuentes, Marisa J. "Power and Historical Figuring: Rachael Pringle Polgreen's Troubled Archive." *Gender & History* 22, no. 3 (2010): 564–84.

Fussell, Paul. *The Great War and Modern Memory*. New York: Oxford University Press, 2000.

Gartrell, Beverley. "Colonial Wives: Villains or Victims?" In *The Incorporated Wife*, edited by Hilary Callan and Shirley Ardener, 165–85. London: Croom Helm, 1984.

Ghai, Yash P., and Patrick McAuslan. *Public Law and Political Change in Kenya: A Study of the Legal Framework of Government from Colonial Times to the Present*. Nairobi: Oxford University Press, 1970.

Ghose, Indira. "The Memsahib Myth: Englishwomen in Colonial India." In *Women & Others: Perspectives on Race, Gender, and Empire*, edited by Celia R. Daileader, Rhoda Barge Johnson, and Amilcar Shabazz, 107–28. New York: Palgrave Macmillan, 2007.

Gikandi, Simon. "Pan-Africanism and Cosmopolitanism: The Case of Jomo Kenyatta." *English Studies in Africa* 43, no. 1 (2000): 3–27.

Greene, Graham. *Ways of Escape*. New York: Simon & Schuster, 1980.

Gregory, Robert G. *India and East Africa: A History of Race Relations within the British Empire, 1890–1939*. Oxford: Clarendon Press, 1971.

Gregory, Robert G. *Quest for Equality: Asian Politics in East Africa, 1900–1967*. Orient Blackswan, 1993.

Gregory, Robert G. *Sidney Webb and East Africa: Labour's Experiment with the Doctrine of Native Paramountcy*. Berkeley: University of California Press, 1962.

Grogan, Ewart Scott. *From the Cape to Cairo: The First Traverse of Africa from South to North*. New and rev. ed. London: Hurst & Blackett, 1902.

Guha, Ramachandra. *Gandhi before India*. New York: Alfred A. Knopf, 2014.

Gupta, Desh. "South Asians in East Africa: Achievement and Discrimination." *South Asia: Journal of South Asian Studies* 21, no. 1 (1998): 103–36.

Hartman, Saidiya. *Lose Your Mother: A Journey along the Atlantic Slave Route*. New York: Farrar, Straus and Giroux, 2007.

Hasian, Marouf. "The Deployment of Ethnographic Sciences and Psychological Warfare during the Suppression of the Mau Mau Rebellion." *Journal of Medical Humanities* 34, no. 3 (2013): 329–45.

Haskins, Victoria K., and Claire Lowrie, eds. *Colonization and Domestic Service: Historical and Contemporary Perspectives.* New York: Routledge, 2015.

Hewitt, Peter. *Kenya Cowboy: A Police Officer's Account of the Mau Mau Emergency in Kenya.* London: Avon Books, 1999.

Hoad, Neville. *African Intimacies: Race, Homosexuality, and Globalization.* Minneapolis: University of Minnesota Press, 2007.

Hoad, Neville. "Arrested Development or the Queerness of Savages: Resisting Evolutionary Narratives of Difference." *Postcolonial Studies: Culture, Politics, Economy* 3, no. 2 (2000): 133–58.

Hodgen, Margaret T. "The Doctrine of Survivals: The History of an Idea." *American Anthropologist* 33, no. 3 (July 9, 1931): 307–24.

Hodgson, Dorothy Louise. *Once Intrepid Warriors: Gender, Ethnicity, and the Cultural Politics of Maasai Development.* Bloomington: Indiana University Press, 2001.

Holman, Dennis, and David Drummond. *Bwana Drum.* London: W. H. Allen, 1964.

hooks, bell. *Black Looks: Race and Representation.* New York: Routledge, 2014.

Huxley, Elspeth. *Red Strangers.* London: Penguin Books, 2006.

Hyam, Ronald. "Concubinage and the Colonial Service: The Crewe Circular (1909)." *Journal of Imperial & Commonwealth History* 14, no. 3 (May 1986): 170–86.

Hyam, Ronald. *Empire and Sexuality: The British Experience.* Manchester: Manchester University Press, 1990.

Hyam, Ronald. "Empire and Sexual Opportunity." *Journal of Imperial & Commonwealth History* 14, no. 2 (January 1986): 34–90.

Hyam, Ronald. "'Imperialism and Sexual Exploitation': A Reply." *Journal of Imperial & Commonwealth History* 17, no. 1 (October 1988): 90–98.

Hyslop, Jonathan. "White Working-Class Women and the Invention of Apartheid: 'Purified' Afrikaner Nationalist Agitation for Legislation Against 'Mixed' Marriages, 1934–9." *Journal of African History* 36, no. 1 (1995): 57–81.

Itote, Waruhiu. *Mau Mau in Action.* Nairobi: Transafrica Book Distributors, 1979.

Jackson, Will. "Bad Blood: Poverty, Psychopathy and the Politics of Transgression in Kenya Colony, 1939–59." *Journal of Imperial & Commonwealth History* 39, no. 1 (2011): 73–94.

Jackson, Will. "Dangers to the Colony: Loose Women and the 'Poor White' Problem in Kenya." *Journal of Colonialism and Colonial History* 14, no. 2 (Summer 2013). https://doi.org/10.1353/cch.2013.0029.

Jackson, Will. *Madness and Marginality: The Lives of Kenya's White Insane.* Manchester: Manchester University Press, 2013.

Jackson, Zakiyyah Iman. *Becoming Human: Matter and Meaning in an Antiblack World.* New York: New York University Press, 2020.

Jeater, Diana. *Marriage, Perversion, and Power: The Construction of Moral Discourse in Southern Rhodesia, 1894–1930*. Oxford: Clarendon Press, 1993.

Kanogo, Tabitha. *African Womanhood in Colonial Kenya, 1900–50*. Oxford: James Currey, 2005.

Kanogo, Tabitha M. *Squatters and the Roots of Mau Mau, 1905–63*. London: James Currey, 1987.

Kariuki, Josiah Mwangi. *"Mau Mau" Detainee: The Account by a Kenya African of His Experiences in Detention Camps, 1953–1960*. Nairobi: Oxford University Press, 1963.

Kennedy, Dane. *Islands of White: Settler Society and Culture in Kenya and Southern Rhodesia, 1890–1939*. Durham, NC: Duke University Press, 1987.

Kenyatta, Jomo. *Facing Mount Kenya: The Tribal Life of the Gikuyu*. New York: Vintage Books, 1965.

Kinyatti, Maina wa. "Mau Mau: The Peak of African Political Organization in Colonial Kenya." *Kenya Historical Review* 5, no. 3 (1977): 287–311.

Koster, Mickie Mwanzia. "Mau Mau Inventions and Reinventions." In *Contemporary Africa: Challenges and Opportunities*, edited by Toyin Falola and Emmanuel M. Mbah, 23–45. New York: Palgrave MacMillan, 2014.

Kuczynski, R. R. *Demographic Survey of the British Colonial Empire*. Vol. 2. London: Oxford University Press, 1949.

Kuklick, Henrika. *The Savage Within: The Social History of British Anthropology, 1885–1945*. Cambridge: Cambridge University Press, 1991.

Lavers, Anthony. *The Kikuyu Who Fight Mau Mau: The Thrilling Story of the Kikuyu Home Guard Told in English and Swahili*. Nairobi: The Eagle Press, 1955.

Leakey, Louis. *Defeating Mau Mau*. London: Methuen, 1954.

Leakey, Louis. *Mau Mau and the Kikuyu*. London: Methuen, 1952.

Leakey, Louis. *White African*. London: Hodder and Stoughton, 1937.

Leopold, Joan. "British Applications of the Aryan Theory of Race to India, 1850–1870." *The English Historical Review* 89, no. 352 (1974): 578–603.

Lessing, Doris. *The Grass Is Singing*. London: MJoseph, 1950.

Leys, Norman. *Kenya*. London: Published by Leonard & Virginia Woolf at the Hogarth Press, 1926.

Lonsdale, John. "Constructing Mau Mau." *Transactions of the Royal Historical Society* 40 (1990): 239–60.

Lonsdale, John. "The History of Swahili." *Journal of African History* 11, no. 3 (January 1, 1970): 452–53.

Lonsdale, John. "Kenya: Home Country and African Frontier." In *Settlers and Expatriates: Britons over the Seas*, edited by Robert A. Bickers, 74–111. Oxford: Oxford University Press, 2010.

Lonsdale, John. "When Did the Gusii (or Any Other Group) Become a Tribe?" *Kenya Historical Review* 5, no. 1 (1977): 123–35.

Lonsdale, John, and Bruce Berman. "Coping with the Contradictions: The Development of the Colonial State in Kenya, 1895–1914." *Journal of African History* 20, no. 4 (1979): 487–505.

Lorcin, Patricia M. E. *Historicizing Colonial Nostalgia: European Women's Narratives of Algeria and Kenya 1900–Present*. New York: Palgrave Macmillan, 2012.

Lowe, Lisa. *The Intimacies of Four Continents*. Durham, NC: Duke University Press Books, 2015.

Lowrie, Claire. "White Mistresses and Chinese 'Houseboys': Domestic Politics in Singapore and Darwin from the 1910s to the 1930s." In *Colonization and Domestic Service: Historical and Contemporary Perspectives*, edited by Victoria K. Haskins and Claire Lowrie, 210–34. New York: Routledge, Taylor & Francis Group, 2015.

Luongo, Katherine. *Witchcraft and Colonial Rule in Kenya, 1900–1955*. Cambridge: Cambridge University Press, 2011.

Lyons, Andrew, and Harriet Lyons. *Irregular Connections: A History of Anthropology and Sexuality*. Lincoln: University of Nebraska Press, 2004.

Macharia, Keguro. "African Queer Studies." *Gukira* (blog), 2014. https://gukira .wordpress.com/2014/08/24/african-queer-studies/.

Macharia, Keguro. *Frottage: Frictions of Intimacy across the Black Diaspora*. New York: New York University Press, 2019.

Macharia, Keguro. "Queer Natives." PhD diss., University of Illinois at Urbana-Champaign, 2008.

Mackenzie, Fiona. "Political Economy of the Environment, Gender, and Resistance under Colonialism: Murang'a District, Kenya, 1910–1950." *Canadian Journal of African Studies/La Revue Canadienne Des Études Africaines* 25, no. 2 (1991): 226–56.

Mamdani, Mahmood. *Citizen and Subject: Contemporary Africa and the Legacy of Late Colonialism*. Princeton, NJ: Princeton University Press, 1996.

Martens, Jeremy C. "Settler Homes, Manhood and 'Houseboys': An Analysis of Natal's Rape Scare of 1886." *Journal of Southern African Studies* 28, no. 2 (June 1, 2002): 379–400.

McCulloch, Jock. *Black Peril, White Virtue: Sexual Crime in Southern Rhodesia, 1902–1935*. Bloomington: Indiana University Press, 2000.

McCulloch, Jock. *Colonial Psychiatry and "The African Mind."* Cambridge: Cambridge University Press, 1995.

Meredith, Martin. *Born in Africa: The Quest for the Origins of Human Life*. New York: PublicAffairs, 2011.

Miles, Tiya. *Ties That Bind: The Story of an Afro-Cherokee Family in Slavery and Freedom*. Berkeley: University of California Press, 2005.

Morgan, Ruth, and Saskia Wieringa. *Tommy Boys, Lesbian Men, and Ancestral Wives: Female Same-Sex Practices in Africa*. Johannesburg: Jacana Media, 2006.

Morgensen, Scott Lauria. "Settler Homonationalism: Theorizing Settler Colonialism within Queer Modernities." *GLQ* 16, no. 1/2 (2010): 105–31.

Morgensen, Scott Lauria. *Spaces between Us: Queer Settler Colonialism and Indigenous Decolonization*. Minneapolis: University of Minnesota Press, 2011.

Morgensen, Scott Lauria. "Theorising Gender, Sexuality and Settler Colonialism: An Introduction." *Settler Colonial Studies* 2, no. 2 (January 1, 2012): 2–22.

Mwangi, Wambui. "Of Coins and Conquest: The East African Currency Board, the Rupee Crisis, and the Problem of Colonialism in the East African Protectorate." *Comparative Studies in Society and History* 43, no. 04 (October 2001): 763–87.

Mwangi, Wambui. "The Order of Money: Colonialism and the East African Currency Board." PhD diss., University of Pennsylvania, 2003.

Nicholls, Christine Stephanie. *Red Strangers: The White Tribe of Kenya*. London: Timewell Press, 2005.

Ocobock, Paul. *An Uncertain Age: The Politics of Manhood in Kenya*. Athens: Ohio University Press, 2017.

Ogot, Bethwell A., and William Robert Ochieng'. *Decolonization & Independence in Kenya, 1940–93*. Athens: Ohio University Press, 1995.

Oyono, Ferdinand. *Houseboy*. London: Heinemann, 1966.

Paxman, Jeremy. *Empire: What Ruling the World Did to the British*. London: Penguin, 2012.

Perham, Margery. *Native Administration in Nigeria*. London: Oxford University Press, 1937.

Perham, Margery. "A Re-Statement of Indirect Rule." *Africa* 7, no. 3 (1934): 321.

Perham, Margery. "Supplement: Some Problems of Indirect Rule in Africa." *Journal of the Royal African Society* 34, no. 135 (1935): 1–23.

Peterson, Derek R. *Creative Writing: Translation, Bookkeeping, and the Work of Imagination in Colonial Kenya*. Portsmouth, NH: Heinemann, 2004.

Peterson, Derek R. *Ethnic Patriotism and the East African Revival: A History of Dissent, c. 1935–1972*. New York: Cambridge University Press, 2012.

Pick, Daniel. *Faces of Degeneration: A European Disorder, c.1848–c.1918*. Cambridge: Cambridge University Press, 1989.

Presley, Cora Ann. *Kikuyu Women, the Mau Mau Rebellion, and Social Change in Kenya*. Boulder, CO: Westview Press, 1992.

Puar, Jasbir K. *Terrorist Assemblages: Homonationalism in Queer Times*. Durham, NC: Duke University Press, 2007.

Radway, Janice A. *Reading the Romance: Women, Patriarchy, and Popular Literature*. Chapel Hill: University of North Carolina Press, 1991.

Rao, Rahul. *Out of Time: The Queer Politics of Postcoloniality*. New York: Oxford University Press, 2020.

Ray, Carina E. *Crossing the Color Line: Race, Sex, and the Contested Politics of Colonialism in Ghana*. Athens: Ohio University Press, 2015.

Ray, Carina E. "Decrying White Peril: Interracial Sex and the Rise of Anticolonial Nationalism in the Gold Coast." *American Historical Review* 119, no. 1 (February 2014): 78–110.

Ray, Carina E. "Interracial Sex and the Making of Empire," In *A Companion to Diaspora and Transnationalism*, edited by Ato Quayson and Girish Daswani, 190–211. Chichester, UK: John Wiley & Sons, 2013.

Regis, Pamela. *A Natural History of the Romance Novel*. Philadelphia: University of Pennsylvania Press, 2003.

Rifkin, Mark. *Settler Common Sense: Queerness and Everyday Colonialism in the American Renaissance*. Minneapolis: University of Minnesota Press, 2014.

Rosberg, Carl Gustav, and John Cato Nottingham. *The Myth of "Mau Mau": Nationalism in Kenya*. Stanford, CA: Hoover Institution Press, Stanford University, 1975.

Roscoe, Will, and Stephen O. Murray. *Boy-Wives and Female Husbands: Studies of African Homosexualities*. New York: Palgrave Macmillan, 2001.

Routledge, W. Scoresby, and Katherine Pease Routledge. *With a Prehistoric People: The Akikuyu of British East Africa*. London: Edward Arnold, 1910.

Rubin, Gayle. "Thinking Sex: Notes for a Radical Theory of the Politics of Sexuality." In *Deviations: A Gayle Rubin Reader*. Durham, NC: Duke University Press, 2011.

Rutherford, J. A. *A History of the Kikuyu Guard*. Edited by David Lovatt Smith. Brighton, UK: D. Lovatt Smith, 2003.

Sarkar, Tanika. "A Prehistory of Rights: The Age of Consent Debate in Colonial Bengal." *Feminist Studies* 26, no. 3 (2000): 601–22.

Sarkar, Tanika. "Rhetoric against Age of Consent: Resisting Colonial Reason and Death of a Child-Wife." *Economic and Political Weekly* 28, no. 36 (1993): 1869–78.

Seligman, Charles Gabriel. *Races of Africa*. London: T. Butterworth, 1930.

Shadle, Brett. "African Court Elders in Nyanza Province, Kenya, ca. 1930–1960: From 'Traditional' to 'Modern.'" In *Intermediaries, Interpreters, and Clerks: African Employees in the Making of Colonial Africa*, edited by Benjamin N. Lawrance, Emily Lynn Osborn, and Richard L. Roberts, 180–201. Madison: University of Wisconsin Press, 2006.

Shadle, Brett. "Bridewealth and Female Consent: Marriage Disputes in African Courts, Gusiiland, Kenya." *Journal of African History* 44, no. 02 (2003): 241–62.

Shadle, Brett. "Debating 'Early Marriage' in Colonial Kenya, 1920–50." In *Marriage by Force? Contestation Over Consent and Coercion in Africa*, edited by Annie Bunting, Benjamin Nicholas Lawrance, and Richard L. Roberts, 89–108. Athens: Ohio University Press, 2016.

Shadle, Brett. *"Girl Cases": Marriage and Colonialism in Gusiiland, Kenya, 1890–1970*. Portsmouth, NH: Heinemann, 2006.

Shadle, Brett. "Rape in the Courts of Gusiiland, Kenya, 1940s–1960s." *African Studies Review* 51, no. 2 (September 1, 2008): 27–50.

Shadle, Brett. *The Souls of White Folk: White Settlers in Kenya, 1900s–1920s*. Manchester: Manchester University Press, 2015.

Shaw, Carolyn Martin. *Colonial Inscriptions Race, Sex, and Class in Kenya*. Minneapolis: University of Minnesota Press, 1995.

Sinha, Mrinalini. "'Chathams, Pitts, And Gladstones in Petticoats': The Politics of Gender and Race in the Ilbert Bill Controversy, 1883–1884." In *Western Women and Imperialism: Complicity and Resistance*, edited by Nupur Chaudhuri and Margaret Strobel, 98–116. Bloomington: Indiana University Press, 1992.

Sinha, Mrinalini. *Colonial Masculinity: The "Manly Englishman" and the "Effeminate Bengali" in the Late Nineteenth Century*. Manchester: Manchester University Press, 1995.

Sinha, Mrinalini. *Specters of Mother India: The Global Restructuring of an Empire*. Durham, NC: Duke University Press, 2006.

Sorrenson, M. P. K. *Origins of European Settlement in Kenya*. Nairobi: Oxford University Press, 1968.

Spillers, Hortense J. "Mama's Baby, Papa's Maybe: An American Grammar Book." *Diacritics* 17, no. 2 (1987): 64–81.

Steinem, Gloria. "If Men Could Menstruate." *Women's Reproductive Health* 6, no. 3 (July 3, 2019): 151–52.

Stocking, George W. *After Tylor: British Social Anthropology, 1888–1951*. Madison: University of Wisconsin Press, 1995.

Stoler, Ann Laura. *Along the Archival Grain: Epistemic Anxieties and Colonial Common Sense*. Princeton, NJ: Princeton University Press, 2009.

Stoler, Ann Laura. *Carnal Knowledge and Imperial Power: Race and the Intimate in Colonial Rule*. Berkeley: University of California Press, 2002.

Stoler, Ann Laura. "Making Empire Respectable: The Politics of Race and Sexual Morality in 20th-Century Colonial Cultures." *American Ethnologist* 16, no. 4 (November 1, 1989): 634–60.

Stoler, Ann Laura. *Race and the Education of Desire: Foucault's History of Sexuality and the Colonial Order of Things*. Durham, NC: Duke University Press, 1995.

Stoler, Ann Laura. "Sexual Affronts and Racial Frontiers: European Identities and the Cultural Politics of Exclusions in Colonial Southeast Asia." *Comparative Studies in Society and History* 34, no. 3 (1992): 514–51.

Stoneham, C. T. *Out of Barbarism*. London: Museum Press, 1955.

Strange, Nora. *The Clinton Heritage*. London: Hurst & Blackett, 1958.

Strange, Nora. *Kenya Calling*, 5th ed. London: Stanley Paul, 1928.

Strange, Nora. *Kenya Dawn*. London: Stanley Paul, 1928.

Strange, Nora. *Kenya Noon*. London: Wright & Brown, 1933.

Strange, Nora. *Kenya Today*. London: Stanley Paul, 1934.

Strange, Nora. *Latticed Windows*. London: Stanley Paul, 1924.

Strange, Nora. *Mistress of Ceremonies*. London: Stanley Paul, 1928.

Strange, Nora. *A Wife in Kenya; a Story of East Africa*. London: Stanley Paul, 1925.

Strobel, Margaret. *European Women and the Second British Empire*. Indiana University Press, 1991.

Stubbs, Richard. *Hearts and Minds in Guerrilla Warfare: The Malayan Emergency, 1948–1960*. New York: Oxford University Press, 1989.

Sutton, John Edward Giles. "Denying History in Colonial Kenya: The Anthropology and Archeology of G.W.B. Huntingford and L.S.B. Leakey." *History in Africa* 33, no. 1 (2006): 287–320.

Tallie, T. J. *Queering Colonial Natal: Indigeneity and the Violence of Belonging in Southern Africa*. Minneapolis: University of Minnesota Press, 2019.

Teo, Hsu-Ming. "Historicizing the Sheik: Comparisons of the British Novel and the American Film." *Journal of Popular Romance Studies*, no. 1.1 (August 2010): n.p.

Thiong'o, Ngũgĩ wa. *Detained: A Writer's Prison Diary*. Nairobi: East African Publishers, 1981.

Thomas, Lynn M. *Politics of the Womb: Women, Reproduction, and the State in Kenya*. Berkeley: University of California Press, 2003.

Throup, David. *Economic & Social Origins of Mau Mau, 1945–53*. London: James Currey, 1988.

Tol, Deanne van. "The Women of Kenya Speak: Imperial Activism and Settler Society, c.1930." *Journal of British Studies* 54, no. 02 (April 2015): 433–56.

Torgovnick, Marianna. *Gone Primitive: Savage Intellects, Modern Lives*. Chicago: University of Chicago Press, 1991.

Tranberg Hansen, Karen. *Distant Companions: Servants and Employers in Zambia, 1900–1985*. Ithaca, NY: Cornell University Press, 1989.

Twaddle, Michael. "Z. K. Sentongo and the Indian Question in East Africa." *History in Africa* 24 (January 1, 1997): 309–36.

Van Onselen, Charles. *Studies in the Social and Economic History of the Witwatersrand, 1886–1914*. New York: Longman, 1982.

Van Tilburg, JoAnne. *Among Stone Giants: The Life of Katherine Routledge and Her Remarkable Expedition to Easter Island*. New York: Scribner, 2003.

Vaughan, Megan. *Curing Their Ills: Colonial Power and African Illness*. Oxford: Polity Press, 2004.

Veracini, Lorenzo. "'Settler Colonialism': Career of a Concept." *Journal of Imperial & Commonwealth History* 41, no. 2 (June 2013): 313–33.

Vint, F. W. "The Brain of the Kenya Native." *Journal of Anatomy* 68 (1934): 216–23.

Voeltz, Richard A. "The British Empire, Sexuality, Feminism and Ronald Hyam." *European Review of History-Revue Europeanne D Histoire* 3, no. 1 (1996): 41–45.

Wallace, Edwin R. *Freud and Anthropology: A History and Reappraisal*. New York: International Universities Press, 1983.

Warner, Michael. *The Trouble with Normal: Sex, Politics, and the Ethics of Queer Life*. New York: Free Press, 1999.

White, Luise. *The Comforts of Home: Prostitution in Colonial Nairobi*. Chicago: University of Chicago Press, 1990.

White, Luise. "Separating the Men from the Boys: Constructions of Gender, Sexuality, and Terrorism in Central Kenya, 1939–1959." *The International Journal of African Historical Studies* 23, no. 1 (1990): 1–25.

Williams, Elizabeth W. "Recipes for Disaster: Cookery Books and the Management of Intimacy in Colonial Kenyan Settler Homes 1919–1944." *Gender & History* 35, no. 2 (2023): 511–27.

Williams, Elizabeth W. "'Stoop Low to Conquer': Race and Sexual Trusteeship in the Kenyan 'Indian Crisis' of 1923." *Journal of Colonialism and Colonial History* 19, no. 3 (2018): n.p.

Wipper, Audrey. "Kikuyu Women and the Harry Thuku Disturbances: Some Uniformities of Female Militancy." *Africa: Journal of the International African Institute* 59, no. 3 (January 1, 1989): 300–337.

Youé, Christopher P. "The Threat of Settler Rebellion and the Imperial Predicament: The Denial of Indian Rights in Kenya, 1923." *Canadian Journal of History* 12, no. 3 (February 1978): 347–60.

INDEX

....

Abraham, Jasper, 128

Achariar, Sitaram, 69, 72, 83–86, 163, 183n5

Adam and Eve analogies, 113, 117, 118, 150, 206n64

administration, colonial, 29; Devonshire Declaration of 1923, 75, 196n104; and import of white women, 45; and interracial rape discourse, 92, 102–3, 108–9, 116; lower levels occupied by Kenyan Indians, 50, 62, 73; women's movement restricted by, 54. *See also* colonialism; Colonial Office (London); Silberrad, Hubert; Silberrad scandal

African Americans, racialization of, 146

African diaspora, 11, 68

Africans, Kenyan: "childlike" nature attributed to, 49, 61, 71, 90–91, 94, 104–5, 110; demands for meaningful representation, 89–90; and ecological disasters, 18, 51; as extension of reparative landscape, 121, 133, 137; feminization of, 71, 82, 87; gaze of, 120, 132–33; morality, sense of, 37–38, 102, 149–50; Native Reserves, segregation on, 18–19; as "not yet ready" for self-rule, 7, 70, 72, 102, 150; as Other, 9, 34, 123; "tribal" populations, segregation into, 18–19; as "uncontaminated," 1–2, 53–54; voices of in Indian Crisis, 87–90, 188n80. *See also* domestic servants, African; Embu, Meru, and Kamba peoples; Gikuyu people; Kipsigis people; Maasai people; Nandi people; primitive normativity; sexuality, African; Somali people; women, African

Ainsworth, John, 20, 52–53, 92, 101, 199n47, 206n64

Aiyar, Sana, 15, 70–71, 74, 82, 88

Amery, Leo, 114

Anderson, David, 208n88; interracial rape, study of, 98, 99; Mau Mau, study of, 140, 142, 144, 147, 154, 161, 203n23, 203n27; on servants' laws, 19–20, 116

anthropology, 21, 25–35, 172n3; amateur, 34; comparative method, 26, 30; functionalist school, 28–29, 36–37; urbanization, views of, 29–30, 123. *See also* evolutionary anthropology

Anti-Slavery and Aboriginal Protection Society (London), 81

Arabs, 5, 18, 73, 133, 135, 184n12

Archer, C. K., 81

archive, 11–14, 50, 56–57, 166; novels as, 119; testimony of colonized women in, 47, 177n34

Arondekar, Anjali, 13–14

Arthur, John W., 79, 89, 115–16

arts, "primitivism" in, 34

Aryan race theory, 78

"backwardness," 11, 25–26, 28, 34, 78, 164–65

Baring, Evelyn, 143

Barth, J. W., 50, 59, 177n36

Berman, Bruce, 36–37, 56, 161–62

biopolitics, colonial, 6–7, 120–22, 137, 161

birth and mortality rates, 104–5, 119

Blackness: negative queering of, 9–10; plasticity of as racial construct, 8, 24

"Black Peril" discourse, 22–23, 46, 85, 93, 131, 189n5; false accusations, 100; Rhodesia, 96, 97, 98–99, 191n32; in United States, 96–97. *See also* rape, interracial

"'Black Peril' in British East Africa. A Frank Talk to Women Settlers, The" (Hinde), 100–101

Blixen, Karen, 128, 199n46, 200n73, 201n87

Boers, migration of, 15, 17, 199n47

Boer War, 15, 123, 196–97n21

"Bokkie" (cartoonist), 151, 152–53, 206n65

Bonaparte, Marie, 33–34, 39

Brickman, Celia, 26, 31–32, 125

bridewealth, 51, 52, 55, 57, 161

British empire: divide and rule policy, 78, 111; historians of sexuality, 46; industrial England, 47; white settlement in Kenya not actively promoted, 123. *See also* colonialism; Colonial Office (London); imperialism; white settlement

Brockway, Fenner, 144

"canker" metaphor, 62–64

Carothers, John Colin (J. C.), 142, 147–50, 204nn42–43, 209n104

Carruthers, Susan, 159–60, 207n83, 208n93

Castle, Barbara, 144, 203n27

"chattel" discourse: agency of African women erased by, 22, 41, 44–45, 49, 54; applied to white women, 86; British officers' "purchase" of women from male guardians, 43–44; colonial interpretations, 52–53; colonial policies enabled by, 55, 56; erasure of girlhood in, 51; and legal policies of colonial government, 54–55; and Mau Mau, 152; and rape, 112–13; "tradition" as central to, 21–22, 43, 50

"chiefs" and "headmen," as colonial construction, 56, 89, 179n65

"childlike" nature attributed to Africans, 49, 61, 71, 90–91; and interracial rape accusations, 94, 104–5, 110

China, General, 143

Churchill, Winston, 184n18

Circumcision Crisis, 147

"civilization": contamination by, 24–25, 71, 99–100, 118, 149–50, 156; degeneration linked with, 6, 11, 26–28, 77–78, 94; detribalization linked with "too-rapid" exposure to, 5, 24–25, 33, 35, 103, 124, 139; deviance linked with, 27–28, 34, 71; homosexuals as uniquely civilized, 32; Indian as more civilized than white, 83–84; "protection" of Africans from, 2, 5, 14, 21, 25–26, 45, 71, 87;

and self-control, 38, 67; sexual development as mirror of, 31; sublimation necessary for in Freud's thought, 32. *See also* progress

"civilizing mission," 25–26, 103, 161; function of domestic service in, 96; in Indian Crisis debates, 76, 79–80, 88; "villagization" as, 161

Clinton Heritage, The (Strange), 135

clitoridectomy, 33–34, 36, 37, 39, 174n66

Cloete, Stuart, 139, 141, 201n1

clothing, 150–51, 205n61, 205n63, 206n64

Cobb, E. Powys, 82, 204n42

Cobb, James, 147

Cohen, Cathy, 9–10

colonialism: biopolitics of, 6–7, 120–22, 137, 161; class discourse, 108; degeneration fears linked to, 123; essentialization of racial difference introduced by, 12–13; Gikuyu disproportionately impacted by, 146, 147; indirect rule, 26, 29, 43, 56, 67; modernization as goal of, 103; panoptic African gaze in service of, 120; queering of, 8; as temporal construct, 3, 5; white belief in benevolence of, 145, 147; white interests prioritized, 14, 18, 20, 25, 54, 70, 114–15, 163. *See also* administration, colonial; British empire; settler colonialism; white supremacy

Colonial Office (London), 14, 17–18, 29; and "Crewe Circular," 46, 60, 175n11, 176n13; and "Indian Crisis," 72, 75; Native Paramountcy policy, 17, 20–21, 75–76; testimony of colonized women in archive, 47, 177n34. *See also* administration, colonial

colonial officials: salary increases suggested, 63–64, 182n107; settlement in Kenya, 16. *See also* Haywood, C. W.; Silberrad, Hubert; Silberrad scandal

Committee to Enquire into the Sociological Causes and Remedies for Mau Mau, 147, 204n37

comparative method, 26, 30

concubinage: African men as "pimps" for colonial officials, 61; as aid to cross-cultural interactions, 45, 46; "canker" metaphor, 62–64; as threat to white prestige, 59. *See also* Silberrad scandal

gendered and racial discourse, malleability of,
8, 24, 80–81, 163, 165

George, Prince of Greece and Denmark, 33

Gikuyu people, 6, 19, 169n6; clitoridectomy
practiced by, 33, 36, 37, 39, 174n66; consent
in Gikuyu society, 57, 179–80n71; as
disproportionately impacted by colonization, 146, 147; education of blamed for
Mau Mau, 147–48; irua (coming of age
and circumcision), 37, 38, 174n66; land
ownership, 37; masculinity, mechanisms for
asserting, 150; nationalism, 25, 35, 54; passive
construction of, 145–47; polygyny practiced
by, 36–37, 40; reproduction as goal of sexual
activity, 38, 40; superior sexuality attributed
to by Kenyatta, 25, 36, 37–38, 163; tensions
among, 143; tri-class reconstruction of
society, 161–62; white settler understanding of, 145–47. See also Africans, Kenyan;
Mau Mau

Grant, Nellie, 107–8

Grass is Singing, The (Lessing), 130

Greene, Graham, 145

Gregory, Robert, 76

Grigg, Edward, 114

Grogan, Ewart, 100, 191n34

Haddon, A. C., 147

Haeckel, Ernst, 30, 31

Hayes Sadler, James, 50, 58, 59–60, 64

Haywood, C. W., 50, 55–56, 58–59

Heterosexual Africa? (Epprecht), 33

Hewitt, Peter, 145, 146, 159

Hinde, Hildegarde, 100–101, 191n37

History of the Kikuyu Guard, A (Rutherford), 156

Hoad, Neville, 10

Hola Massacre of 1959, 144, 203n27

homes, settler, 91, 93; as bastion of British
values, 103; as contact zones, 96; "native
lines," 95; spatial arrangements of farms,
95; and "White Peril" discourse, 103–4.
See also domestic servants, African; domestic sphere; white settlement

homophobia, 10, 174–75n69; as colonial
import, 164–65

homosexuality, 135–36, 174–75n69; and anti-
imperial rhetoric, 164; as colonial import,
10, 136, 156; as un-African, 164

hooks, bell, 153

Hosking, E. B., 5

Houseboy (Oyono), 130

Hull, Edith Maud, 133, 200n64

"Hut Tax," 19, 54, 171nn65–66, 178n57,
201n84

Huxley, Elspeth, 35–36, 107, 142

Hyam, Ronald, 46–47, 48, 58, 176n23

Imperial British East African Company,
14–15

Imperial Indian Citizenship Association, 74

imperialism, 48, 63, 121; domestic sphere's
role in, 94, 96; image of Other used to
legitimize, 34; in India, 77–78; queer
temporality of, 4–5. *See also* British empire;
colonialism

incest, 67, 84, 95, 157

India, 185nn24–25; Aryan race theory applied
to, 78; civilizational claims, 83; construction of sexual immorality by imperialists,
77–78; indentured laborers imported
from, 15, 73, 183n7; noncooperation movement, 74–75; Raj, legitimacy of, 76; and
World War I, 74

Indian Crisis of 1923, 18, 22, 68, 69–91; Achariar's arrest, 85; African-authored sources,
87–88, 188n80; African demands for
meaningful representation, 89–90; deviance
attributed to Kenyan Indian settlers, 22,
69, 71, 77–82, 90–91, 186n46; Devonshire
Declaration, 75; feminization of Africans,
71, 82, 87; gendered and sexual dimensions
of, 70–71, 77, 83–87; hartal strike action, 85;
Native Paramountcy policy, 17, 20–21,
75–76; rebellion threatened by white
settlers, 18, 75–76, 185n28; sexual deviance
attributed to white women by Kenyan
Indians, 22, 69, 84–88; "trusteeship" of
African sexuality, 22, 70–72, 77, 79–80,
82–83, 87, 90–91; white women's prestige as
threatened, 84–86

35–41; education of, 36, 173–74n48; *Facing Mount Kenya,* 36, 37, 41, 173n39; functionalist anthropology used by, 36–37; masturbation, explanation of, 38–39, 174n64; and Mau Mau rebellion, 144; *Muigwithania* paper, 36, 86; polygyny, defense of, 36–37, 40; on prostitution, 40, 54; superior sexuality attributed to Gikuyu people by, 25, 36, 37–38, 163

Kenyatta, Uhuru, 164

Kikuyu. *See* Gikuyu people

Kikuyu Central Association, 36, 149

Kikuyu Guard, 152, 156

"Kikuyu Tribe and Mau Mau, The" (Elector's Union paper), 150, 151

Kings African Rifles, 75

kipande pass laws, 5, 20

Kipsigis people, 19

Kubai, Fred, 143

Kuklick, Henrika, 27, 29

labor: involuntary servitude, elements of, 19–20; Kaffir farming, 19; laborers imported from India, 15, 73, 183n7; Masters and Servants ordinances, 19–20; preservation of Indigenous populations for, 7, 8; "squatted," 19, 73, 122, 171n62, 171n68, 184n14; waged, forcing of African men into, 20, 54

Lamark, Jean-Baptiste, 30, 31

land ownership: African claims to nullified, 121; appropriation of African lands, 18–19, 73–74; Crown Lands Ordinance of 1903, 18, 73; Crown Lands Ordinance of 1915, 19; gendered and sexual valences, 122–23; Gikuyu, 37; sharecropping ("Kaffir farming"), 19; "squatted labor," 19, 73, 122, 171n62, 171n68, 184n14; "White Highlands," 19, 73–74, 171n59, 184n15

landscape: as agential character, 122; Kenya as "eugenic landscape," 119, 127, 133–34, 163; noble, 146. *See also* reparative landscape

Lari massacre of 1953, 143

Latticed Windows (Strange), 126–27, 128, 199n37

Lavers, Anthony, 152–53

Leakey, Louis, 125, 174n64, 204n37, 204n39, 208n88, 208–9n103; as "expert" on African mind, 142, 147–50; preoccupation with oathings, 157, 208n85; primitive normativity embraced by, 147–48; publications, 147, 149; solutions to Mau Mau proposed by, 161, 208–9n103; stages of development used by, 204–5n53

Legislative Council (LegCo), 18, 73, 74, 79; debate on interracial rape, 112, 115; Devonshire Declaration of 1923, 75, 196n104

Lessing, Doris, 130

Leys, Norman, 67

Livingstone, David, 62–63

Lizo wa Ndegwa (Gikuyu "headman"), 55–57

Lonsdale, John, 14, 36, 56, 146, 158, 196n2, 209n104

Lowe, Lisa, 166–67

Lowrie, Claire, 96

Loyalist Guards, 162

Luongo, Katherine, 34, 140

Lyons, Andrew, 27, 28

Lyons, Harriet, 27, 28

Maasai people, 57–58, 145, 146, 200–201n78, 203n34

Macharia, Keguro, 5, 9, 10, 11, 21, 38, 165

Malaya, 47

Malinowski, Bronisław, 28–29, 33, 35–37, 173–74n48

Marett, R. R., 29

marriage: bridewealth, 51, 52, 55, 57, 161; colonial view of wives as property, 54–55; detribalization linked to decline in, 149; disrupted by ecological and economic changes, 51–52; pawnship arrangements, 52, 55–56

Masters and Servants ordinances, 19–20

masturbation, 38–39, 174n64

Matenjagwo, General, 156

Mathari Mental Hospital, 147, 204nn42–43

Mau Mau, 6, 13, 139–62, 169n6, 202n18, 203n31; background, 142–44; cannibalism attributed to, 1, 156, 158, 159; cartoons of, 151, 152–53; Corfield Report, 35, 142, 202n6; degeneration linked with, 141,

Native Reserves, 18–19, 21, 35, 70, 73; Manifesto circulated to, 108–9; overcrowding in, 161

neurosis, sexual, 31–33, 119, 123–24, 137, 140; as impossible for Africans, 2, 25; Mau Mau accused of, 140; neurotics = children = primitives analogy, 31–32

Nguni peoples (South Africa), 8

ngweko (ombani na ngweko, platonic love and fondling), 37–39, 174n58

noblesse oblige references, 61

normativity: deviance produced in relation to, 2–3; as opposite of queerness, 9; and power, 10. See also primitive normativity

Northey, Edward, 16

novels: and Mau Mau discourse, 150. See also romance novel genre; Strange's novels

Nyakayena (Maasai girl), 50, 55, 57–59, 67, 177n34

Nyambura (Gikuyu girl), 50, 55, 58–59, 67, 177n34

Nyeri District Council, 109

oathing rituals. See Mau Mau oathing rituals, white mythologies of

Obama, Barack, 163–64

Oldham, J. H., 29

oral fixation, 31–32

orgasm, "mature" vaginal, 33, 39

"Oriental despot," figure of, 63, 82

Other: consumption of racialized difference, 153–54; eroticization of racial, 153; produced by degeneration discourse, 123; used to legitimize slave trade, 34

Out of Africa (Blixen), 128, 199n46

Outpost Wooing, An (Strange), 118

Oyono, Ferdinand, 130

panoptic disciplinarity, 120, 132–34

paternalism, 5, 18, 88

pawnship arrangements, 52, 55–56

Pease, Joseph, 60, 181n88

Pease family, 60

Perham, Margery, 35–36

"periodicity," hypothesis of, 172n12

Pick, Daniel, 29–30, 123

polygamy, 80

polygyny, 36–37, 40, 63

"poor whites," 7, 63, 131–32, 170n51, 207n81; as cause of contamination, 105–6; discouraged from settlement, 16–17, 94, 106, 108; "Distressed British Subjects" deported, 17, 108, 199–200n54; eugenics thinking applied to, 107–8, 116; as likely to engage in interracial sex, 98, 108, 131; and "White Peril" discourses, 93, 107–8

prestige, white, 17, 51, 194n83; and degeneration discourse, 120, 133, 136; and homosexuality, 136; and Indian Crisis of 1923, 84–86; and "White Peril" discourse, 99–100, 107

primitive normativity: Africans racialized by proxy, 22, 71; as alibi of empire, 162; applied to domestic context, 93–94, 100–105, 112–13, 115; "childlike" nature attributed to Africans, 49, 61, 71, 90–91, 94, 104–5, 110; deviance as absent in "traditional" African society, 2–3, 25, 34, 40–41, 53–54, 92, 94, 101, 109–10, 124, 156, 163–65; "deviance" not possible for Africans, 28–29, 81, 162; and "Indian Crisis," 70, 77, 81–82; Indian "deviance" contrasted with, 77, 81, 82; Kenyatta's use of, 35–41; malleability of, 8, 24, 163, 165–66; and Mau Mau rebellion, 23, 140–41, 148–49, 156, 158, 162; premarital sex play as "characteristic" of, 53; as prominent narrative in Kenya, 20–21, 124; as proof of political unfitness, 22, 25, 27–28, 34, 83–84, 87; queerness of, 8–11; as reversal of standard narrative, 8, 21, 111, 137, 163; settler interests advanced by, 25, 70, 114–15, 163; in sexology and anthropology, 25–35; as sexually healthier, 28, 137, 172n14; and social control, 40, 101–3, 149, 207n80; temporality linked with, 3, 113, 125; used to assign asexuality to African women, 43–44, 60, 68, 98; white supremacy enabled by, 21. See also normativity; sexuality, African

primitivity: artistic and social movements linked with, 6; concept of, 24; and fertility, 6, 123–24 progress, 26–27, 32, 146; degeneration linked with, 29–30; narrative of, 26; "too-rapid" for Africans, 25, 33, 35, 103, 140, 141. *See also* "civilization"

prostitution, 198n23; detribalization blamed for, 149, 157; Kenyatta's view of, 40, 54; Mau Mau linked with, 151–52, 157; in Strange's nonfiction, 124; during times of economic change, 52, 207n81; urbanization linked with, 36, 43, 53–54, 156; women's choice to engage in, 52–54

"protection" of Africans, 20–21, 29; in anthropology and sexology, 26; from "civilization," 2, 5, 14, 21, 25–26, 45, 71, 87; from colonial officials, 45, 49

psychoanalytic theory: in colonial sources, 34–35; doctrine of survivals, 30–31; and Mau Mau oathing mythologies, 157–60; "primitive" as term in, 125; regression, 31–32, 39

queerness, 8–10; queering of temporality, 4–5, 8, 9

queer settler sexuality, 119–21, 123–24, 131; curing through reparative landscape, 121, 125–30, 137, 198n30

queer studies, 3, 166; Black, 11, 164–65

race: normativity produced through, 2–3, 165; as temporal category, 32

racial boundaries: blurred by interracial sexual relations, 67, 130, 131; and domestic sphere, 93–94, 96, 106, 108; white European women imported to maintain, 45–48, 66

rape: "chattel" discourse, 112–13; hunting metaphor, 128; Kenyan African understandings of, 194–95n91; linked to "civilization," 94; marital, 119–20, 126–28; as more harmful to white women, 112; "reparative," 125–28; by whites, blamed on servants, 95

rape, interracial, 92–116; adolescent African boys accused of, 105; of African women by white men, 113; children and fears of, 93–94, 101, 104–6, 109, 111; death penalty advocated, 113, 114–15; harsh measures ad-

vocated, 105, 110–15, 191n32, 195n99; Indian views of, 115; metropolitan British debates about, 130; policies implemented, 111; as rare, 92, 95, 110–11, 114, 189–90n5; and settler homes, 91, 93; and social class of white woman, 97–98; Special Committee on Sexual Assaults of Natives upon Europeans, 22, 92, 105, 109, 113, 114; tribal punishment of, 115; white women blamed for, 91, 93–94, 97–98, 99–106, 114, 116. *See also* "Black Peril" discourse; "White Peril" discourse

Registration of Domestic Servants Ordinance (1926), 116

Registration of Natives Ordinance (1915), 20

reparative landscape, 7, 23, 119–20; Africans as extension of, 121, 133, 137; as cure for settler queerness, 121, 125–30, 137; eugenic elimination of the unfit, 120, 127, 132–34, 136–37; near-death experience in, 120, 127

"repatriation" of urban Africans, 5, 116, 178n56

reproduction, as stated goal of Gikuyu sexual activity, 38, 40. *See also* futurity, settler reproductive

Resident Native (Squatters) Ordinance of 1918, 19, 171n62, 184n14

"responsible self-rule," 74–75, 122

Rhodesia, 96, 97, 98–99, 191n32

romance novel genre, 47, 116, 198n27; near-death experiences in, 120, 127; "reparative rape" in, 125–26; used to explore sexual themes, 124–25. *See also* Strange, Nora; Strange's novels

Routledge, Katherine Pease, 42–43, 49–50, 59–61, 176–77n31, 179n65, 181n88

Routledge, W. Scoresby, 42–43, 49–50, 59–60, 66–67, 176–77n31, 179n65, 180–81n86

rural areas: "repatriation" of urban Africans to, 5, 116, 178n56; as "safe" for Africans, 6–7

Scott, Francis, 112

Seely, Colonel, 60, 65

Sekanyolya (Luganda-language paper), 87

self-control, 64, 66, 67, 103, 115; and ngweko, 38; white middle-class, 107, 123, 129–30, 136–37

Seligman, Charles Gabriel, 29, 173n21, 201n83

Sentongo, Z. K., 87–88, 188n80

settler colonialism: biopolitical project of, 7; in Kenya, 14–23; North American model, 8; preservation of Indigenous populations for labor purposes, 7, 8; "settler sexuality," production of, 124; Silberrad scandal at beginnings of, 45; specificities of, 120–21. *See also* colonialism

"settler colonial phenomena," 122

settler colonial studies, 3

sexology, 21, 25–35

sexual development theories, 29–31, 38–39, 157–58

sexuality: culture as disseminated through, 45; of "overcivilized" Europeans, 7, 23, 24, 118–21, 126–27, 137; as temporal category, 3–5, 24

sexuality, African: age of maturity for young men and women, 37–39, 51, 174n66, 177n36; as both backward and normative, 27–29, 34, 165; debate over guardianship by "immigrant races," 70, 72, 90–91; "free love," 92, 101–2, 124, 189n4; as healthier than European, 28, 137, 172n14; as monotonous, 28; nineteenth-century view of, 27; polygyny, 36–37, 40, 63; as pure and unrepressed, 24; representations of not based on empirical research, 34; timescape of as queer, 9; turn of the century view of, 27; vulnerability, discourse of, 67–68, 78, 90–91. *See also* Africans, Kenyan; primitive normativity; vulnerability, discourse of; women, African

"Sexual Threat and Settler Society: 'Black Perils' in Kenya, c. 1907–30" (Anderson), 98, 99

Shadle, Brett, 7, 17, 43, 51, 70, 84, 98, 183n5

Shambulia ("Bokkie"), 151, 152–53

Shaw, Carolyn Martin, 146, 147

Shaw, W. H., 83, 187n60

Sheik, The (Hull), 133, 200n64

Silberrad, Hubert, 163; "customary law" not followed by, 56–57, 59; "customary law" used to mitigate misconduct of, 21–22, 43, 51, 56–57; jailing of Mgulla, 42, 50, 182n112;

positioned as guardian of African tradition, 57–58; punishment reduced, 66, 182n112; white wife, 65

Silberrad scandal, 42–68, 152, 163, 179n68, 180–81n86; aftermath of, 66–68; ages of Gikuyu girls, 50, 177n36, 181n91; attempts to keep quiet, 59–60; in British metropole, 48, 49, 60–66; commonalities between vision of white and colonized women, 45; detractors positioned as "trustees," 61–62; girls' interpretations not considered relevant, 50, 61; historiography of, 46–49; indirect rule applied to sexual realm, 43, 56, 67; Kenyan judicial inquiry into, 50; parliamentary debates, 43, 50, 61, 65–66; at periphery, 49–60; Silberrad said to have "purchased" women, 21–22, 43–44; *Spectator* articles and letters, 61–63; support for, 181n89, 182n112; testimony of girls, 56–57, 179n68, 179n70, 180n74; translations of testimony, 50, 179n70, 180n74

Sinha, Mrinalini, 74, 77, 78

slavery: concubinage compared with, 62–63; women ungendered under, 44

slave trade, 34, 62–63

"sleeping dictionaries," African women portrayed as, 44

social control: detribalization's effect on, 156–57; and primitive normativity, 40, 101–3, 149, 207n80; and "White Peril" discourse, 93–94, 97, 104, 110, 116

Soldier Settlement Scheme of 1919, 16, 123

Somali people, 135, 201n79, 201nn83–84

South Africa, 17, 75, 97

South Africans, migration to East Africa, 15, 17, 199n47

Special Committee on Sexual Assaults of Natives upon Europeans, 22, 92, 105, 109, 113, 114

speculative approaches to history, 166

Spencer, Herbert, 30, 31

Spillers, Hortense, 22, 44

"spivery," 150–51, 205n61, 205n63

"squatted labor," 19, 73, 122, 171n62, 171n68, 184n14